DORCHESTER LIBRARY
COLLITON PARK
DORCHESTER DT1 1XJ
01305 224440 / 224652

Dorset Library Service

- Please return items before closing time on the last date stamped to avoid charges.

- Renew books by phoning 01305 224311 or online www.dorsetforyou.com/libraries

- Items may be returned to any Dorset library.

 Dorset Library HQ, Colliton Park, Dorchester, Dorset DT1 1XJ

DL/M/2372
dd03517

THE BOOK OF
STINSFORD

Thomas Hardy's Mellstock

KAY KEARSEY AND MIKE COSGROVE

HALSGROVE

Title page: *A stylish Dorothy Blackaller at Bockhampton crossroads, 1930s. Dorothy was the daughter of Henry and Emma Blackaller whose other children were Gladys and William (Bill). Henry was employed by the Webers of Birkin House and lived at Birkin Cottages. All three children went to Bockhampton School.*

British Library Cataloguing-in-Publication Data.
A CIP record for this title is available from the British Library.

ISBN 978 1 84114 786 4

HALSGROVE

Halsgrove
Halsgrove House
Ryelands Industrial Estate
Bagley Road
Wellington
Somerset TA21 9PZ

T: 01823 653777
F: 01823 216796

e: sales@halsgrove.com
www.halsgrove.com

Printed in Great Britain by CPI Antony Rowe, Wiltshire

Whilst every care has been taken to ensure the accuracy of the information contained in this book, the publisher disclaims responsibility for any mistakes which may have been inadvertently included.

Preface: Stinsford Parish Today

Stinsford parish includes the hamlets and settlements of Bhompston, Higher and Lower Bockhampton, Higher Kingston, Kingston Maurward, Stinsford and Waterston Ridge. Coker's Frome and Frome Whitfield were attached to the parish in 1894 having previously been part of All Saints' parish, Dorchester. The parish covers 1,352 hectares of agricultural land and woodland at Grey's Wood, Yellowham and Thorncombe Wood and parts of Puddletown and Bhompston heaths.

There are two conservation areas: Stinsford with Lower Bockhampton and Higher Kingston. Kingston Maurward House, its gardens and park with the Old Manor House are recognised as a historic park and garden. There are several scheduled monuments in the parish: Grey's Bridge, Bockhampton Bridge, the Roman Road and two barrows near Waterston Ridge. The River Frome and its river banks have Site of Special Scientific Interest status and the water-meadows have land of local landscape importance. The chalk quarry just north of the Tincleton Road at Dark Hill is a Regionally Important Geological Site. There is a large number of listed buildings in the parish and five country houses, Birkin House, Frome House, Kingston Maurward House, the Old Manor House and Stinsford House.

The parish is a popular place for tourists, particularly those with an interest in the poet and novelist Thomas Hardy who was born at Hardy's Cottage, Higher Bockhampton, now owned by the National Trust. This site is visited by thousands each year from across the world. Kingston Maurward attracts many visitors to the beautiful gardens and the Animal Park. Accommodation is available in holiday cottages, a hotel and two country houses.

Kingston Maurward College and its estate occupies 750 acres in the centre of the parish. There are 600 full-time students, some living on the college site, and up to 4,000 part-time students of all ages studying horticulture, agriculture, equestrian studies, animal care, outdoor leisure and recreation, as well as business-related courses.

Mellstock Farm and Hampton Farm are two business parks at Higher Bockhampton on the site of the chicken units.

The population of the parish in 2001 was 346 but was at its highest in 1851 at 373, slowly dropping to 278 by 1891. In 1901 with Coker's Frome and Frome Whitfield added to the parish the population was 350. The number of dwellings in the parish between 1851 and 1891 was between 58 and 67, whereas in 2001 there were 148. The average number of people in each dwelling in 2001 was 2.3 compared to 5.5 in 1851, reflecting the smaller families of today and the disappearance of extended families sharing a cottage. In 1851 46 percent of the people living in the parish had been born here, which dropped to 17 percent in 1891. If this data was available for 2001 the figure would probably be lower still. A study of all the surnames occurring in the parish census returns from 1851 to 1901 reveals that the only one which occurs in all is Hardy. Members of the Bishop and Squibb families appeared in all years between 1851 and 1891.

Left: *William Purseglove, butler to the Fellowes and then the Balfours with his wife Alvina, daughters Mary Ellen and Alice who were born at Bockhampton. This photograph was taken in front of their retirement home in Upwey, near Weymouth. Their son Henry became a carpenter and lived at Higher Bockhampton in 1909.* Standing left to right: *Mary Ellen, William Purseglove, Alice;* seated: *Alvina.*

Right: *Bob Holt in 1931, possibly in Scotland. He was a servant of the Hanburys who went on to be butler to a family in Hampshire. He volunteered for the RAF in 1940 but having completed his training in 1941 he was taken ill with rheumatic fever and died whilst on leave in Dorchester. Lady Hanbury attended his funeral at Stinsford where he was buried in the Hanbury cemetery. For many years Mr and Mrs Farr of Stinsford cared for his grave for the Commonwealth War Graves Commission.*

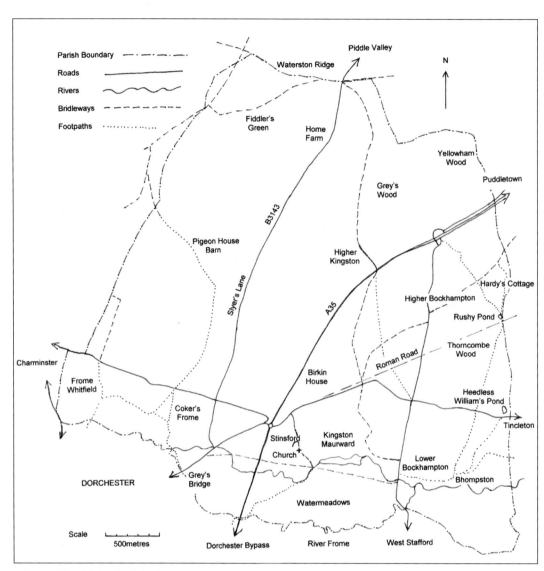

The parish of Stinsford, 2007.

Members of the hunt on the steps of Stinsford House, 1940s, with Mary Newcomb Higginson on the left and Henry Higginson in the second row, third from the left.

Off-duty housemaid Beatrice Parratt enjoying the sunshine in the gardens at Stinsford House, c.1935.

Contents

Acknowledgements

Without the participation of the hundreds of marvellous people who have contributed material, taken time to talk about the past, come to the exhibitions and encouraged us to continue there would be no book to share.

We would like to thank the following individuals for loaning us photographs, other material and for information. Nigel Allen, David Ashford, the late George and Cyril Atkins, Nicholas Balfour, Julian and Sophie Bailey, Isabel Bearpark, Vicky Bevan, Sylvia, Les and Rod Blackaller, Geraldine Burrows, Alan Butler, the late Clare Carey, David Chant, the late Mary Clark, Bob Clarke, Michael and Susan Clarke, Peter Crabbe, Sheila Crocker, Rosanna Dawson, Elsie Dean, Dennis Dunford, Douglas Eaves, Alan and Doreen Ferris, Liz Ferris, Peggy Fowler, Betty Friend, Sylvia Goddard, the late Mabel Goldsworthy, Richard Gooch, Michael Graham Jones, Hugh Grenville-Jones, Caroline Hanbury, the late Jean Hansell, Shirley Harris, Daphne Styan and Margaret Hill, John Herring, the late Mrs Winifred Hopkins and Ruth Axtell, Harry and Celia Hounsell, Wendy Hunt, Oliver Hurden, Denis and Betty Jenkins, Bill and Vera Jesty, Richard and Gillian John, Philip Jones, Ron, Dorothy and Ian Karley, Jim Keble-White, Roy and Eve Kellaway, Claire Kendall-Price, John Kennedy, Nicholas Lee and the late Muriel Burnett, Shirley Legg and Margaret Thorne, Deidre Levi, Terry and Rob Linee, Tim Loasby, Donald Mackenzie, Woodford McClellan, Marian Marsh, John and Irene Mayo, Alan J. Miller, Simon Mills, Diane Morgan, Bernard and Marion Mussell, Beatrice Parratt, Bob Pinnow, Anthony Pitt-Rivers, Derek Pride, Paul Pritchard, 'Busty' Read, Mina Rich, Tom and Maureen Rimmer, Phil Roberts, Bob Salway, Roger and Sue Samways, Frances Sanders, John and Ruth Seal, Jan Simmonds and Mark Needham, Jeff St Aubyn, Doris Street, Lilian Swindall, Frank Tapper, The Honourable Mrs Townshend, Stuart Turner, Kate Webb and Markus Stickelberger, Andrew and Mulu Thomson, June Thompson, Ernie Thorne, Brenda Tunks, David and Daphne Vulliamy, Tony and Jean Wakely, Ron Webb, Pamela Wenden, Mrs J. and Fay White, Lona White, Hugh Willis, Jim and Diana Wilson, Norrie Woodhall, Doris Wray, Gwen Yarker.

We also thank the following organisations: Allhallows Museum, Honiton, for permission to reproduce images of lace from its collection; Awards for All for financial support to mount exhibitions in 2000 and 2005; Berkshire Record Office for access to Benyon documents; Dorset County Museum for permission to reproduce images from the Moule, photographic and Thomas Hardy Memorial and Lock collections; *Dorset Echo* for publicity; Kingston Maurward College for support with reproduction fees and access to photographs and maps; Stinsford Parish Council for support to mount the millennium exhibition; the Dean and Chapter of Exeter Cathedral for permission to reproduce the Bockhampton Manor map; Revd Janet Smith and the churchwardens of St Michael's Church, Stinsford, for permission to include photographs of the church; The Dorset Federation of Women's Institutes for permission to reproduce images of documents of the Mellstock branch of the WI; The Dorset History Centre staff for their help and support during the past ten years of research and for permission to reproduce documents and maps from the archives.

Finally, we would like to thank fellow members of the Stinsford and Bockhampton Village History Group for their encouragement, support and contributions towards reproduction fees.

Left: *Gardeners, c.1930s. Arthur Tizzard is on the right.*

Right: *The days of hand milking, with pails and three-legged stools at the ready, 1930s. No names are known.*

Introduction

Soon after moving to Lower Bockhampton in 1995 I began to hear stories and recollections from neighbours about life in the parish since the 1920s. I decided to record them as they were so interesting and explained what life was like then – so different from today.

With my appetite whetted I asked people to tell me what they could remember and to lend photographs to be copied for my collection. I discovered that Thomas Hardy was the parish's first local historian as he had recorded the stories he had heard from his parents, grandparents and neighbours in his notebooks, including extracts from past copies of the *Dorset County Chronicle* newspaper which he read at the Museum. Information from his notebooks and extracts from conversations he had with a number of people appear in many chapters of this book.

As part of the millennium celebrations in 2000 an exhibition of photographs and documents from my collection was displayed with the help of a neighbour, Claire Kendall-Price. In 2004 the Stinsford and Bockhampton Village History Group was formed, which brought together a small group of people with an interest in the history of the parish. In the following year exhibitions were shown at St Michael's Church and the Old Manor House to share the results of research since the millennium. Lots of people asked if we were going to write a book about the parish, which seemed daunting but also a good idea. Work started on the text in January 2006 and Mike Cosgrove has scanned, repaired and prepared all the photographs and created the comparative maps showing how the hamlets have changed, or not!

This is a patchwork of Stinsford history pieced together from research, reminiscences, maps and photographs. There will be things we have not heard about that we would have included, people we did not find who could have told us more. It has been particularly difficult to collect photographs and information about the last 50 years but is probably because no one seems to think of the period 1950 to the present as history – though of course it will be one day. We hope everyone with connections to and affection for the parish will find something of interest and hopefully something new!

When he spoke at the opening of the Bockhampton Men's Reading Room in 1919 Thomas Hardy said: 'There would be many things to interest us in the past of Bockhampton if we could only know them, but we know only a few.' We hope we have put that right, not just for Bockhampton, but for the parish of Stinsford as a whole.

Kay Kearsey,
Chairman,
Stinsford and Bockhampton Village History Group

Dressing up for amateur theatricals seems to have been a favourite activity in the 1940s and 1950s. None of these performers from the Mellstock Drama Group have been identified.

A special day for evacuees Doreen and Molly Ferris when their mother was able to travel from Southampton to visit them at Higher Bockhampton, c.1940.

George and Agnes Lee with their daughter Pamela, son Ernest and Ernest's daughter Vivienne, c.1933. Ernest was killed in 1940 whilst attempting to defuse an enemy torpedo which had been washed ashore near Alexandria, Egypt.

Cyril Atkins, Bill Blackaller and George Atkins enjoying a holiday at Butlins with the help of Muffin the Mule, 1950s.

An outing to the seaside and the only photograph found of Aileen Graham-Jones who is sitting just right of centre in a dark hat and dark cardigan. She and her husband Dr Graham-Jones lived at Bockhampton House and were active in many aspects of parish life including the school, the church and the WI.

Chapter 1

Landscape and Geology of the Parish

The parish of Stinsford occupies the northern slope of the River Frome valley to the north and north-east of Dorchester. Its boundary in the north is along the Ridge Way of Waterston Ridge (height above sea-level approximately 125 metres) and to the south its boundary is essentially the course of the River Frome (the 50-metre contour crossing the valley just south of Stinsford church). The west boundary follows a somewhat erratic route from Three Cornered Copse in the north to join the River Frome on the outskirts of Dorchester between Frome Whitfield and Burton. The east boundary, equally erratic, passes through Yellowham Wood, takes in the western fringe of Puddletown Forest, just includes Rushy Pond and Heedless William's Pond and runs south to join the River Frome just west of Duddle Farm.

Within the parish, from west to east, the landscape changes from classic chalk downland slope to classic heathland formed on Tertiary sands and clays. The River Frome valley reflects this change, being approximately ½ kilometre wide at Frome Whitfield in the west to over 1 kilometre wide at Bhompston in the east.

The chalk here is part of the Portsdown Chalk Formation and is about 75 million years old. The overlying sands and clays are part of the London Clay and Poole Formations and are about 60 million years old. During the time gap of about 15 million years, the chalk was eroded to become an irregular plane surface on which the sands and clays were deposited. Such a feature is called an unconformity.

Thus, in Stinsford parish we have the feather-edge of a deposit of Tertiary sands and clays that thicken to the east forming the well-known Dorset heaths. This edge runs approximately north–south from Waterston Ridge, through Thorncombe Wood to just east of Bhompston.

Later geological upheavals, together with an Ice Age and its various advances and retreats have super-imposed a series of approximately north–south valleys (now dry) in the chalk (e.g. through Pigeon House Barn and south parallel to the B3143 to join the Frome valley at Coker's Frome; through Higher Kingston to Kingston Maurward; from Higher Bockhampton to Lower Bockhampton just east of Bockhampton Lane, and just west of the eastern parish boundary) all now intersected by the west–east flowing River Frome. This has been the major drainage channel in the area, established during the Ice Age and leaving a series of terraces as it cut down through the chalk and Tertiary sediments.

The British Geological Survey has recognised 15 terraces in the Stinsford area. The highest (terrace 15) occupies the high ground in Puddletown Forest (about 120 metres above sea-level); Bhompston Heath is terrace 14 (about 115 metres). At the other extreme, terrace 1 is between Coker's Frome and just south of Stinsford church (just over 50 metres). Terraces 7, 8 and 9 are the more prominent of the intermediate ones occupying the high ground between the north–south dry valleys.

Of much later formation are the dolines or sink-holes prominently displayed in Thorncombe Wood and Puddletown Forest. These features form on the feather-edge of the Tertiary sands and clays where seeping acidic waters (acidified by passage through the sands) have dissolved away the underlying chalk, leading to collapse of the overlying material.

Outcrops of the geology can be seen just north of the Tincleton Road where the bridleway from Kingston Maurward to Higher Kingston crosses (SY718917). Here chalk is exposed in a small quarry, still in occasional use. The irregular top surface of the chalk, with solution hollows, is well displayed. This outcrop has been designated a Regionally Important Geological Site. A good outcrop of gravel from terrace 9 can be seen alongside the footpath from Bhompston to Heedless William's Pond (SY728909). Good examples of dolines can be found immediately east of Hardy's Cottage at Higher Bockhampton.

It was the landscape, essentially determined by the River Frome, rather than the underlying geology, that influenced the orientation of the manors that became established in the parish. They all occupied a north–south strip of land containing high terraces in the north, valley slopes with intermediate terraces in the middle and valley bottom, later developed as water-meadows, in the south. All the manors, except Bhompston, were on chalk. Bhompston Manor was set across the feather-edge of Tertiary sediments, leading to a landscape ranging from heathland to rolling downland.

Left: *Evidence of early human activity: a Neolithic flint tool which was discarded when the tip was broken and found in the garden of a cottage in Lower Bockhampton 5,500 years later in 1998! It was dated to c.3500BC.*

Below: *The earliest surviving Manor Court Rolls for Bockhampton begin in 1376. This fragment of rim from a storage jar found under flagstones in a cottage at Lower Bockhampton has been dated to the thirteenth or fourteenth century so may well have been in use at the same time.*

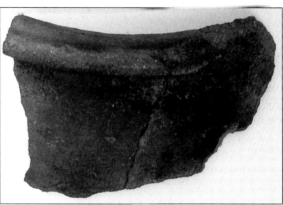

Below: *The reconstructed neck and shoulders of a jug which has been dated to about 1450. It was discovered under the flagstones of a cottage at Lower Bockhampton.*

Stinsford's Early History

The parish of Stinsford has an abundance of prehistoric sites just beyond its borders. The nearest of these is Mount Pleasant Henge just south of the River Frome on the opposite bank to Stinsford itself.

This structure is believed to date from the late Neolithic period (about 3000BC). The Tudor Arcade Timber Circle in Dorchester is also only a few 100 metres from Stinsford's southern boundary. This has been radiocarbon dated to 2100BC. Even Maiden Castle, the largest Iron Age hill-fort in Europe sited on a Neolithic causewayed enclosure of about 3800BC is less than 7 kilometres to the southwest. Poundbury hill-fort, early Iron Age, is just to the southwest of the Frome Whitfield corner of the parish.

With the proximity of such sites it is not surprising that there have been significant prehistoric finds within the parish. The earliest relics are flints believed to be Mesolithic (pre-4000BC) found in the Frome valley at various sites between Frome Whitfield and Coker's Frome. Also of this age is a sandstone saddle quern from the Coker's Frome area. An early Neolithic flint blade has been found in a garden in Lower Bockhampton. Later Bronze Age finds include flints (Slyer's Lane), Beaker pottery (Frome Whitfield) and bell barrows (Fiddler's Green) from the period 1500–1100BC. Other barrows, probably of a similar age occur, near Home Farm and Higher Kingston Farm.

The late Iron Age in the area was dominated by Maiden Castle, occupied by the Durotriges tribe. This was conquered by the Romans under Vespasian in AD43 who then established Durnovaria (Dorchester) on the south bank of the River Frome. Of the Roman roads radiating from Durnovaria, the one to Badbury Rings slices through the parish of Stinsford giving some fine displays of the original structure particularly just to the north of Dark Hill (the Tincleton Road) and in Thorncombe Wood nature reserve. An old milestone, now re-sited to the west of Stinsford roundabout, was on this road and is believed to be Roman in origin. In 1988, an excavation in the grounds of Kingston Maurward College found evidence of an older Roman Road connecting Durnovaria with Lake Farm (Wimborne). This road aligns with London Road in Dorchester and the Grey's Bridge crossing of the Frome, exiting the parish on the Tincleton Road by Heedless William's Pond.

Roman pottery has been found in the Slyer's Lane area, and Romano-British pottery and ditches have been noted near Coker's Frome and in Exhibition Field. Inhumations of this period have been unearthed near Waterston Ridge as well as at Frome Whitfield and Coker's Frome.

At the same time as the Roman developments in the area, the native population was very active with extensive 'Celtic Fields' and settlements on the high ground in the north of the parish from the Fiddler's Green area northwards across the parish boundary into Charminster, Piddlehinton and Puddletown parishes. This activity dating from the first to fourth centuries occupies an area of over 600 acres (240 hectares).

There is little evidence of activity in Stinsford parish during the long period from the end of the Roman occupation (AD410) to the Norman Conquest (1066), often called the Dark Ages or the Anglo-Saxon period. However, it was during this period that the manorial system became established, a social system that was to feature strongly in our parish history until quite recent times. Its roots were in the Romano-British period and it was flourishing by the eighth century. Typically the manor consisted of peasant dwellings, usually clustered together to form a village, often with a church and possibly also a mill. Nearby would be the manor house, usually fortified in early times, occupied by the lord or his steward. In Stinsford parish, the manors of Stinsford, Kingston, Bockhampton and Bhompston became established each occupying essentially a north–south territory across the northern slopes of the River Frome valley. The manor of Frome Whitfield in the west was only added to the parish in 1894. During the tenth century shires (counties) became established with their subdivisions, the hundreds. Stinsford is in George Hundred.

The relief carving of an angel once on St Michael's Church and only recently (1996) moved inside to protect it from further weathering dates from the late-tenth or early-eleventh century. The church, however, dates from the early-thirteenth century so it would seem reasonable to assume that the angel was transferred from a pre-existing Saxon church on the same site.

The Domesday Book, produced in 1086, records information on Stinsford, Bockhampton and two Frome localities – Frome Whitfield and Bhompston. The data includes population, land resources, who held (owned) the localities before 1066 and to whom they were allocated after that date by King William. A monetary value was also given. From such data, Frome Whitfield and Bockhampton Manor would seem to have been of similar importance. Both had mills and paid taxes for four hides (a hide was approximately 120 acres). Bhompston also paid taxes for four hides, but Stinsford only paid taxes for two hides and 2½ virgates (a virgate was approximately 30 acres).

The next 500 years or so are generally referred to as the medieval period. There is limited evidence of this period in our parish although thirteenth- and fourteenth-century pottery has been found in the Frome Whitfield, Coker's Frome and Lower Bockhampton areas.

Recent excavations by a local group of archaeologists have uncovered medieval pottery in sites around Lower Bockhampton. Of particular interest is the discovery of a substantial (broken) part of a jug dated at approximately 1450, found beneath the flagstone floor of Molehill Cottage, whilst next door at Roller Cottage earlier floors have been discovered with medieval pottery shards beneath the present-day flagstones. It seems evident that the site of the existing terrace in Lower Bockhampton has been occupied for many centuries. Additionally, excavations north of the lane to Lower Dairy to investigate the site of the poor house in 1839 (occupied by James Dawe as a farmhouse in 1774) uncovered evidence of that building and beneath it the remains of an older structure. In Stinsford the church dates from the early-thirteenth century and there is a history of Stinsford House dating back to 1470.

Throughout Tudor times (sixteenth century) there was a growth of country estates and it was during this period that the Old Manor House, Kingston Maurward was built. The Georgian manor house at Kingston Maurward followed this in the eighteenth century... but details of the history of these buildings and related matters follow in later chapters of this book.

St Michael's Church

St Michael's Church from the southeast, 2007.

The church is next to Stinsford House, so close that the door in the garden wall of the house is opposite the church door. The oldest parts of the church have been dated to the thirteenth century and the oldest object is the carving of St Michael in Ham Hill stone, dated to the Saxon period. This was originally outside on the west wall of the tower but was moved inside to the south aisle in 1996 to protect it from further damage by frost. The font is also very old, dating from the Norman period.

In 1335 the church at Stinsford was granted to the prior and brethren of the Order of St John of Jerusalem who had a base at 'Mayne', probably Friar Mayne, near Broadmayne. It is not thought that the brethren were ever based at Stinsford but they were responsible for providing the vicar to serve the parishioners.

Following the dissolution of the monasteries the right to appoint the vicar and the tithes passed to the Crown and was subsequently leased or sold to the highest bidder. In 1562 Queen Elizabeth leased this right to Robert Jacob and his sons, William and Jacob. It seems likely that the Jacobs lived in Lower Bockhampton as a stone with Robert's name and the initials AJ and WJ is set in the centre of the front wall between the Old Post Office and Greenwood Cottage. In 1665 the right to select the vicar and tithes was sold to Giles Strangways for £1,000 and his descendants have been the patrons of the church ever since.

The restored Norman font was found in 1920 in several pieces buried in the churchyard. It was discovered when the earth that had accumulated against the church wall was removed in an effort to deal with the damp, which was damaging the walls. A simple new base for the font was designed by Thomas Hardy and was given to the church by Mrs Ethel Cowley, the vicar's wife.

An undated drawing made by A. Crane for the Revd W. Floyer who was vicar between 1784 and 1820, which shows the north door of the church. Stinsford House on the right appears to have a very elaborate chimney.

The carving of St Michael, dated to the Saxon period, which was originally outside on the west wall of the church tower but thanks to a gift from Mrs Jean Hansell is now inside the church in the south aisle, safe from further damage from rain and frost. This photograph was taken in 1940, unfortunately some of the detail of the carving has been lost since then due to damage from the weather.

St Michael's Church, Stinsford and the chancel arch, pictured in 2007.

The Building

The rather plain tower dates from the fourteenth century. It appears to be rather short now but this is because the roof of the nave was raised during the restoration work of 1868. Photographs from the early years of the twentieth century always show the tower almost completely covered in ivy. There are three bells in the tower, the treble originally cast during the fifteenth century, the tenor cast in 1616 and the third bell dated 1663 has the initials of William Chamberlain, Thomas Griffin (both churchwardens) and Thomas Purdue the bell founder cast into it. The bells were re-hung in 1927 when the ancient treble had to be recast as it was badly cracked, it is said after some over-enthusiastic ringing at a wedding!

Inside the simplicity of this country church is reflected in the chancel arch with plain mouldings along its almost horseshoe shape. The Visitors' Book often includes comments on the tranquillity and beauty of the church.

The north side of the church in 2007. The vestry on the left was added in a major restoration in 1868. At the same time the roof of the nave was raised and the remains of the blocked north door were removed. The windows in the north aisle which commemorated members of the Pitt family were very faded and have recently been replaced with plain glass and some small fragments of the old glass incorporated.

Above: *The beautiful set of silver-gilt communion vessels made by Paul Lamarie, a famous eighteenth-century silversmith. It was given by the patron of the church, Mrs Strangways Horner in 1737, who also owned the Stinsford House estate. The Revd Medway worried about its safekeeping during his time as vicar when it was regularly used for communion services. His solution was to hide it in the bottom of the family's laundry basket each week! As it is now literally priceless it is in the care of Salisbury Cathedral and is usually on display in the chapter house.*

Left: *The large marble vase given to the church as a font by Lora Pitt of Kingston House.*

'Directions to keep the gilt plate clean from the silversmith that made it. Clean it now and then with only warm water and soap, with a spunge [sic], and then wash it with warm water and dry it very well with a soft linnen [sic] cloth; and keep it in a dry place for the damp will spoyle [sic] it. June 1737.' Some have suggested these instructions were written by Mrs Strangways Horner but it seems more likely they would have been written by someone from Paul Lamarie's workshop and, if so, possibly makes this small sheet of paper particularly interesting.

In 1630 changes were made to the north aisle and probably also at this time a door was added to the north wall, possibly for the convenience of the Grey family of Kingston Maurward who had their pew in that part of the church. A pen and ink drawing that hangs in the church shows the position of this north door.

Music for church services was provided by a choir accompanied by a small group of musicians playing violins and bass viols. Members of the Hardy family, the first Thomas, his sons Thomas and James and son-in-law James Dart, were the musicians for many years. In 1843 the churchwardens decided not to pay the musicians in future, possibly one of the changes made under the influence of the Revd Arthur Shirley, and the group of musicians were disbanded. From that time the choir were accompanied by a barrel organ, itself eventually replaced by a harmonium. The story of the musicians' demise was used later by Thomas Hardy for the theme of his novel *Under the Greenwood Tree*. The churchwarden's accounts for 1844 include payment of £45 for the barrel organ which was operated by James Hardy whose daughter Teresa was later to become church organist. The front of the west gallery where the musicians and choir had stood was removed in 1843 and the remaining floor in 1911.

In 1868 a major restoration of the church took place and the vestry was added. The door in the north wall, which had already been blocked up by then, was completely removed. Sadly by this time the original roof of the nave with its bosses was badly damaged and was replaced with one made of pine. The height of the roof was raised at the same time.

Top: *A telegram dated 13 November 1930 from Dorchester West railway station staff alerting Revd Cowley to the arrival of the Hardy Memorial Window which had been made in Scotland by Douglas Strachan.*

Above: *The Hardy Memorial Window, in the south aisle, which was unveiled in 1930. It is pictured here in 2007.*

The large altar piece which had been given by Mrs Strangways Horner in 1751 was removed and replaced with a mid-Victorian reredos which in turn was replaced in 1939 by the present oak one given by Mrs Benita Weber of Birkin House in memory of her husband Colonel Frank Weber.

By 1910 the building was found to be very damp and in a state of decay. The chancel roof was restored at the expense of the Earl of Ilchester. The oak box pews were removed, having been patched and repaired for many years, although Thomas Hardy thought they could have been repaired with new oak. He believed that they were Georgian or even older. However, this was not possible except at great expense and so it was decided that they should be replaced with chairs. Some of the oak from the old pews was used for panelling the aisles and Major Balfour, then owner of Kingston House, donated oak panelling from the Old Manor House for the entrance under the tower.

Sometime before 1748 Mrs Lora Pitt had given a large white Italian marble vase as a font, which was used for almost 200 years. Thomas Hardy was one of those christened in it. In 1920 the old Norman font was found in pieces buried in the churchyard. It was restored to use with a base designed by Thomas Hardy, paid for by Mrs Ethel Cowley, wife of the vicar. The vase given by Lora Pitt was kept in the north aisle until 1948 when it was donated to the diocese after an appeal for surplus ecclesiastical furniture to help refurbish war-damaged churches. Its fate remained a mystery until 2004 when, following an appeal on local radio by Bill Jesty, churchwarden, it was traced to St Luke's Church in Winchester.

On the south side of the chancel there is a window in memory of Revd William Floyer, vicar from 1784–1819. The windows in the north wall commemorated members of the Pitt family but over the years they became very faded and indistinct and have recently been replaced with mostly plain glass which has improved the level of light in the church and allows a glimpse of the churchyard beyond. Mr James Fellowes of Kingston House presented the east windows of the two aisles and the chancel.

When a window in memory of Thomas Hardy was proposed his widow suggested the theme of 'the still small voice', one of his favourite passages from the bible. It was designed and made by Douglas Strachan, and Cecil Hanbury and the Earl of Ilchester visited the artist's studio in Edinburgh as work progressed. In 1930 the window was unveiled by the Countess of Ilchester and dedicated by the Archdeacon of Sherborne. Funds for the window had been raised by public subscription, from the church box, from an appeal in *The Times* newspaper and from a village sale. In all, £327.13s.6d. was raised, which was just sufficient to cover all the costs. Mrs Cowley had organised the village sale and in her letter to Colonel Weber, Honorary Secretary of the

Parochial Church Council, enclosing the proceeds she added an amusing postscript: 'Miss Weber's evening dresses and your pyjamas sold splendidly. This needn't be entered in the receipt!' Were they silk, or monogrammed pyjamas? Who bought them?

Perhaps a little ironically in view of the fate of the Hardy musicians, replaced by a barrel organ about 100 years earlier, Miss Kate Hardy gave an organ to the church in memory of her parents, sister Mary and brothers Thomas and Henry in June 1931. Several people have recalled that as children they pumped the organ during Sunday services including 'Busty' Read, who lived at the Old Manor House in the 1940s and 1950s, when the organist was Miss Lang, affectionately nicknamed by the children Mary Poppins because when it rained she often rode her bicycle with her umbrella up.

Richard Little Purdy of Yale University, a Thomas Hardy scholar and writer, endowed the church and churchyard in commemoration of the life and work of Thomas Hardy's second wife Florence. As a result, a new gallery was constructed under the tower, this time including an organ which replaced the one given by Miss Kate Hardy, although the front of the old organ was kept in place. A service of dedication took place at a special choral evensong in December 1996.

The new gallery of St Michael's Church, 2007.

The Vicarage

The earliest reference to a vicarage at Stinsford is on a map of Stinsford Manor and farm dated 1759. An earlier document of 1713 refers to oats grown on Stinsford parsonage but not to a vicarage or house. The present house has been dated to the eighteenth century with a Victorian extension next to Church Lane.

Following Revd Medway's death in 1973 there was no resident vicar and the Salisbury Diocese decided that the vicarage should be sold. Plans were drawn up for a modern, smaller vicarage to be built somewhere in the parish but this idea was abandoned and

Tea at the vicarage between 1944 and 1950. The picture includes: *Eustace Brutton, Muriel Gooch, Mrs Gwendoline Gooch and Revd Gooch.*

Revd H.W. Gooch, vicar between 1944 and 1950, enjoying some refreshment at the wedding reception for Bob Dean and Elsie 'Bubbles' Farr which was held in the vicarage garden just across the lane from the church in 1947. The bride and her parents lived in part of the vicarage.

South-facing Stinsford vicarage in summer with well-tended lawns, 1920s. By 1944, when the Revd and Mrs Gooch arrived, the house and garden were in a sorry state having been empty for some time.

The vicarage, looking much as it did in the 1920s, was sold by the diocese in 1977 and is now a private family home. It is pictured here in 2007.

a property in Dorchester at 10 Treves Road was purchased for the vicar who had responsibility for a number of other scattered parishes. The vicarage was sold by auction at The Antelope Hotel, Dorchester in March 1973. It seems that although 75 people attended the auction the Diocese were disappointed that it only realised £33,000. The vicarage has remained in private hands ever since. Soon after the sale, the Parochial Church Council expressed a preference to join with the parish of St Mary's, Charminster, if it was necessary to share a vicar with another parish and since the linking of the parishes the vicar has always lived at Charminster vicarage.

Church Registers

The earliest entries in the registers for St Michael's, Stinsford, are the burial of Alice Gryffin, daughter of Robert, on 8 August 1577 and the marriage of Richard Stanley and Christian Hillarye on 8 June 1579, possibly the daughter of the vicar. The first christening recorded is of Priscilla, daughter of Robert Honiborne, on 16 March 1631.

The entries seem to be rather sporadic in these early years and some years are without any entries at all, but this may be an accurate record even so. A surprise in some of the registers from 1800 onwards are comments written by Thomas Hardy, in his distinctive handwriting, identifying members of his family.

Churchwarden's Accounts

Two churchwardens for the parish were appointed or re-appointed each year at the Easter Vestry meeting. Their duty was to care for the church building and the church services so their accounts include expenditure on wine and bread for communion, cleaning the church, building materials, the washing of surplices, and oil for bells. Payments to ringers also appear in the Stinsford accounts most often at Christmas but also on 5 November and for coronations.

As a consequence of regulations introduced much earlier in the sixteenth-century the churchwardens were still paying parishioners for vermin such as stoats, sparrows and hedgehogs as late as the eighteenth century. It is rather sad to see that hedgehogs were considered as much of a pest as stoats.

Extracts from payments for year from Easter 1753
Pd John Coxe for a Stotshead 2d.
Pd John Vie for three higgogs heads 6d.
and for 6 doz. sparoes hds. 1s.
Pd Wlm West for 3 doz. ditto 6d.
Pd John Seward for 8 stotes and a polecates head 1s.4d.
Pd Robert Coward for 12 stots and polcats heads 2s.0d.
Pd Clerk is bill and wages £2.5s.2d.
Pd for the ringers on the 5th of November 5s.0d.

Records of the Overseers of the Poor

Until the workhouse was opened in Dorchester in 1836 rates were collected in the parish and used to help the elderly, the sick, orphaned children, unmarried mothers and occasionally poor people passing through the parish. In 1798 during the war with France, for example, there is an entry 'Gave a sailor in distress to help him on the road being come out of a French Prison 1s.0d.' Like the churchwardens the two overseers of the poor were appointed for the coming year at the Easter Vestry meeting. They were responsible for supporting the poor and needy, keeping an account of how they spent the money raised by the rates. The earliest records of the overseers for Stinsford are in the Poor Rate Book beginning in 1772 where the first entry on May 12 reads 'Bout a New Book for Stinsford at cost 2s.3d.'

A great deal of the overseers' time was taken up by checking the right of individuals to settle in the parish, particularly if it seemed they were likely to need financial support from the parish rates. Under the Act of Settlement the rate payers were only expected to support people who could prove they were entitled to it. A child's place of settlement at birth was the same as the father's and on marriage a woman took the place of settlement of her husband. Illegitimate children were granted settlement in the place where they were born, which sometimes meant that unmarried pregnant women were encouraged to 'move on'. If a boy or girl became an apprentice, possible from the age of seven, their parish of settlement was the place of the apprenticeship. Settlement could also be gained in other ways, for instance by renting a property for at least £10 a year, but this was beyond the means of any poor person, or by being in continuous employment for at least a year. Many employers, who were of course rate payers, offered jobs for 11 months, or 364 days, to deny the chance of settlement in the parish.

Justices of the Peace examined anyone whose place of settlement was unclear or contested. If it was decided that a Removal Order was needed it was signed by the JPs and required the local overseers to return the person or family to the parish deemed to be their place of settlement. Overseers of that parish were ordered to receive them, find somewhere for them to live and give them support in money or goods.

Poor Houses

In 1774 the parish poor house was in Lower Bockhampton at the northern end of the hamlet on the site of 'Martins' and the cottage 'Bockton'. By the first half of the nineteenth century the poor occupied an old farmhouse on the left-hand side of the lane leading down to Lower Farm. The overseers' accounts show that each year reed was bought to repair the thatch on the poor house and also turf and furze from the heath, which was used for fuel.

In the period from 1774 to 1803 there were usually 10 or 12 people receiving weekly 'pay' from the overseers with occasional extra payments for clothes or bread. Some people received help when it was particularly needed, due to illness or temporary unemployment. Clothing for the poor was regularly made by the village tailor, Henry Coward and his wife Mary who lived opposite the turning down to Lower Farm. Shoes were made by Robert Reason who was the model for Thomas Hardy's Mr Penny in his novel *Under the Greenwood Tree*. He lived in the last cottage at the northern end of Lower Bockhampton beyond the original poor house.

Most poor people were widows left without an income and often with a number of young children to feed. Once these children reached the age of about 12 they were found apprenticeships, the indenture fees being paid by the overseers who also provided the tools for the child's new trade. Poor women were often paid to look after the sick or injured and a daughter might be paid for looking after her elderly mother or father.

The overseers paid the local surgeon, Mr Arden, for treating and caring for the poor and for medicines. In 1785 they paid him £4.6s.9d. for 40 visits to the poor during the year. In 1794 he was paid for inoculating the poor, almost certainly against smallpox.

Stories From the Overseers' Accounts

The Dart Family

In February 1782 the overseers paid James Dart 9s.6d. when he had a bad arm and in December he was paid 12s. as he was sick. If he was close in age to his wife who was born in 1759, James was probably less than 30 years old in 1782. Three years later in January 1785 Mary Dart, James's wife, was paid 6s. for four weeks and in December another entry reads 'Paid Dart two times at 1s.' Similar payments were made in the next two years, most probably at times when James was unable to work. By 1788 the family appear to be totally dependent on parish pay of 2s.6d. a week. On 5 October 1791 James Dart was buried at Stinsford church and in the following month a bill of 2s. was paid for his laying out. His widow was about 32 years old. During December the family were given furze for fuel, two payments of 3s. and one of 6s.

In the following year Mary Dart continued to receive weekly pay and the family were given another load of furze, which cost the overseers 8s. They were paid £5.4s.0d. for gristing that year, which meant working in the fields at harvest time collecting up the spilled grain. On 23 December a bill of £5.10s. was paid for 'dowlais for Darts children', James about six years old and John three. Dowlas was a cloth similar to coarse sheeting often used for shirts. Robert Reason the village shoemaker made shoes for the Dart children and another boy for which he charged 12s.7d. Mary Coward the tailor's wife made them clothes, probably with the dowlas mentioned above.

Mary Dart continued on monthly pay but in September 1797 she received extra sums, her son 'having his thigh broke', although which son is not mentioned. She received more payments for this reason three years later so he must have been badly incapacitated. In 1802 Mary was paid two shillings for two weeks 'her daughters being out of work at the Spinning School'. The parish registers only include one daughter, Rebecca, who was about 12 in 1802. The factory is probably the one set up in 1795 in Fordington, Dorchester, by William Morton Pitt, owner of the Kingston estate, as one of his philanthropic efforts to help the poor.

In 1802 Mary's son James, then aged nine, was apprenticed and the overseers paid 1s.4d. for 'indenchings' – the indenture formally setting up the apprenticeship. Unfortunately in this instance the accounts do not reveal to whom he was apprenticed, where he went, or if he was the boy who broke his thigh. Mary Dart lived on until 1833 when the registers record her burial at Stinsford aged 74 years old.

Eve Trevelyan

Eve is first mentioned in 1784 when the Stinsford overseers reimbursed £2.2s.5d. to the overseers of Caundle Marsh in north Dorset where she must have been living at the time. In that year she had a son George, possibly an illegitimate child. She then returned to live in Stinsford and her rent was paid by the overseers. In 1791 Eve had another illegitimate son she named Job and received weekly 'pay' as well as blankets and sheets which cost £1.0s.3d. Catherine Oliver, who lived in the parish and was also receiving help from the overseers, was paid 1s.6d. for looking after Eve probably when she had her baby. In February 1795 Eve's older son George, aged about 12 years old, was apprenticed to Thomas Standish, a hairdresser, who received £9 from the overseers for taking him. They also bought George two pairs of stockings for 3s.6d., shirts at 6s.5d. and other clothes for £1.4s.9d. Eve continued to receive regular pay and in September 1795 she had an illegitimate daughter she named Honour.

She was still on parish pay from March to May 1796 and was paid to look after the Oliver children whose father had died. In January 1797 David West admitted that Eve's two-year-old daughter Honour was his child and he paid the overseers £5.13s.9d. towards the expenses incurred in supporting her. He may be the David West baptised at Stinsford church in 1772. Meanwhile, Eve continued to care for the Oliver children whilst receiving monthly pay. In April and May 1800 she was given 4s.6d. for breeches for Job aged nine and in September 7s.10d. for a jacket and 4s. to buy him shoes. Two years later the accounts include an entry for the cost of a hat he was given.

Eve continued on monthly pay but in September 1802 she was given an extra 2s. 'being ill in the masels' (measles). The accounts for 26 October read 'Paid Katherine Oliver for looking after late Eve Trevelyan's children.' Her son George was already apprenticed, Job was about 11 and would probably be apprenticed following his mother's death. Honour was aged about seven when she was given a 'duch pick' by the overseers, probably a Dutch hoe, before she went to live with her natural father David West who may have been a gardener – if so, the Dutch hoe would enable Honour to work with him. The parish registers for Stinsford include the marriage of a Hannah Trevelyan on 1 March 1825 to John Vincent of Dorchester. Trevelyan is not a common name in the parish so perhaps this was a happy ending for Honour/Hannah.

It is said that in Thomas Hardy's poem 'Voices From Things Growing in a Churchyard' Eve Greensleeves is Eve Trevelyan and here is his description of her in a short extract:

... I am one Eve Greensleeves, in olden time
Kissed by men from many a clime,
Beneath sun, stars, in blaze, in breeze,
As now by glow worms and by bees...

It is quite likely that he would have heard about Eve from his grandparents and he is known to have looked through the parish registers. Perhaps he read the overseers' account books too!

William Bishop

As late as 1836 people were still being examined to determine their place of settlement if they fell on hard times and needed financial support. William Bishop appeared before Henry Frampton, JP, on 2 July 1836. Unusually Henry Frampton came to Stinsford for the interview as William was ill.

In reply to questions William said that he had heard his father say that he had been born in the parish of Worth Matravers where he was brought up, his father having an estate he rented at £100 a year. He had worked for his father, living at home until he was 24 years old when in 1819 he married Sarah Theobald. From February 1819 he had rented a dairy at Aflington Farm, Corfe Castle, with 35 cows at £9.10s. a cow in the first year and afterwards at £9 a cow. He had stayed at this farm for three years and a quarter, moving from Corfe Castle to Chaldon where he rented another dairy of 45 cows from May 1822. He returned to Corfe after two years to join his father who had moved there. He worked for his father for a year on weekly wages, living in a part of his father's house. From May 1826 until 1830 his next dairy was at Turnerspiddle where he had 24 cows. He then moved to Eastnor near Ringwood but stayed less than a year, returning to work for his father as a labourer until leaving to work at Tincleton. After less

than a year he moved to Stinsford to work for Mr Harding again as a labourer but he became ill and was unable to work to support his wife, daughters Eliza aged nine, Mary Ann aged seven and son John aged four. As a result they had become dependent on the parish and had been given money by the Relieving Officer.

William Bishop must have been really very ill as the parish register records his burial on 28 July 1836, aged 41, less than a month after his examination. No records have been traced to show what happened to his widow Sarah and the children.

An explanation of the reference to renting dairy cows: in Dorset, farmers often had a dairy attached to the farm run by a dairyman who rented the cows, paying the rent from the sale of milk, butter and cheese. The dairyman's wife and daughters usually made the butter and cheese.

After 1836

Once the new Dorchester Union Workhouse opened in 1836 a payment was made by the parish to the workhouse to provide for the poor there rather than in a village poor house. A surprising number of people from the parish ended their days in the workhouse. They were brought to Stinsford for burial and their names and the fact that they had been in the workhouse is recorded in the register: George Churchill, aged 74 in 1865; Jane Keats, aged 64, in 1867; George West, aged 76 in 1874; George Bishop, aged 67, in 1876; Christiana Coward, aged 82 in 1876; William Coward, aged 89, in 1884; William Randall, aged 80, in 1885. Although their marital status is not given in the burial registers, a search of the census returns from 1871 to 1891 reveals that the men and women were most likely to be widows or widowers. Census returns for Stinsford have also been checked for these people when they were younger, which shows that the men had worked for many years, supported growing families as well as they could but found themselves in old age with no means of support. Widows were often in an even worse situation. The workhouse was their fate.

The Parochial Church Council

The PCC held its inaugural meeting in 1921 and the minute books show how its members organised events to raise the money always needed for repairs to the church. Great efforts were also made to raise money for church work overseas, particularly in the countries of the Empire. Representatives attended diocesan meetings in Salisbury. It seems that keeping an up-to-date list of those entitled to be included on the parish electoral roll was always a bit of a challenge!

Church sales and fêtes took place during the summer of most years usually at Mrs Weber's home, Birkin House, but also in the gardens of Stinsford House, home of Henry Higginson and his actress

Left: *The beautiful embroidered banner of Stinsford Mothers' Union which hangs in the church. The last meeting in the parish was held at Kate Wyatt's home in Lower Bockhampton in December 1992. From January 1993 the Stinsford group joined with the Mothers' Union at St George's at Fordington.*

Left: *The declaration made by members of the Mothers' Union, which belonged to Mrs Ethel Dunford of Stinsford, March 1952. The border is made up of names of all the countries in the empire and beyond where the Mothers' Union was active.*

Right: *Members of the Mothers' Union at Knapwater, late 1970s. Left to right, back row: Kate Wyatt, Eric Sandling?, ?, Ruby Dacombe, Frances Saunders, ?, Jean Wakely; seated on chairs: ?, Sheila Sandling, Ethel Dunford, Evelyn 'Dolly' Kellaway, ?, Amelia Farr, ?, ?, ?; seated on grass: John Oliver (Archdeacon of Sherborne), Gillian Greening (Warden from West Stafford) and Clare Carey (Warden at Knapwater).*

The Mothers' Union was very popular. This photograph was taken at Mellstock House, Higher Bockhampton in about 1950. Standing left to right: Mrs Marjorie Pride, Mrs Mabel Parsons, Mrs Beatrice Hyde, Rene or Norah Bowles, Mrs Crabbe, Mrs Gooch, Mrs Atkins from Stinsford, ?, Mrs Elsie Stockley, Mrs Elsie Fost, Miss Jones, Mrs Flora Rimmer, Kathleen Thorne, Mrs Jane Symes, Mrs Amelia Farr. Seated left to right: ?, Mrs Margaret Thorne, Mrs Miller and baby, ?, ?, Mrs Christopher, ?, Mrs Atkins from Lower Bockhampton. Children left to right: Derek Pride or Alan Stockley, Shirley Hill, Marion Farr.

wife Mary Newcomb Higginson. The proceeds helped to keep the church finances on an even keel. It seems that for many years there was a skittles competition held in the week before the church fête organised by George Wakely of Bhomston Farm. In 1972 an alternative to a fête was arranged when Rohan Sturdy who had rescued the Old Manor House, gave a talk at the college about the restoration, followed by supper and wine at the Old Manor House which raised £121 from ticket sales. Some income was used to pay for annual school and Sunday school outings to Weymouth, Swanage, Bournemouth and Weston-super-Mare.

In 1939 at the beginning of the war, council members welcomed the idea that a Christmas gift should be sent to each of the men from the parish who were serving in the Armed Forces. A house-to-

Revd L.J. Medway, vicar from 1950 to 1973, photographed at a church fête during the 1960s. He was to be the last vicar solely working in Stinsford.

house collection was made which raised over £8 and the vicar wrote letters to accompany the small gift of money. He later reported letters of appreciation from most. Closer to home, in 1940, Mrs Higginson donated a stirrup pump and buckets of sand to protect the church should incendiary bombs fall on it. Gifts continued to be sent to servicemen from the parish each Christmas during the war and when peace came the council agreed to collect money again so that a leather wallet could to be given to each man on his return home from war, in appreciation of what they had done.

The work of the Parochial Church Council continues and so do the popular and successful annual fêtes, again held for some years at Birkin House. Improvements to the church continue too with new lighting the very latest addition.

The children are entertained by Punch and Judy at St Michael's Church fête, June 2007.

Stinsford Maps Showing the Changes of 250 years

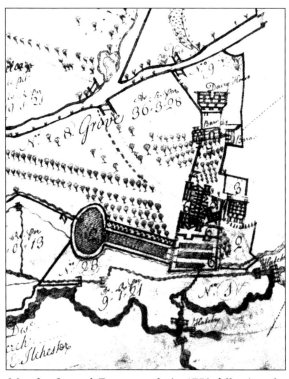

Map by Samuel Donne made in 1759 following the convention of showing buildings as if lying on the ground rather than in plan.

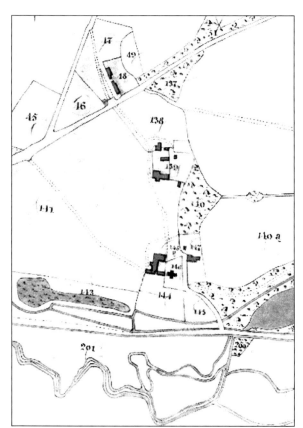

Tithe map, 1839.

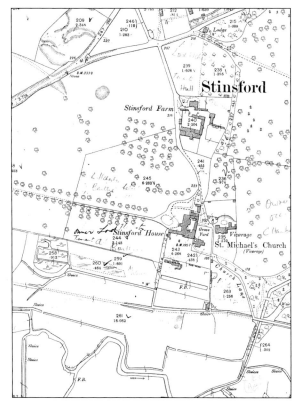

Above: *1902 Ordnance Survey map.*
Right: *Stinsford in 2007.*

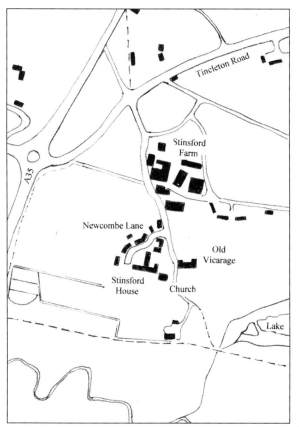

Chapter 4

Stinsford House

Stinsford House was built just to the west of St Michael's Church and Stinsford farmhouse is to the north. The house has a grand entrance portico which faces west, originally approached along the avenue of sycamore trees from the London Road. The Dorchester bypass has now cut off this route. The house has a pale grey stone façade and high ceilings on the ground floor with long sash windows which are very striking particularly when seen from walled garden to the south. At the east end of the house, nearest the church, the windows are gothic in style and were created in the nineteenth century.

The manor of Stinsford is mentioned in the Domesday Book of 1086 and during the twelfth and thirteenth centuries a number of charters identify changes in its owners and occupiers. From 1405 until 1470 the manor was owned by members of the Stafford family and when the Earl of Stafford died the estate became the property of his cousin and co-heiress Eleanor Talboys who had married Thomas Strangways of Melbury House, Dorset. Fragments of the medieval house, probably built by the Stafford family, survive within the present house. It seems that the Strangways family used Stinsford House either as the residence of eldest sons until they inherited and moved to Melbury House near Evershot, or as a home for widows who moved from Melbury to Stinsford when their sons inherited.

An inventory of the property of Sir Giles Strangways, made after his death in 1546/47, includes the contents of Stinsford House. Amongst the rooms mentioned are the hall, buttery, day house, broad chamber with a chamber within it, a chamber over the day house, another over the porch, a napery (for linen), the armoury and kitchen. The furniture of the broad chamber included 'a grete bestede, a cobbered of oke, nineteen joined stowles and a form'. The napery contained 'eight pere of sheets, one playne table cloth, one towel, four napkins and one cubborde'. Try reading the words above phonetically and hear the Dorset dialect! The armoury was well stocked compared to the napery with 86 pairs of 'almayne ryvetes with splyntes and gorgets', suits of armour for as many men, two pairs of harness covered with black velvet, five coverlets for servants, two poll axes, a battle axe and six javelins. Just two years earlier in 1544 Henry VII had invaded France and Henry, the son of Sir Giles Strangways, was killed during the siege of Boulogne. A token dating between 1490 and 1550 was found quite recently in the garden of Stinsford House, a Nuremberg 'ship

penny', made for the French market and known as a 'jetton'. Is it too fanciful to think that one of Henry's retainers returned to Stinsford after the siege and lost the token in the garden?

In the seventeenth century the house was extended to include a high-status chamber, possibly a long gallery with a barrel vaulted ceiling in part of the south-facing wing. Later the medieval hall was demolished leaving the southeast end of the building nearest the church, as a service wing. The house was 'U' shaped in plan at this period.

The Strangways family supported the King during the Civil War and suffered the consequences during the periods of Parliamentary power. Giles and James, sons of Sir John Strangways, were both colonels in the King's Army and fought at Worcester early in the war. In 1642 a garrison of parliamentary men was sent to Stinsford House. Soon after, following some sort of incident, Giles Strangways wrote to the Parliamentary Committee for Dorset to defend himself insisting that he had done nothing against the garrison. He said that there was no significance to his 'opening a door in dead of night'! The authorities were not convinced and shortly after, an order from the Council of War was issued to remove him and his servants from Stinsford House immediately. Later Sir John and Giles Strangways were imprisoned for several years in the White Tower of the Tower of London, having been captured at the fall of Sherborne Castle in 1645. Much of the Strangways land was seized by Parliament and a fine of £10,000 was set for its return. The fine was intended to help pay for the Navy. Sir John's wife successfully petitioned for the return of some land, part of her marriage settlement. During the Civil War wives were entitled to one-fifth of their husbands' estates. Her success was probably due to the support of her kinsman Sir Thomas Trenchard of Wolfeton House near Dorchester and other friends who petitioned on her behalf.

During the Monmouth Rebellion in 1685, Wadham, the son of Giles Strangways, was killed in a skirmish when a group of rebels attacked an inn at Bridport where he was staying. His body was brought to Stinsford and he was buried in his wife's grave at St Michael's. It seems probable that Stinsford House had been their home.

Thomas, the nephew of Wadham Strangways, born in 1682, also lived at Stinsford House. He and his wife Mary extended and improved the house installing the fashionable sash windows on either side of the entrance and along the south front of the house. When he died at Melbury in 1726 aged 42 he left his wife Mary his coach and horses, jewels, plate and the furniture of Stinsford House during her lifetime. It seems to have been his plan for widowed Mary to return to Stinsford, as on his death his sisters Susanna and Elizabeth inherited Melbury and his estates as he and Mary had no children.

Extensive inventories of each of Thomas's houses were made following his death. The contents of just two rooms at Stinsford House show that the house was quite lavishly furnished. The main bed chamber was called the 'yellow callimancoe room' (callimancoe was a brocaded shiny material). It contained a sacking bottom bedstead with yellow callimancoe furniture, presumably upholstered furniture, a feather bolster, one pillow, four blankets, two pairs of callimancoe window curtains and hangings, four chair covers also of callimancoe, a looking glass in a walnut frieze and an oval wainscot table. The great dining-room contained eight hollow-backed jacquard chairs, two stools covered with velvet loose covers, two pairs of blue mantua silk window curtains, a large looking-glass in a filigree frame, a table, three pieces of tapestry hangings and a walnut card table covered with velvet. The total value of the contents of Stinsford House was £338.13s.8d. compared with £982.16s.0d. for Melbury House and £91.10s.0d. for Abbotsbury. These were huge sums of money compared with the inventory of the goods and chattels of Peter Green from Bockhampton who died in 1722. Unfortunately the inventory does not give his occupation. The valuations for his property were his clothes £2, a chest and coffer and pair of old sheets £2, plus two pieces of gold worth £2.6s.0d.

Thomas Strangways's sister Susanna had married Thomas Horner of Mells in Somerset in 1713 and when she became joint heiress of the Strangways family's estates in 1726 she and her husband changed their surname to Strangways Horner. Following her sister's death in 1729 Susanna became sole heiress.

Susanna Strangways Horner was described as a strong-willed woman and her inheritance gave her enormous financial independence from her husband for whom she had little time. Thomas and Susanna had one child, a daughter Elizabeth born in 1723, and Susanna and Elizabeth spent many years travelling on the continent, some of the time with Henry Fox a young man making a Grand Tour of Europe. Susanna may have become his mistress.

On her return to this country she arranged the secret marriage of her daughter to Henry's brother Stephen Fox who had an estate at Redlynch, Somerset, not far from the Strangways Horners' estate at Mells. Elizabeth was only 13 years old when the marriage took place in 1736, and Stephen was about 30. Being completely unaware of his wife's plan, Susanna's husband was understandably furious. As she was so young Elizabeth returned home to live with her feuding parents after the ceremony. Susanna and Elizabeth stayed briefly at Stinsford House around this time, perhaps a place of retreat! When she reached the age of 16 Elizabeth moved to Redlynch to live with her husband who then changed his surname to Fox Strangways. Thomas Hardy knew this Strangways family story and wrote *The First Countess of Wessex* based on the events surrounding Elizabeth's marriage.

After 1736 Stinsford House appears to have been abandoned as a residence. The family did, after all, have the grander Melbury House and Stephen Fox Strangways and Elizabeth had their house at Redlynch as well as a home in Great Burlington Street, London, where their secret marriage had taken place. In 1741 Stephen Fox Strangways was created Lord Ilchester and became Earl of Ilchester in 1756 mainly thanks to the influence of his brother Henry who had been created Lord Holland.

Stephen and Elizabeth's first child, born in 1743, was named Susanna Sarah Louisa, but was usually known as Susan. She was the first of nine children and was the next member of the family to live at Stinsford House. The story of how she came to do so is a colourful one.

In 1759 when she was 16 years old, Lady Susan Fox Strangways was invited to stay at Holland House in London by her uncle Henry, Lord Holland and his wife Caroline. The house was at the centre of whig political life in London at the time. Lady Holland's youngest sister Sarah Lennox, whose mother had died, was being cared for by the Hollands and they felt she was in need of a companion of her own age. When Lady Susan was asked to be Sarah's companion she must have relished the prospect of life in London rather than the quiet life at Redlynch in Somerset. She and Sarah became close friends and confidantes. In the spring of 1760 it was anticipated by her family that Prince George, Prince of Wales and Sarah would marry. In October the Prince became King George III and in July 1761 chose Princess Sophie Charlotte of Mecklenburg-Strelitz as his bride. Sarah, who said she had not loved the King, and Lady Susan were invited to be bridesmaids at the royal wedding and were among the attendants at the coronation which followed soon after.

At Holland House, private theatricals were very popular and Lady Susan, Sarah, Charles James Fox, Lord Holland's son and family friends performed popular plays of the time. William O'Brien, an actor and protégé of David Garrick, was asked to help produce the plays. Lady Susan was attracted to the good looking William O'Brien and his way of life in the theatre which seemed to her to be full of glamour and freedom compared with her own life and prospects. They secretly exchanged letters and found ways to meet also in secret but her parents discovered their affair. Despite this and their absolute disapproval, Lady Susan decided to follow her heart

Portraits of William and Lady Susan O'Brien painted in 1762 and 1764. Having eloped in 1764 and been banished to America for five years the O'Briens moved to Stinsford House in 1774 where they lived for the rest of their lives.

and in April 1764, having reached the age of 21, she and William eloped, marrying at St George's Church, Covent Garden. She must have known her family would be shocked but perhaps because of her privileged life she seems to have completely under-estimated the consequences. Her parents publicly denounced them and as a result they could not be received by anyone in society. The scandal was the subject of much comment. Lady Susan's uncle and aunt, Lord and Lady Holland, were more sympathetic, probably because they too had eloped and married against the wishes of Lady Holland's parents many years before.

William O'Brien was considered to be completely unsuitable as a husband for Lady Susan because he had no fortune, was Irish and an actor and by the values of aristocratic society of the time, fortune, family and status were everything. The situation was only resolved by the O'Briens reluctantly agreeing to be exiled to New York having refused to go to India. They sailed from Falmouth in the autumn of 1764 and lived in New York and later in Quebec, Canada. Before they left for America the plan had been to acquire land there as the King had ordered that 20,000 acres be made available for the Earl of Ilchester (Susan's father) but once William and Lady Susan arrived they discovered that the best land had been taken so the plan was abandoned. Instead her family used their influence to find appointments for William which together with annuities from Lord Holland and her mother provided a small income, certainly small compared to the wealth Lady Susan had previously experienced.

In 1771 the O'Briens returned to England against the wishes of the family. Lady Susan and her mother gradually became close again but she and her father were never really reconciled. In 1774 the house in Wiltshire where they were staying was destroyed by fire and on a visit to Weymouth soon after, the O'Briens called at Stinsford House, which had been inherited by her mother in 1758 as part of the

Strangways estate. Although it was in a poor state of repair they were very attracted to the house and its surroundings and soon it was leased to them by Susan's mother, who agreed to pay for repairs to make it habitable. The O'Briens lived at Stinsford for the rest of their lives and Lady Susan's journal makes is clear that she was very fond of Stinsford House.

In 1800 the O'Briens had to move to London for three years to allow William to take up government work. Lady Susan wrote in her journal in April 1801 that she was homesick. 'Oh Stinsford, Stinsford! When shall I regain happiness, liberty and health. When shall I return to your beloved shades?' Her brother, the second Earl of Ilchester, threatened to pull down Stinsford House if they were not going to return, intending to keep just a small portion of it for the tenant farmer. She responded:

We are so attached to [the house] the happiness of our lives depends so much on our living there, that we cannot give it up without expressing with how much regret it must be.

No doubt the cost of keeping the house repaired was a drain even on the income of an Earl but fortunately he changed his mind and they were able to return after their stay in London. William O'Brien was later appointed Receiver General for Taxes in Dorset thanks to the support of his neighbour William Morton Pitt of Kingston House. The income from this appointment greatly improved their situation. Even so, they had few servants, usually just two upper servants, a man to act as butler and valet, and a woman as housekeeper and personal maid. Two of the servants, Thomas de Borgi and his wife, are remembered on a gravestone in St Michael's churchyard. Andrew Vacher, their gardener for 23 years who died in 1812 is also buried there but has no headstone (these were not common for ordinary working people then).

Lady Susan loved her garden at Stinsford House and in spring she had displays of crocuses. As now, the garden had a terrace below the south frontage but then had two more terraces below. Later in the year there were displays of roses, stocks, carnations and pinks. In 1825 she visited the 'Pink Feast' in Dorchester where many varieties of pink were available but with her small income she often accepted cuttings from relatives and friends rather than buying plants, 'cast offs' she called them. She grew myrtles and orange trees so presumably had a greenhouse. In winter, if the pond at the lowest level of the garden froze, skating was always popular.

Writing in her journal in 1819 she recalled how in their early years at Stinsford she and William would sit in the porch to look west at the beautiful sunsets and plan improvements to the house, its garden and surroundings.

Lady Susan's journal includes notes about their

The west front of Stinsford House during the 1940s, with the grand entrance portico where Lady Susan O'Brien and her husband William sat between 1774 and 1815 to watch the setting sun. In the twentieth century the staff of the house sat on top of the portico to enjoy the sun when they were off duty and their employers were away.

social life, dining with near neighbours the Pitts at Kingston House and the Floyers at the vicarage. Being so close to the turnpike road between Dorchester and London, the house was often full of members of the Fox Strangways family travelling to and from London – a fact about which Susan complained, particularly in later life, as she felt the house was treated like an inn.

King George III was a frequent visitor to Weymouth for sea bathing during the summer months and in 1789 he told Mrs Pitt, of Kingston House, that he had looked out for Lady Susan O'Brien as he had passed by Stinsford House on his way to Weymouth but had looked at the wrong side of the road 'which he was sorry for'.

In 1804 a great ball was held at Stinsford House, by the O'Briens, for the Hanoverian Officers of the King's German Legion. Ten years later the house was the setting for celebrations in July 1814 to mark the abdication of Napoleon. The local farmer gave a supper for the work people while the O'Briens entertained the rest of the inhabitants. As it rained, everyone moved into the servants' hall where between 80 and 90 people enjoyed a good meal of strong beer, beef and pudding!

William O'Brien was unwell for some years and died in 1815 aged 77. The local mason, the first Thomas Hardy of Higher Bockhampton, was asked by Lady Susan to build a vault in the church 'just big enough for ourselves alone'. His grandson, Thomas Hardy the poet and writer kept the page from his grandfather's daybook showing the cost of the vault at £4.10s.0d. In his will William encouraged his wife to sell her investments or belongings if she needed to

raise her income, 'This was and is my first and last and only object.' He also refers to William Morton Pitt, as his dearest and best friend of nearly 40 years. It does seem that the O'Briens' was a happy marriage despite their relatively small income and the family hostility in the early years.

In 1816 a large branch of the plane tree her late husband had planted was torn off during a storm. Susan's journal reads:

... It was O's planting and he loved it much – used sometimes to say, if anything happened to it, he should hate the place. I cannot say that I have too many ties to it, but it grieves me in every way. It quite disfigures the garden, its dear shade, my summer retreat is ruined.

She had some of the wood from the fallen branch made into a table. Despite the damage, it seems the tree must have survived as a magnificent plane tree is a feature of the gardens nearly 200 years later.

Lady Susan recorded another feast in her journal, held to mark the coronation of King George IV in 1821. This time children were treated by Mrs Floyer of the vicarage to 'gooseberry pies, enough for near a hundred, on a long table in her field'. Afterwards there was dancing and singing.

As a widow, Lady Susan stayed on at Stinsford but also spent time elsewhere with her younger relatives and at Melbury. A workman told Thomas Hardy the writer that:

Lady Susan kept a splendid house... A cellar full of home-brewed strong beer that would almost knock you down; everybody drank as much as he liked. The head gardener was drunk every morning before breakfast. There are no such houses now.

Thomas Hardy's father recalled how on Christmas Eve the church choir would visit Stinsford House to sing in the hall at the bottom of the staircase by the terrace door and that Lady Susan would speak to them from the top of the stairs.

Following Lady Susan O'Brien's death in 1827 the house was subject to major repairs and changes. The north wing was demolished leaving it with a slightly lopsided appearance. Thomas Hardy, the builder, undertook much of the work and accounts for just a part of it amount to £533.18s.3d. The house was later occupied by the Revd Edward Murray, vicar of Stinsford and relative of the Earl of Ilchester. He was a firm supporter of the Stinsford church musicians who often practised at Stinsford House. Thomas Hardy senr played the bass viol, his sons Thomas and James and son-in-law James Dart all played violins. In 1836 Jemima Hand was employed by Revd Murray as a cook and as a result met her future husband, the second Thomas Hardy. Their son, the third Thomas, wrote the poem 'A Church Romance' recalling his parents' first sight of each other.

Herbert Williams, a Dorchester banker, lived at Stinsford House after Revd Murray. It must have been during his occupation of the house that the lodge was built on the London Road. When Captain Llewellyn Parry and his family lived at Stinsford a serious fire broke out on 22 September 1892 which was reported in the *Dorset County Chronicle*. The fire started in the late afternoon and once discovered the coachman was sent on horseback to Dorchester and 'in his haste rode a horse with only a halter on'. He was sent from the police station to fetch horses from the Antelope Hotel stables and soon after the fire-engine was speeding along the London Road. The fire had taken a firm hold by 6p.m. with three-quarters of the roof alight. Water was taken from the river with 300 or 400 yards of hose and two relays of men needed to pump enough water. As the fire was mainly on the roof and top floors at this stage servants and helpers were able to remove almost all the furniture. Bedding was thrown down from the top floors to cushion the fall of trunks and boxes.

Amongst those who arrived to help was Thomas Hardy who had been on his way home from Dorchester to Max Gate when he saw the fire. He walked across the water-meadows to help carry out some of the books and furniture and met his sister Mary who had been laying flowers on their fathers' grave in the churchyard next door. At 7p.m. a fire-engine from the Artillery Barracks and soldiers from the Depot Barracks joined the firefighters. The church was thought to be in danger for a while. Between 9p.m. and 10p.m. crowds from Dorchester drifted away, though the firemen continued to pump until dawn when the fire was finally extinguished.

There was more drama in February 1894 when the house was burgled by James Steward who stole a revolver. He had been the Parrys' butler until two weeks before. He was arrested by two policemen who followed him from Dorchester; one of them was PC Alfred Frederick Pride, a distant relation of Derek Pride, who grew up in Lower Bockhampton 50 years later. When James Steward appeared in court he explained what had happened. The day before the burglary he had asked Mr Parry to reimburse his expenses in coming to Stinsford from his previous job but Mr Parry had refused. Having gone to Dorchester and 'got tipsy' he walked to Kingston House with the coachman there and then left again for Dorchester. Passing Stinsford House he saw that a window was open and he told the court he had intended to take some silver but once inside he saw a light in Mr Parry's study and ran away to the front door snatching the gun as he went. He was committed to appear at the June assize but the outcome and his fate do not seem to have been reported.

In 1921 Colonel Woodall moved to Stinsford House because of his love of hunting. The Woodalls kept eight horses so that he and his wife could hunt every day of the season. They had an indoor staff of valet, parlour maid, cook and two housemaids, whilst in the gardens the head gardener, Frederick Marsh, worked with a journeyman gardener and a garden boy, Percy Parker son of the shepherd at Stinsford Farm. Frederick Marsh, his wife, daughter Marian and his mother lived in the gardener's cottage, now much extended and known as Three Bears

Watercolour painting by Henry Moule of the back of the gardener's cottage south of Stinsford House, 15 March 1900. The cottage faces the water-meadows to the south.

Above. *The cottage now very much extended and called Three Bears Cottage. The original part of the cottage is now the central portion.*

Left: *This cottage, seen here in the 1940s, was often the home of the waterman for Stinsford Farm, being situated so close to the water-meadows. During the 1920s and early 1930s it was home to the head gardener at Stinsford House, Frederick Marsh and his family.*

Stinsford House with meticulously kept gardens extending down towards the river path which runs along the bottom of the photo, pictured here in 1931. In the bottom right corner is the cottage used by the head gardeners and waterman at different periods, now called Three Bears Cottage. The church is in the centre with the vicarage, tennis-court and garden on the right. The huge London plane tree in the garden of Stinsford House, which may have been planted by William O'Brien in the eighteenth-century, is in the centre of the photograph.

Cottage. Marian Marsh remembers that on Saturday afternoons everyone from Lower Bockhampton and beyond walked past their cottage to shop in Dorchester and on Sundays many people from Dorchester walked out along the river path.

An aerial photograph, probably taken in 1931 from an aeroplane belonging to Barnard's Flying Circus, shows the house and its meticulously kept gardens. Flying circuses were very popular at the time and during one visit to Stinsford flights from a field north of the present-day bypass roundabout were offered to the public for a few pence. It is said that Alan Cobham's famous Flying Circus also visited the area.

Stinsford House had a second resident with theatrical connections long after William O'Brien's time. The American couple Henry Higginson and Mary Newcomb Higginson arrived from Cattistock in the 1930s. As Mary Newcomb she was a successful actress in America, had been on the stage at The Old Vic in London and in a number of films. Henry Higginson came from a wealthy Boston banking family and was enthusiastic about the English way of life and very keen on hunting. He was a successful writer of books on hunting and fishing. He was appointed Master of Foxhounds to both the Cattistock and South Dorset Hunts at different periods. Eventually he had to give up riding with the hunt but undeterred he followed the hounds in his Jaguar car. When entertaining friends to dinner he had his own way of calling for each course by blowing his hunting horn.

The Higginsons' staff included Madame Charlotte, lady's maid; two footmen, Fred and George Dennis; their sister Hilda was the housekeeper assisted by maids Margaret Gibbs and Beatrice Parratt, who later married Fred Dennis. The housemaids were paid £1 a week, whilst the footmen were paid £1.10s. (£1.50p). Once the Second World War broke out the staff sometimes had to wait a while for their wages as the Higginsons' money came from the family bank in America and could take some time to arrive. As a treat on summer evenings, when the Higginsons were away, the staff sat on top of the entrance portico to enjoy the afternoon sun.

Mary Newcomb retired from the stage in 1937 but during the war she formed the Mary Newcomb Players using a mobile theatre to perform for men and women in the Armed Forces. One of her assistants was Guedreda Graham Jones the daughter of Dr and Mrs Graham Jones of Lower Bockhampton. In January 1942 a performance of *Jealousy* was staged at the Corn Exchange in Dorchester to raise funds for the work of the players with leading roles played by Mary Newcomb and Dennis Price.

By the 1950s there was a staff of 13 at Stinsford House. Miss Shaw was Henry Higginson's secretary, Mary Newcomb had a lady's maid and John Payne was butler and lived in the lodge. There was a chef, and housemaids, as well as a footman/valet and

chauffeur, William Blackaller. Doreen Woodsford was pantry maid and Sylvia Hawkins who later married William Blackaller, was a housemaid. She remembers she had alternate Sundays off and a half day off each week though this didn't start until 3p.m.! The 'living in' staff had rooms on the top floor of the house.

The basement running below the front portico and the rooms on either side of it, was called 'Piccadilly' by the staff, presumably because like Piccadilly it was often a busy place. Beneath the south-facing rooms were the kitchens, staff hall, flower room and cold room. It is said there was a blocked passageway which once linked the house and the church.

Henry Higginson's study and office was to the left of the front portico. Colonel Julian Chamberlain, an American friend, assisted him with his writing and acted as a personal assistant, though they seem to have had heated differences from time to time.

Henry Higginson's father founded and financed the Boston Symphony Orchestra in 1881 and when the Dorchester Music Club was wound up in 1951 due to financial difficulties Henry Higginson followed his father's example, albeit on a different scale, by financing its successor, the Dorset Music Society. As a result the society was able to invite famous international singers and musicians to Dorchester to perform at the Plaza Cinema, which then had 1,000 seats, or at the Corn Exchange. Artists included Elizabeth Schwarzkopf, Gerald Moore, Dame Myra Hess, Peter Peers, Benjamin Britten and Joan Hammond. It was thanks to the financial support from the Higginsons that such very famous names appeared in a small town like Dorchester. Many of them stayed overnight at Stinsford House and the grand piano was regularly transported to Dorchester for performances!

With their connections to the film industry in America the Higginsons' guests and staff were treated to viewings of American films in colour, long before they were on general release and when most people saw them in back and white.

Henry Higginson died in 1958 aged 82 and was buried at Stinsford. Afterwards his widow spent more time in America with her family and in the autumn of 1959 she announced that she was closing the house and moving abroad for a time. When she returned she left Stinsford House to live in Puddletown where she died on Boxing Day 1966. Although originally a catholic she had been confirmed as a member of the Church of England at Stinsford in December 1937 and was buried with her husband in the grave just to the right of the path leading to the church door, below the wall of their old home.

In 1963 Stinsford House became a boarding-school for about 50 secondary school boys with emotional and behavioural problems, most from outside Dorset. The house provided rooms for teaching in small groups, an assembly hall, library and dormitories. George Rigger, the headmaster, was able to

Left: *Henry Higginson of Stinsford House, 1930s.*

Right: *Mrs Mary Newcomb Higginson photographed on the day she was confirmed as a member of the Church of England at Stinsford church 14 December 1937. The Daily Mirror also reported that Mary Newcomb and Mrs Ruxton, Joint Masters of the Cattistock Hunt, both Americans, had set a new hunting fashion that year, wearing smart black peaked hunting caps instead of the bowlers usually worn by women.*

Above: *A meet at Stinsford House, home of the Master of Foxhounds, Henry Higginson and his wife Mary Newcomb, late 1940s.*

Left: *The Higginsons' domestic staff at Stinsford House taking a break in May 1935. Left to right: Beatrice Parratt (kitchen maid), George Dennis (chauffeur), Hilda Dennis (George's sister, housekeeper), Margaret Gibbs (maid), ?, ?, ?.*

Right: *Mary Newcomb, glamorous movie star in the film* The Marriage Bond *in 1932.*

Below: *A January 1942 advertisement for a perform-ance of* Jealousy *performed to raise funds for the work of the Mary Newcomb Players who provided enter-tainment for men and women in the Armed Forces.*

ONE PERFORMANCE ONLY!!!!

CORN EXCHANGE, DORCHESTER

THE

Mary Newcomb Players

WILL PRESENT

'JEALOUSY'

The famous West End Thriller

ON

Thursday, January 1, 1942

at 2.30 p.m. Doors open at 2 p.m.

For the Benefit of their Mobile Theatre for the
Free Entertainment of H.M. Forces.

NUMBERED and RESERVED SEATS, 7s 6d and 5s

RESERVED SEATS (not numbered), 3s 6d.

ADMISSION 2s.

Tickets obtainable from Henry Ling, Ltd. Dorchester,
where the plan of Room may be seen.

Right: *When he left the Army after the Second World War William 'Bill' Blackaller became chauffeur to Henry Higginson and his wife Mary Newcomb at Stinsford House. As a boy he had worked at harvest times for Mr Wyndham Hull at Stinsford Farm who said in 1932 that he was 'a very good chap at cleaning a car'. Here he is with his son Rod, c.1950.*

Above: *The south front of Stinsford House, 1940s, as it had been for many years with the orangery to the left. The principal rooms all had tall sash windows with the lower floor containing kitchens and other service rooms.*

Work being done on the interior of Stinsford House during its conversion into apartments in 1998.

The south front as seen in 2007, without its orangery but with the terraced gardens below. One or two additional dormer windows are the only visible changes.

The modern cottages and houses built in Newcombe Lane, Stinsford, as part of the development of the site in 1998. The lane, seen here in 2007, was named after Mary Newcomb who lived at Stinsford House with her husband Henry Higginson from the 1930s until 1958.

purchase the house, in about 1969. The school held regular sports days and put on theatrical productions at open days. It closed in 1984 because fewer boys could be funded by their local authorities. George Rigger pointed out that a total of 460 boys had attended the school.

Once the school closed Stinsford House only just withstood the following 14 years of neglect and vandalism. Various owners submitted planning applications, including conversion to a hotel, but nothing came of them and the house continued to decay. In 1819 the elderly Lady Susan O'Brien, contemplating the fate of the house after her death had written prophetically in her diary:

... I see all that is neat and handsome destroyed, the grass full of cart ruts, pigs grubbing about the house and shrubbery – everything obliterated but our monument in the church.

Both the house and grounds were eventually purchased by a developer and by 1997 consent was given for the house to be divided into ten dwellings, with a dozen houses built within the grounds. However, this aroused strong feelings both locally and nationally. Once the development was complete the new road off Church Lane needed a name and Newcomb Lane was suggested, though it became Newcombe in the process!

Chapter 5
Birkin House

This country house was built in 1874, on land from the Ilchester estate, for Mr Reginald Thornton who before moving to Dorset had served in the Indian Civil Service. In 1859 he joined the Dorchester banking firm Williams and Company. In 1871 he and his family were living at Frome Whitfield House which belonged to Major General Henning. An intriguing advertisement has been found in the *Dorset County Chronicle* for September 1892 for Stinsford Ceylon Teas and Stinsawella Teas being sold by Alfred G. Tizzard, tea specialists of Weymouth and Dorchester. The grower of the Stinsford Ceylon Teas is shown as H.L. Thornton Esq. Given Reginald Thornton's connections with the administration of India and that his wife was born there, it seems likely that there was a family connection.

Reginald Thornton's son Douglas inherited Birkin House when his father died in August 1895. He was

Above: *The main entrance to Birkin House, built in 1874 for Reginald Thornton, a banker. The house was inherited by his son Douglas and then occupied by his granddaughter Benita following her marriage to Colonel Frank Weber. The house was sold in 1977 following Mrs Weber's death. It has been a hotel and wedding venue for some years and is pictured here in 2007.*

Right: *The west front of the house, 2007, the backdrop for St Michael's Church fête each year.*

Ladies setting off from Birkin House, October 1901. Left to right: *Miss Benita Thornton, a manservant, Mrs Emily Thornton and Mr Douglas Thornton.*

Birkin Cottages built in 1913 to accommodate some of the staff of Birkin House, seen here in the 1950s. The Blackaller family lived in the left-hand cottage and the Foot family in the other.

Right: *Henry Blackaller with his wife Emma and children in 1915. Dorothy was born in 1910, Willie in 1912 and Gladys in 1914. The children attended Bockhampton School. Henry worked for the Webers at Birkin House, and Willie went on to work for Henry Higginson and his wife Mary Newcomb Higginson in the 1940s and 1950s.*

Left: *Mrs Benita Weber (c.1920) married Colonel Frank Weber in 1902 and when he retired from the Army they returned to Dorset, eventually to Birkin House. Following her husband's death in 1936 Mrs Weber continued to live at Birkin House until 1977.*

Brownies enjoying themselves on the lawn in front of Birkin House, 1974.

also a partner of the bank which eventually became a part of Lloyds Bank. He went on to become a JP like his father, served as High Sheriff of Dorset and was one of the first members of Dorset County Council. He died as a result of an accident whilst shooting rabbits in the garden of Birkin House in 1915. The funeral was a quiet one but amongst those attending was Thomas Hardy who had been a frequent and welcome visitor to Birkin House and was particularly popular with the children. Among the staff who attended were Frederick Hold the butler; William Goldring, groom; Ernest Godfrey, chauffeur; Leonard Haynes, head gardener and Edwin Shepard, David and Reginald Hall, gardeners.

Douglas Thornton's daughter Benita lived at Birkin House for many years with her husband Colonel Frank Weber following their return to Dorset probably after he left the Army in 1921. They had a number of servants, amongst them Henry Blackaller, a manservant and chauffeur, who lived at Birkin Cottages with his wife Emma, their son William and daughters Dorothy and Gladys. These cottages were built for the Thorntons in 1913 to accommodate Birkin House staff.

The Webers were both active in public life. Frank Weber raised funds for the new nurses' home at the Dorset County Hospital and he and his wife were both churchwardens at St Michael's in Stinsford for many years. He was involved in raising funds for the Thomas Hardy memorial window, which was installed in 1930. They were both keen followers of the hunt and Benita often rode to pay visits in the parish, always riding side-saddle. She finally gave up riding when she was in her eighties because, she said, her horse was too old! Following her husband's death in 1936 she continued to live at Birkin House.

She worked with the Voluntary Aid Detachments and Red Cross serving as Commandant and was happy to allow the Brownies to hold their summer meetings at her home. Many remember her attending church accompanied by her dog.

Birkin House was the venue for the annual church fête for many years. In the late 1960s Tommy Trinder opened the fête, boosting the funds raised to £500, which went towards the £4,000 needed for the church roof fund at the time. The house has been the venue for successful fêtes in recent years energetically organised by Sue Dodd.

Following Benita Weber's death in 1977 Birkin House was sold a number of times and more recently has been run as a country house hotel and venue for weddings.

In 1974 Mrs Weber kindly loaned the grounds of Birkin House for 'Brownie Revels'. Here she is being presented with a 'Thanks Badge' by the Brownies.

Frome House, previously Frome Whitfield House, was built in 1799. It is pictured here in 1999.

Chapter 6
Frome House, Frome Whitfield

Frome House, previously known as Frome Whitfield House, was built by William Henning in about 1790 having purchased Frome Whitfield from a Francis Browne Esq. He built the new house on the site of three labourers' cottages but to the south of the house is the site of the medieval church of St Nicholas which the historian Hutchins says was decayed before 1549. It had served a hamlet or village which was deserted by 1610 when Frome Whitfield became part of Holy Trinity Church, Dorchester, until 1894 when it was attached to Stinsford parish, with Coker's Frome.

In 1842 the house and its farm were left to a son William Lewis Henning who married Anne Rose Shurlock in 1825. All their children were born in Guildford, Surrey, with the exception of Shurlock Henning the eldest son who was born at Frome Whitfield in 1829. He in turn inherited the house, which was called Froome Mansion at the time of the 1891 census. Lieutenant General Shurlock Henning was 61 years old and had retired from the Army. On the day the census was taken his wife Frances Amelia and daughter Frances Margaret aged 16 were at home with Frances Wilson the General's mother-in-law. Like other grand houses there was a large staff, who lived at the house, a butler, lady's maid, a German governess, footman, cook, housemaid, under housemaid and kitchen maid.

General Henning has been referred to as the most unpopular man in the British Army but he was honoured by being made a Commander of the Bath. To be eligible a man had to have the rank of at least Major and to have been mentioned in despatches. After being made a CB General Henning had a stained-glass window made in 1890 to commemorate the honour and at the same time had the CB crest engraved on all the barns and cattle shed on his 1,000-acre estate.

The General pursued the churchwardens of Holy Trinity Church with considerable vigour when a brass plate was removed from the family pew in the church. He refused to attend the church until it was eventually reinstated.

By 1901 Mrs Frances Henning was a widow, sharing the house with her daughter Ursula and mother Lady Frances Wilson.

A directory for 1907 includes Captain and Mrs Charles Henning at Frome Whitfield and for 1920 Lieutenant Colonel Henning and Mrs Henning. By 1935 Mrs Henning alone is listed.

During the Second World War Frome House entertained troops returning from Dunkirk in 1940 and at the time of writing there are old soldiers who remember having tea in the orangery and playing croquet on the lawns.

The house remained in the Henning family until 1974.

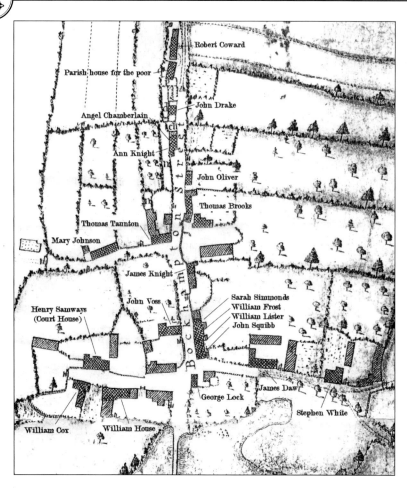

Left: *Part of the 1774 map of the manor of Bockhampton showing the hamlet of Lower Bockhampton with the houses that stood in the paddock of what is now Bockhampton House including the Court House where meetings of the Court Baron were held. The lane from Kingston Maurward on the west of 'Bockhampton Street' was further south than it is now so that the buildings on the corner of this lane and the main street are now the site of the playing-field. In 1847 the school was built on the gardens opposite John Oliver's house. The only buildings which remain from 1774 are Bridge Cottage, parts of the Terrace, the eastern half of Bockhampton House and probably the central wall of the Old Post Office and Greenwood Cottage. Buildings shown without the name of a tenant or occupier were farm buildings.*

Right: *Part of the 1774 map of the manor of Bockhampton showing the hamlet of Bockhampton and some of the many strip fields to the north in Lower and Middle fields.*

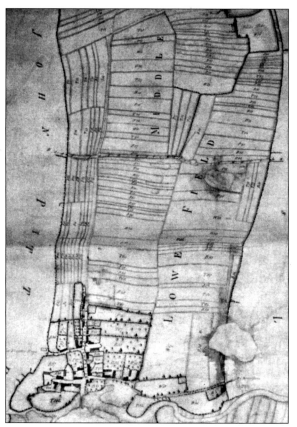

Above: *This cottage was the home of Robert Reason the shoemaker of Lower Bockhampton, painted by Henry Moule, 11 November 1856. Thomas Hardy used the cottage as the model for the home of Mr Penny, the shoemaker, in his novel* Under the Greenwood Tree *published in 1872.*

Chapter 7

The Manor of Bockhampton

The manor of Bockhampton is mentioned in the Domesday Book of 1086 as having 480 acres of land, including 20 acres of meadow, an area of woodland and a mill. Although the river frontage of the manor is small it is difficult to say where the mill might have been located in 1086 as there have been many changes in the course of the river since that time. The manor was held by the Countess of Boulogne in 1086 and later passed to the Priory of Wast or le Vast, near Boulogne in northern France.

The Manor Court

The Court Rolls recorded the decisions made at meetings of the Court Baron, which tenants were expected to attend. Here disputes were settled, tenancies surrendered and new tenants 'admitted'. Each year one tenant was chosen to act as the hayward to oversee haymaking and the harvesting of crops and another was responsible for reporting tenants who broke the customs of the manor, for example by overstocking the common land or allowing property to fall into disrepair. He was called the tythingman.

Medieval period

The earliest surviving Manor Court Rolls are for the years 1376 and 1493-4. In January 1376, during the reign of King Edward III, the Court Roll recorded the absence of a serf, Thomas Bardolf, who had gone away and was ordered to return 'on pain of a fine of 12d., to be paid by his heirs'. John Corn had been catching fish in the lord's warren, which is strange as a warren was usually thought of as a place where rabbits were kept as a source of meat in winter. Robert Gladman had pastured his sheep on the lord's land for nine weeks without permission but no mention is made of any fine or punishment. Elianor Carnes paid a fine of 12d. for her residence in a tenement. Fines were often paid at the beginning of a tenancy, or when a tenancy was transferred. Three months later Thomas Bardolf was still missing and John Veyse had dug a ditch next to the highway 'to the harm of travellers'. He was instructed to put this right or pay a fine of 40d., the highest amount mentioned as a fine.

Some 117 years later in November 1493 during the reign of King Henry VII a list of tenants is included on the Court Roll. This is long before parish registers were kept and gives an opportunity to see who lived in the parish 500 years ago. The tenants were Johanna Cookes, John Poket, Robert Cady, John Snell,

Thomas Tope and John Hogyn. Katherine Piper, John Mason, William Dewland, Thomas Norys, John Hogyn senr, John Cherwyn and William Cremel were all told to repair their tenements. John Hays was Steward to the lord of the manor in charge of the meetings of the court.

The manor of Bockhampton belonged to the Crown after the dissolution of the monasteries and in 1583 Queen Elizabeth granted it to the Dean and Chapter of Exeter Cathedral, which is why documents relating to the manor are amongst the archives there.

1750 to 1848

There are no records for Bockhampton Manor from 1493 until 1750 when the 'Court Book for the Manor of Bockhampton' begins. At Bockhampton the land was still farmed under the old manorial system, a method of farming which had generally disappeared by 1750, although the great fields south of Dorchester were still farmed in this way. The manor was divided into 23 'half places' most tenants having between two and five 'half places'. A half place entitled the tenant to keep one cow, one horse and 21 sheep on the common ground. Arable land was divided into many hundreds of narrow strips, grouped in three great fields, North, Middle and Lower field. Tenants had a varying number of strips in each field, not necessarily next to each other. These fields appear on the map of 1774 rather like a patchwork quilt of strips, each one colour coded to show the name of the tenant. Some tenants such as John Pitt of Kingston, let their land or cottages to under-tenants. There were three tenants with cottages who worked as a tailor, a shoemaker and a blacksmith.

Rules regulating the way the land was farmed in the manor ensured that everyone planted the same crop and harvested it at the same time so that sheep or cattle could graze on all the strips in a particular field at the same time, or the next crop be sown. It was not possible for tenants to farm their land independently; this would have been chaotic. Use of the common land was also regulated, limiting the number of animals tenants could graze there, which sort of animals and the times when they could, or could not be kept there.

The map made in 1774 shows the extent of the manor, occupying a relatively narrow area of 426 acres stretching from the River Frome in the south almost to Waterston Ridge in the north. There were 252 acres of arable land, 6 acres of pasture, 35 acres of meadow, 21 acres in The Moor and 91 acres of heath.

Bockhampton Moor still exists today, south of Bockhampton Bridge, now two fields divided by the road to West Stafford. An eighteenth-century definition of a moor is 'a low marshy meadow by the water-side' which describes it exactly. The field to the east of Bockhampton Moor between the footpath to Bhompston and the River Frome was called The Mead. There is no indication of water-meadows on the map but in 1769 the Manor Court agreed that one person would be employed to take care of them and the moors, indicating that they did exist at this time. The first water-meadows in Dorset appear at Puddletown, not far away, first mentioned in 1629.

There is no reference to a manor house in 1774 probably because the lords of the manor always lived elsewhere. The nearby Elizabethan Manor House, at Kingston Maurward served as the manor house for the manor of Kingston.

The only hamlet in the manor was Bockhampton, with the first cottage at New or Higher Bockhampton not built until 1800. Cottages in Bockhampton were built along the lane running north from the river but a group of cottages, farm buildings and the Court House were grouped on the western side of the road in the paddock between the river and the house now called Bockhampton House. Meetings of the Court Baron were held in the Court House, usually once a year but less frequently after 1800. The main business, as in earlier years, was the transfer of tenancies and the admission of new tenants under the copyhold system. The name 'copyhold' refers to the fact that the tenant received a copy of the entry in the Court Book. By 1750 tenants paid rent in money whereas in earlier times they might have had to work on the lord's land or undertake military duties in exchange for the tenancy. A copyhold tenancy was normally for three lives and a new tenant would name the two others who would succeed him. A man might name his wife and a child, a child and brother or sister, or two children. The advantage of the system for the tenant was that he or she and the family had the security of renting land for a considerable number of years.

In 1774 Thomas Taunton of Charminster was lord of the manor, leased from the Dean and Chapter of Exeter Cathedral. That year John Pitt inherited the Kingston estate from his brother William and was obviously keen to extend his land to include the whole of Bockhampton Manor, particularly as the eastern boundary of his estate was a common one with the western boundary of Bockhampton Manor and he already held 26 acres as a tenant of the manor. After negotiations with Thomas Taunton it was agreed that Fossil Farm at Winfrith and a farm at Askerswell, both owned by John Pitt, would be exchanged for the manor of Bockhampton. A condition of the exchange was that a full survey of the manor should be made, which was undertaken in 1774 by Benjamin Pryce of Dorchester and it is his map and the accompanying schedule with the names of tenants, under-tenants and their holdings that have helped with research of the history of the manor.

In September 1803 the Dean and Chapter leased the manor for 21 years to John Pitt's son, William Morton Pitt but in December that year he purchased the manor outright. From that time Bockhampton Manor was always linked with the Kingston estate. In the years up to his death in 1836 William Morton Pitt gradually retained the land and property of his tenants as it was surrendered and some time between 1800 and 1825 the strip fields disappeared and the land was incorporated into three farms on the estate, which were leased to tenant farmers.

The last Manor Court meeting was held on 4 February 1848 following an Act of Parliament which abolished copyhold tenancies and made Courts Baron and the manorial system irrelevant.

Included below are the stories of two tenants who appear in the Court Book.

Angel Chamberlain 1719–83

Angel Chamberlain was baptised in 1719 at St Michael's Church, Stinsford, the son of another Angel Chamberlain and his wife Rebecca. In January 1750 the younger Angel Chamberlain, a shoemaker, married Ann Symons, a Stinsford girl, when he was about 30. He and Ann had five sons, Richard, Mark, Angel, Isaak, Samuel and a daughter Rebecca. In 1764 disaster struck the family during an outbreak of smallpox in the parish. Angel's wife Ann died and was buried on 2 April, one-year-old Isaak was buried on 10 April and their four-year-old son Angel died three weeks after his mother. In just a few months eight people from Stinsford died of smallpox. It is almost impossible to imagine how anyone might come to terms with such tragedy, particularly as in November 1770 Angel's daughter Rebecca died aged 16. The only child known to survive to adulthood seems to have been Mark and possibly Richard who disappears from the records after his baptism.

Angel regularly attended the meetings of the Court Baron and in October 1777, when he was about 57 years old, he took his son Mark to the meeting of the Court where Mark was nominated to be the next copyholder of the cottage where they lived. In other words Mark would follow his father as tenant with his uncle James Chamberlain named as the third tenant. A fine, or fee, of £2.2s.0d. was paid and the rent was fixed at 6d.

Angel attended the Manor Court for the last time five years before he died in October 1783. The burial register gives the cause of death as 'the bloody flux' which we know as dysentery. Mark would then have become the tenant of their cottage but he survived his father by less than a year. In September 1785 James Chamberlain, Mark's uncle, went to the Manor Court meeting to claim his right to the tenancy of the cottage but an entry in the Court Book shows that the copyhold was cancelled for some reason. No Chamberlain family members are mentioned in the Court Book again but branches of the family did thrive and appear in the census returns for the parish until 1861.

Robert Coward 1741–91

Robert was baptised in August 1741, the son of Robert and Mary (née Travers) who were married in May 1735 at St Michael's Church. A second son, Henry, was baptised in November 1746 and a daughter Celia in August 1750. At a meeting of the Manor Court in May 1758 Robert senr was granted the tenancy of a plot of land in Bockhampton north of the poor house where he built a house. Robert named his sons, Robert and Henry, as future tenants and the rent was fixed at 2s.6d.

In May 1766 young Robert married Mary Voss from Broadmayne and in the same month his grandmother Elizabeth Coward died. In her will dated 11 August 1765 she left her grandsons Robert and Henry £10 each and Henry was also left, '… my bed and all the things that I have except the chest of drares [drawers] and that I give to my granddaughter Sealey Coward [Celia].'

She left Robert and Henry another £10 to repair the house as their father had died in 1763. Her final wish was that 'If any of the money should be left they most all be alouance to it not for won to have all and the rest none.' As Mary could not write, her will was written for her and she made her mark, a cross, at the end of the page.

In October 1777 the old copyhold of 1757 was cancelled and by this time the dwelling built by the deceased Robert senr is referred to as two dwellings. His son Robert, a tailor, became tenant of the north end of the building which was 40 feet long and 16 feet wide with a small garden. Robert named his daughter Elizabeth then aged ten and his brother Henry, aged about 31, as the future tenants. At this same time Henry a gardener took the tenancy of the smaller south dwelling which was 28 feet long and 16 feet wide. Henry named his own son, also Henry, aged ten and his brother Robert aged 37 as future tenants. The brothers Robert and Henry attended many meetings of the Manor Court from this time on.

Robert and Mary Coward's only child Elizabeth was married to Robert Reason, a shoemaker, in February 1786. He must have come to Bockhampton before their marriage, succeeding Angel Chamberlain as the village shoemaker, because he was paid a guinea by the overseers in 1785 for shoes he made for the poor .

In February 1796 Elizabeth and Robert Reason attended the meeting of the Manor Court to surrender her right to the north dwelling under the old copyhold of 1777 taken out by her father and uncle. It was replaced with a new one in the names of Robert Reason aged about 33, Elizabeth aged 'twenty-nine or thereabouts' and Henry Coward, Elizabeth's uncle who still lived next door in the south dwelling. Robert Reason died in December 1819 aged 56 years. He and Elizabeth had no children so that in his will he gave Elizabeth the use of the house and household goods for her life and appointed his friend Benjamin Bowering of Kingston and a brother William Reason of Dorchester, a coach maker, as trustees of £1,000, a great deal of money at the time. Benjamin Bowering was a tenant farmer of some standing which reinforces Robert's position as a relatively wealthy and successful man who could count someone like Benjamin Bowering as a friend. Robert's nephews and nieces, his sister's children, were the main beneficiaries. James, another of Robert's brothers and sister Catherine Reason were left income from investments in Navy stock. Nephew Robert Godden was left the house, shop and garden on Elizabeth's death but when she died in January 1832 the house was not offered for lease but was retained by William Morton Pitt.

In his novel *Under the Greenwood Tree* Thomas Hardy modelled the character of Mr Penny the shoemaker on Robert Reason. Born in 1840, 20 years after Robert Reason's death, Thomas Hardy must have heard about the shoemaker from his grandmother, Mary Hardy who would have known Robert Reason from 1800 when she and her husband first moved to their cottage on the edge of the heath.

Robert Reason's cottage no longer exists; The Mellstock Hut, was built on the site in 1919 but by 1957 it too had been demolished and the house called 'Martins' was soon constructed to replace it.

Lower Bockhampton Maps Showing the Changes of 240 Years

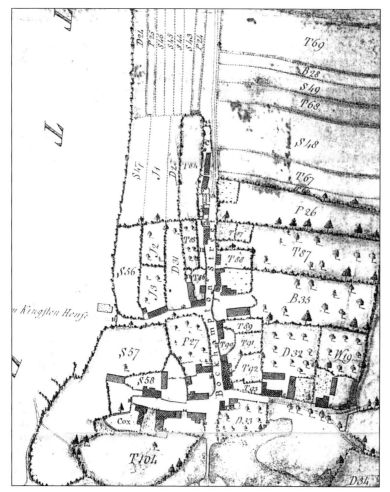

Left: *Part of the 1774 map of the manor of Bockhampton.*

Bottom left: *Ordnance Survey map, 1928.*

Bottom right: *Bockhampton in 2007.*

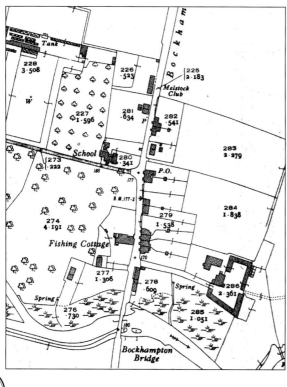

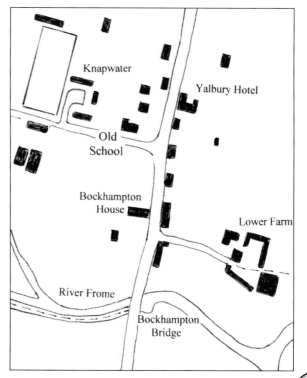

Chapter 8

Lower Bockhampton and House Histories

Two of the cottages which once stood next to the river at Lower Bockhampton painted on 16 February 1897 by Henry Moule. The bridge is just to the right of the cottages.

Lower Bockhampton was the biggest hamlet in the parish for many years though since the recent development at Stinsford the two now have a similar number of inhabitants. The plan of the hamlet has remained much the same since 1774, the date of the earliest map found, with cottages on either side of the lane running north from the river.

A wider view of the group of cottages which stood between the river and the building now called Bockhampton House, 4 December, year not given but probably in the late-nineteenth century. The cottages all appear on a map of 1774. The last cottage went in the 1930s.

The differences between then and now are the absence of the cottages and farm buildings in the paddock below Bockhampton House and the lane which led to them. In a speech made in 1919, Thomas Hardy mentioned his own recollections of this part of Lower Bockhampton.

> ... the village contained several old Elizabethan houses with mullioned windows and door [ways] of Ham Hill stone. They stood by the withy bed. I remember seeing some of them in process of being pulled down, but some were pulled down before I was born. To this attaches a story. Mr Pitt, by whose orders it was done, came to look on and asked one of the men several questions as to why he was doing it in such and such a way. Mr Pitt was notorious for his shabby clothes and the labourer, who did not know him, said at last. 'Look here, old chap, don't you ask so many questions and just go on. Anybody would think the house was yours!' Mr Pitt obeyed orders and meekly went on murmuring, 'Well, 'tis mine after all!'

As William Morton Pitt was owner of the whole estate the buildings were indeed his! It is intriguing to see that some blocks of Ham Hill stone are incorporated into the wall of Bockhampton House facing the lane. The last cottage on the site was still occupied by the Wallis family in the 1930s but it was not long before it crumbled away and fell down.

The last cottage in the paddock of Bockhampton House which was demolished in the 1930s. A group of cottages, farm buildings and the Court House which were on the site by 1774 were gradually demolished during the course of the nineteenth century. Sitting on the railings are two of the Wallis children, probably Archie and Trixie, the last family to live in the cottage.

The last remaining cottage between Bockhampton House and the river, 1920s or 1930s.

Another change is the disappearance of the farm buildings grouped around some of the cottages and the slightly different route of the lane coming into the hamlet from the direction of the Old Manor House. Until the school was built in 1847 this lane crossed the field behind the Construction Department of the college, then the present playing-field, and joined Bockhampton Lane opposite Morello and The Cottage.

Lower Bockhampton was probably chosen as the site for the school and the Post Office because it was the place where most people lived. Incidentally, in the 1840s and 1850s there was a beer shop in the cottage, now Bridge Cottage, the closest the parish has ever come to having a pub!

Memories of Life at Lower Bockhampton

A number of people who have lived in Lower Bockhampton since the First World War have shared their memories of a very different way of life compared to today. Almost everyone was employed by the Hanburys who owned the Kingston estate until 1947 and most of the cottages belonged to them too. They were 'tied cottages' occupied so long as a man worked on the estate. Employees were addressed by their surname only and they were expected to 'doff' or lift their caps to the squire or vicar. All the ladies referred to each other as Mrs, never by first names, however good or longstanding their friendships. Hats were worn much more frequently than now and were always worn to church. Some housewives apparently kept an old hat which was worn for dusting out the porches, known as 'cobweb hats'. Most wore cross-over pinnies for housework and cooking.

Although the rents were low and rates were paid by the Hanburys the condition of the cottages and the facilities are remembered as 'primitive'. Until the 1950s none of the cottages had names as they do today; they were simply known by the surname of the family living in them.

The gravel lane through the village was not surfaced until Eddison's workmen came with steam rollers in the 1930s to lay tarmac. The tar used came in large round galvanised containers, which once empty were soon put to good use by the resourceful men of Lower Bockhampton who hammered the sheets flat to make garden sheds.

Everyone used paraffin lamps and candles at bedtime. What heating there was downstairs came from the kitchen range and a fire in the sitting-room. Bedrooms were not heated, although some had small fireplaces, and were often very cold in winter with ice on the inside of the windows in the early morning. So until 1937, when electricity became available, there were no cables zig-zagging busily across the lane!

In 1947 piped water was laid on, which meant each cottage had just one tap, usually outside the back door. Until then those who lived at the northern end of Lower Bockhampton fetched water from the pump whilst at the southern end it was collected from brick-lined dipping pools, one near the lane to the dairy and another south of Bockhampton House. George Critchell, who lived in one of the cottages that now forms part of Yalbury Cottage hotel and restaurant, preferred to drink the water from the dipping pool which he collected everyday in two buckets carried on a yoke across his shoulders. The water there came from a spring and was always very cool even in summer. The dairy at Lower Bockhampton, the school and Bockhampton House had their own wells.

Two trees that once grew at Lower Bockhampton

Left: *The splendid beech tree often called the 'Greenwood Tree' across the lane from the school, c.1912. In summer children were taught beneath its shady boughs.*

Above: *Estate workers in the process of felling the 'Greenwood Tree' in the playing-field at Lower Bockhampton, 1930s. To the right is The Cottage which at the time was occupied by the Lee family.*

Left: *Mrs Agnes Lee lived in the cottage opposite the 'Greenwood Tree' in Lower Bockhampton, early 1930s. A photographer asked her to sit on the tree to show just how big it was.*

Bockhampton Bridge, c.1904, with Riverside House, now Bockhampton House, in the centre. On the right is the workshop of Stephen Whitaker the shoemaker, with his thatched cottage beyond, now Bridge Cottage. The gate to the ford across the river which no longer exists can be seen behind the children.

The western parapet wall of the bridge was completely removed and scaffolding erected prior to its being rebuilt in as close a match to the original brick as could be found, 1999.

COUNTY COUNCIL OF DORSET.
TAKE NOTICE THAT THIS BRIDGE
(WHICH IS A COUNTY BRIDGE) IS INSUFFICIENT
TO CARRY WEIGHTS BEYOND THE ORDINARY
TRAFFIC OF THE DISTRICT; AND THAT THE
OWNERS AND PERSONS IN CHARGE OF
LOCOMOTIVE TRACTION ENGINES AND OTHER
PONDEROUS CARRIAGES ARE WARNED AGAINST
USING THE BRIDGE FOR THE PASSAGE OF
ANY SUCH ENGINE OR CARRIAGE.
E. ARCHDALL FFOOKS
CLERK OF THE COUNTY COUNCIL OF DORSET

DORSET
ANY PERSON WILFULLY INJURING
ANY PART OF THIS COUNTY BRIDGE
WILL BE GUILTY OF FELONY AND
UPON CONVICTION LIABLE TO BE
TRANSPORTED FOR LIFE
BY THE COURT
7 & 8 GEO 4 C30 S13   T FOOKS

Left and above: The replica notices which were reinstated on the bridge at Lower Bockhampton following the completion of strengthening work, 1999.

The Lee family lived in Lower Bockhampton from before 1914 until about 1936. Here they are standing outside their cottage, c.1925, now called The Cottage. From left: George Lee, visiting relatives Mervyn and Ada Weller, Agnes wife of George and Hilda Lee, daughter-in-law, later Hilda Burnett.

are often mentioned with affection in reminiscences. One was a huge chestnut tree that grew at the north end of the hamlet in the field now occupied by Spring Glen. It was so large that its branches formed a canopy across the lane. The other was a beech tree, often referred to as the Greenwood Tree, which grew in the plot opposite the school. Children who attended the school in the 1930s remember lessons in its shade in summer. It too cast a huge shadow across the lane to the Post Office. Of course, it was called the Greenwood Tree because Thomas Hardy set a large part of his novel *Under the Greenwood Tree* in Lower Mellstock, his name for Lower Bockhampton. When the two main characters Fancy Day, the schoolteacher, and Dick Dewey married there was dancing 'under the greenwood tree' and so many assumed that the tree opposite the school was the one Thomas Hardy had in mind. However, Mrs Jenkins, wife of the head gardener at Kingston Maurward in the 1920s overheard Thomas Hardy's reply when he was asked if the tree in Lower Bockhampton was the Greenwood Tree. He said not and that the tree was in Yellowham Wood near the gamekeeper's cottage, just beyond the parish boundary. The tree in Lower Bockhampton was felled in the 1930s and a replacement was planted in 1935 to mark the silver jubilee of King George V but it did not thrive. Large elm trees once lined the lane north from Lower Bockhampton to the crossroads. Fortunately their replacements, an avenue of small leaf lime trees, are now large enough to give a hint of how the lane will look when they are fully mature.

Bockhampton Bridge

The foundation-stone for the bridge at Bockhampton was laid by Mrs Morton Pitt in July 1823. The idea for a new and wider bridge had been suggested to the authorities by her husband William Morton Pitt who offered to contract for the rebuilding of the bridge at a cost of £300. It was to have brick arches and be wide enough for carriages. He described the old bridge as much decayed and damaged by floodwater, only wide enough for a horse or pedestrian to cross.

It is not certain that Thomas Hardy senr built the new bridge but it does seem a distinct possibility as he was often employed by the estate. A clue that he was the builder may be the inscribed copy of the Book of Common Prayer which was presented by Mrs Morton Pitt to his 11-year-old son, also Thomas Hardy, when the foundation-stone was laid.

The new bridge was built just as William Morton Pitt had described. He and his wife must have found it very much more convenient to be able to use a carriage to visit friends and acquaintances in West Stafford and beyond.

In 1999 the bridge was renovated and strengthened at a cost of £18,000 and following a campaign two signs which had once been attached to the bridge

were replaced with replicas. One threatens transportation to anyone damaging the bridge and the other warns the owners or persons in charge of locomotive traction engines and 'other ponderous carriages' against using the bridge which was 'insufficient to carry weights beyond the ordinary traffic of the district.'

Reminiscences of the 1930s From Hilda Lee (later Burnett)

Hilda Burnett wrote her memories in 1989. In the 1930s she lived in a house now called The Cottage with her husband Ernest's parents George and Agnes Lee. George was employed on the estate as a hedger. Her memories remind us just how completely things have changed:

Away from the main road, no gas, electricity, pub or bus service, it was a haven of peace and tranquillity. It was part of the estate belonging to Sir Cecil Hanbury who, with his wife, kept an eye on the inhabitants.

The 'Hut' is gone, where men from far and near gathered to play billiards and dominoes, mostly on winter evenings. Very little time could be spared in good weather as everyone had a large garden to tend, which made each family self-sufficient. Any surplus was exchanged with neighbours after enough was bottled or made into pickle or wine. The latter was simply made but very potent! Fruits or vegetables were cut up into a large earthenware pan, covered with water and a cloth and left for two or three weeks. Then yeast on a piece of toast was floated on top. After fermenting it was strained and bottled and left to mature. Visitors partaking of this brew departed in an extremely happy frame of mind! I remember one man who rode a large tricycle falling off his machine and remounting with inebriated giggles!

The few cottages were thatched, with stone-flagged floors, a living-room with closed door to the staircase and a pantry with shelves all around housing all the produce laid in for the winter. Milk fetched from the farm stood in a bowl of water on the cold floor. Milk and meat were covered with net weighted down with beads sewn along the edges. My mother-in-law's cottage floor was covered with coconut matting and bright rag rugs made during the winter. There was always plenty to do: oil-lamps to be filled, wicks to be trimmed, lamp glass to be polished and candlesticks to be cleaned for carrying to bed. There was a large cooking range in the room gleaming from vigorous brushing with black lead, the hearth cleaned with whitening and steel fender rubbed with emery paper. A brick was always in the oven during the winter. This, wrapped with paper and a piece of blanket, served as a hot water bottle in the feather bed and kept lovely and warm all night. It was a wrench to rise and break the ice in the water jug before washing!

A few fowls were kept in the garden and when one

was killed for the pot Ma plucked it, rolled the feathers in paper and put them under the stove to dry. When enough had been saved they were made into pillows and cushions. I am still using some after all these years. Surplus eggs were 'put down' (usually put in a bowl with isinglass as a preservative) and used as needed when the laying season was over.

In the summer when the stove was not used, Ma would don an old hat and clear out the flu; a dirty job with soot settling everywhere. Then, to save work and make more time for other jobs, the cooking was done on a small primus stove in the woodhouse. This had to be continually pumped up as the flames died down. Ma worked wonders with it, cooking several vegetables in the same saucepan, each kind tied in muslin and in the afternoon delicious large cakes were cooked in a biscuit tin on top. I remember her posting a Christmas cake made in this fashion to her son in the Royal Navy, who I married the following year.

The woodhouse was a sort of utility room which held everything: fowls, wood, coal and on several wide shelves were the vegetables and fruits which had to be picked over from time to time and potatoes 'chimped' (growing shoots rubbed off) otherwise they grew soft. Very small ones and all peelings were boiled in an old saucepan and mixed with bran for fowls' food. They loved it. Below the small window under the eaves was a mirror where Pa washed and shaved with a cut-throat razor, the strop hanging alongside and the bench containing enamel bowls in which hands were washed and vegetables strained, the water carefully poured into pails for other uses.

Everybody's door was left open until nightfall. Gipsies called with handmade clothes pegs and tinkers with pockets and bags full of gadgets to sell; tin kettles and saucepans hanging around their waists clanking as they walked along. Sometimes they brought rabbits, poached no doubt, which Ma deftly skinned and pulled. Once she had a cat which caught rabbits and brought them to lay at her feet, mewing while they were skinned so that he could have his share. 'Gentlemen of the road' also called asking for hot water to make their tea and were invariably given bread and cheese or homemade cake to go with it. They were polite and never a nuisance.

Mr Crabbe next door used to cut the men's hair with a pair of sheep shears. He also kept bees and would sometimes give us a honey-comb when collecting honey out the hives, which was sheer nectar. Mrs Crabbe made bee wine and I was always fascinated by the 'bees' floating up and down the jar in the window. She kept me guessing for a long time before admitting that it was yeast! The wine tasted something like mead.

... Few trades people called. When time permitted we took the shortcut into town, over the bridge, along the path by the stream and across the meadow, sometimes flooded by the rising River Frome, whereupon we removed shoes and black woollen stockings and waded

Bert Crabbe, a keen beekeeper, ready to collect a swarm of bees from an apple tree, 1940s. He lived in the cottage now called Morello in Lower Bockhampton with his wife Dora and sons Victor and Peter. He never wore any protective clothing when working with bees and was once photographed in a national paper covered in bees but unscathed. Sadly the photograph remains untraced.

Here he is gathering the swarm into a skep.

The river path from Lower Bockhampton to Stinsford and Dorchester. This undated postcard shows a man working in the river cutting weed just to the west of the bridge at Lower Bockhampton. The branch of the river from Kingston Maurward joins the main river to his right and beyond is a bridge from the path to the island called Dog Kennel. The bridge is a bit of a mystery, it doesn't appear on maps and nobody can remember it now.

to the gate at the junction with the main road. Shopping finished and baskets loaded, we fortified ourselves on the return journey with lardy buns, fat oozing down our chins. Money was not always available and Ma told me that once, having no money to pay the butcher, he accepted a silver shilling set in a brooch.

The 'Big House' was only a few minutes away. There the men were allotted their tasks. In the winter two would arm themselves with a two-handed saw and working in harmony saw up tree trunks, while others made faggots and logs for lighting fires. To a small degree I made use of the sawing block in the garden to get through a few logs before going indoors glowing with warmth – well recommended for healthy exercise in cold weather! Not much coal was used as there was plenty of wood to be picked up and dragged in from the fields. During summer Pa usually took a bottle of cold tea and bread and cheese in a cloth if working on the hedges or ditches, bringing home perhaps mushrooms or blackberries and sometimes an eel or two, making a welcome change from a mainly vegetarian diet. He was very good at hedging and won several certificates over the years.

No water was laid on in the village so two large galvanised buckets were filled from the pump up the road, one in each hand. They were very heavy on the return journey and we tried to make do with two trips a day so every drop was precious and used over and over again to wash hands, before being put on the garden to nurture growing plants. The garden could be a great problem in very dry weather the family depending on it for all their vegetables and fruit throughout the year.

Once a week the tin bath hanging under the thatch was brought in, kettles put on the fire and a few inches of water, just enough to sit in, had to suffice for one's ablutions. Our long hair was not washed very often and even then with as little water as possible. One depended on the hair brush to keep it sleek and clean. It was dried by sitting with backs to the fire and constant running through of fingers.

For laundering, extra water was fetched to fill the

high brick copper in the woodhouse, a fire lit beneath, hot water ladled out with a dipper into a laundry bath and Hudson's soap and soda added. Each item was well scrubbed with a stiff brush on a board before boiling, rinsed with clean water, then again in water in which a blue-bag had been squeezed, then starch added. Finally all was put through the mangle, a tall monster with wooden rollers which were turned with a large handle while water cascaded into a bath beneath, frequently also dousing the turner. One had to be careful to fold shirts with buttons inside or they popped all over the place. During the next day or so flat-irons were put on the range and to find out if they were hot enough one spat on the base. Once the laundry was pegged on the line and propped up with a forked sapling, brought from the field beyond the garden, the precious hot soapy water was used in every possible way after the fire was cleaned out and ashes spread over the garden. Benches and floor were scrubbed, also the pantry and the bare boards of the staircase. The final cleaning was that of the 'privy' which was at the bottom of the garden and consisted of a wooden seat with two holes, the smaller one for children. Underneath was bare earth and on a shelf was kept a canister of carbolic powder, for sprinkling over, and a pile of paper and scissors – so as not to waste time. This was used as toilet paper and one sat and cut squares to add to those hanging on the door from a piece of string. People who have never known such a Spartan way of life would hold up their hands in horror, yet I never knew of any illness arising from this crude sanitation. Many times have I gone shivering down there on a cold winter's night, trying to shield a candle which invariable went out (no torches then), and sitting petrified at the furtive scuttle of some nocturnal creature or sudden hoot of an owl much too close.

Every so often the privy was cleaned out, when everybody either went out wood gathering, or shut themselves indoors. Pa would dress in old rags kept for the occasion, dig a trench in the garden, take off the lavatory seat, arm himself with an old saucepan or *suchlike on the end of a long pole and begin. When it was all over he threw fresh sweet earth into the trench so that it covered well and came back to the woodhouse where the copper of hot water was waiting for his bath. As he stripped he pushed each garment into the fire beneath and, after a decent interval, cleansed and purified with hair and moustache slicked into shape, he emerged smelling strongly of carbolic soap.*

All these things are now a distant memory for with the passing of time has come to the village sanitation, water and electricity. It is still a peaceful place, very rural, the only sign of the times being a car or two behind the side hedge, the gateway being widened to facilitate matters. There I used to recline in the sun on the garden seat made specially for me by my kind father-in-law. I also made myself useful there preparing vegetables, cutting up blocks of salt into an earthenware jar (no table salt in those days) or cutting into sizeable chunks very long hard bars of household soap, which was not at all kind to the hands.

The village pump still stands, but as an ornament and everything appears unchanged. I was recently invited into The Cottage. What a transformation. Gone is the old black range and in its place a smart fireplace with raised curb which only needs a wipe over. The corner holds a television set where once stood the gramophone with its trumpet. There is wall-to-wall carpet upstairs and down but the staircase door still stands. The pantry is now a kitchen with all mod cons and, by all that's wonderful, the woodhouse is a luxurious bathroom with flushing toilet. The garden no longer needs to be sown to feed the family all the year round and the privy is a garden shed.

Marjorie Pride first came to teach at the school in 1930 as Miss Coombs and later married Mr Alf Pride. They lived in one of the cottages in the Terrace for many years. Mrs Pride said that although there were no gadgets such as washing machines and fridges everyone enjoyed village life, everyone was so friendly. She recalled Sunday evenings when:

... we walked along the path to Stinsford church. When Revd Gooch was the vicar we acted nativity plays at Christmas time and the church was full of happy people singing carols.

Her booklet *Memories of Bockhampton and Bockhampton School* was the first in the collection of parish history that eventually led to exhibitions and this book.

Bockhampton House

In 1774 this house and garden with a smith's workshop attached was occupied by John Voss, an under-tenant of John Pitt, owner of the Kingston estate. The house was about half its present length. As no earlier maps have been found it is not possible to verify the exact age of the house, which was extended some time between 1839 and 1880.

On the 1839 tithe map schedule it is listed as Kingston Home Farm with a garden and stables occupied by Thomas Lock who later became the tenant of Higher Kingston Farm. In November 1883 James Fellowes let this farm and Higher Kingston Farm to James Symes Hull of Tyneham.

It seems that by 1900 the house was no longer needed as a farmhouse and that year it was let to a Miss Mabel Inglis from Puddletown for a rent of £31.10s. a year and re-named Riverside Cottage. Other members of the Inglis family appear in a photograph with the Hardy family at a picnic on the heath at Higher Bockhampton in 1917.

By 1911 Brigadier General John Balguy had retired to live at Riverside Cottage following a distinguished career in the Royal Artillery. He is always referred to as Col Balguy in reminiscences and even occasionally as Col Bogey! In January 1916 his daughter Dorothy married Philip Egerton of West Stafford at Stinsford church. Children from the 1930s remember Col Balguy's old donkey in the paddock which they passed on their way to school and which a few have confessed to teasing.

Dr John Graham Jones and his wife bought the house in 1934. They involved themselves in many aspects of village life. He was Honorary Secretary to the Parochial Church Council, correspondent for the school managers and an active member of the Kingston Park Tennis Club. Mrs Aileen Graham Jones started the Mellstock branch of the Women's Institute and the Horticultural Society. Bockhampton House was the venue for some of the first Horticultural Society Shows and in 1953 the parish Coronation Day celebrations took place in a marquee in the gardens.

As a young woman Mrs Graham Jones was something of a pioneer which she spoke about on the radio programme 'Woman's Hour' in 1962:

I believe I was the first woman to take up motoring as a career. Social standards were different in 1911 and there was much raising of eyebrows and cold disapproval when I announced my intention to go into a motor works to learn how the wheels went round. Driving lessons followed and in the slow-moving and infrequent traffic driving was far less terrifying than it would be today. I successfully took my RAC certificate; I think I was the first woman to apply for this. After that came the serious question of a job. In those days the Morning Post *was the recognised medium so into that respectable paper, under 'Personal' I put the startling advertisement: 'Lady Chauffeuse, RAC certificate, can do running repairs. What offers?' To my surprise I had three replies. The one that appealed to me most was from Mrs Pankhurst's secretary, a request to drive the great leader of the Militant Suffragette Movement for five months on a campaign through England, Wales and Scotland. Up I went for the interview and at once found myself pledged to drive the famous Mrs Pankhurst and her staff in an enormous car at £1 a week all found.*

In about 1958 the house was bought by Mr Thomas Illingworth on his retirement from the photographic film company Ilford. He was keen on fishing and so renamed the house Fishing Cottage. Mrs Paddy Illingworth was also a great supporter of the Horticultural Society and helped raise money towards the cost of repairing the church roof by selling miniature slates at 2s.6d. each during the fête in 1968. She sold the house in about 1970 which has been occupied by the same family since.

Bridge Cottage

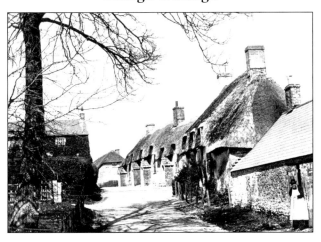

Above: *Stephen Whittaker outside his workshop, c.1890s. Beyond is his cottage and the Terrace of four cottages which had thatched roofs and stone fronts then. To the left is the farmhouse of Lower Kingston Farm and in the background beyond the Terrace is another thatched worker's cottage.*

Below: *The scene in 2007 with Mike Cosgrove standing by the old workshop which is now part of the cottage. Beyond the Terrace now has slate roofs. When the thatch was removed in the 1890s the ceiling height of the bedrooms was raised and Broadmayne brick extensions were added at the back to give each cottage a new kitchen downstairs and bedroom above. Just beyond the Terrace is Morello. The farmhouse on the left, now Bockhampton House, is obscured by the walnut tree planted in 1953 to commemorate the coronation.*

This is one of four buildings in the village today which appear on the earliest map of Bockhampton dated 1774. The building then is described as a house and old smith's shop occupied by G. Lock, though no trace has been found of this man.

In December 1832 the Court Book for the manor of Bockhampton records that James Moors, blacksmith of Bockhampton took the dwelling-house, garden and premises late in the occupation of William Oliver, shepherd, for a rent of 10s. yearly. He held the tenancy for his own life and those of his sons Walter aged 11 and George James aged seven 'or thereabouts'. James Moors was born in the parish in 1795, the son of James and Margaret Moors who also had a daughter Martha Maria. She married William Oliver in 1820, possibly the same William Oliver who occupied the cottage before James Moors.

In 1839 James attended the Manor Court and was granted a licence to let all or part of the cottage to Charles Eldridge of Dorchester, 'common brewer' for 60 years or less. James had a beer shop on the premises at the time of the census of 1851 and 1861 when his occupation was given as blacksmith and beer-shop keeper. A beer shop was different from a pub or inn, as only beer was sold, usually from the licence-holder's home. For those who can remember them, this was probably like buying from the 'jug and bottle' of a pub. Presumably James's job as a blacksmith would have combined well with a beer shop as customers would be able to quench their thirst whilst waiting for horses to be shod! Interestingly the garden

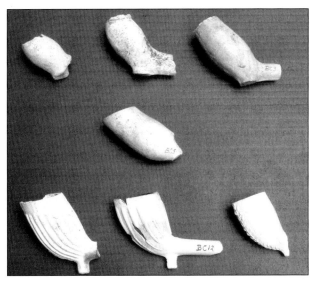

A selection of clay pipe bowls found in the garden of Bridge Cottage, the home of blacksmith and beer-shop keeper James Moors from 1832 until c.1861 when another blacksmith, Thomas Gillett occupied the cottage from c.1871 until 1878. The garden has produced dozens of pipe bowls and pieces of pipe stem suggesting that a pipe and a pint were popular with customers of the forge! Top row left to right: *Very small bowl 1610–40, two larger bowls 1660–80;* middle: *1700–70;* bottom row, left to right: *decorated bowls, one from 1770–1800 and two from 1810–40.*

Above and left: *The roof of Bridge Cottage was exposed when the thatch was removed, 2002. As the pictures show the roof was made of unprepared tree trunks and branches, some of them were surprisingly small and many were reduced to powder within the shell of the bark.*

The Post Office and the adjoining cottage viewed from the gated entrance to the Kingston Maurward estate. In the foreground is the shadow of the Greenwood Tree, 1930s.

The Old Post Office and Greenwood Cottage, 2007. The gates from Kingston Maurward House have gone and a 30 mile an hour sign has replaced the old sign and there is no shadow from the Greenwood Tree.

The boots from 1892 found in the bread oven of the cottage now called Greenwood Cottage in Lower Bockhampton, 2007.

has produced a huge collection of fragments of clay pipe stems and bowls suggesting that customers also enjoyed a smoke. In his novel *Under the Greenwood Tree* set in Lower Bockhampton, which he called Lower Mellstock, Thomas Hardy has the character Enoch say that he 'had a pint o' small down at Morrs's...'.

In 1871 another blacksmith, Thomas Gillett, occupied the cottage and adjoining forge but with no mention of the beer shop. By 1878 the property was let to Stephen Whittaker, a boot- and shoemaker who was born in Somerset though his wife Sarah was born nearby at West Stafford and their children at Fordington and Dorchester. He continued as boot-maker for 35 years and he died in May 1913 aged 72. His wife had predeceased him and so their daughter Emily continued to live in the cottage with two other ladies, Teresa Hardy, cousin of the author who moved to Lower Bockhampton from her family home at Higher Bockhampton, and Jane Plowman who had come to Lower Bockhampton with her mother in the 1850s. She had lived at the Old Manor House for many years before moving in with Emily and Teresa. Emily Whittaker and Teresa Hardy both died early in 1928 and Jane Plowman in 1930 aged 85.

The cottage was included in the sale of the estate to Dorset County Council in 1947. A contract to sell the cottage to the tenant Mr Jones was completed in 1960 but the survey revealed it was 'unfit and requiring structural repairs'. The repairs were estimated as likely to cost £2,300 and the sale fell through. The cottage was purchased in the same year by Mrs Illingworth of Fishing Cottage (Bockhampton House) who renovated it and used it to accommodate her staff. A Dorchester architect then bought the cottage and during that time the old access to the ford across the river, at the side of the bridge, was incorporated into the garden.

The cottage has come to be used as 'Farmer Shiner's' in the biennial December re-enactments by the Hardy Society and The Madding Crowd group of musicians and singers of 'Going the Rounds'. Recent research suggests that Thomas Hardy probably based Farmer Shiner's on a farmhouse that once stood opposite Bridge Cottage in the paddock of Bockhampton House.

Greenwood Cottage

Greenwood Cottage is one of a pair with the Old Post Office. In the centre of the front wall is a carved stone with the name Robert Jacob and the initials AJ and WJ and the date 1565. In 1562 the rectory of Stinsford was leased to Robert Jacob and his sons William and Robert. The wills of Robert and William Jacob made in 1585 and 1595 include bequests of land, silver and money, showing how wealthy they were compared with most of the other inhabitants of the time. It has been suggested that the carved stone may have come from an older building,

possibly on the same site, and incorporated into the wall of these later cottages. The dividing wall between the two cottages has been identified as being older than the rest of the building so the stone may just belong here.

In 1881 at the time of the census the Elsworth family lived here. Charles Elsworth, a groom, his wife Harriett and oldest son John aged seven, were all born at Mappowder but William aged five and three-month-old Catherine, or Kate, were both born here in the parish. Annie aged eight, called Alice in the school records, and Martha aged three were also born in Lower Bockhampton and were included in the census for 1891.

Some interesting finds were made in the bread oven of the cottage when the old inglenook fireplace was opened up in the 1980s, including a collection of well-worn button boots. One pair perhaps belonged to Kate or Annie, a right boot of a slightly larger size might also have belonged to one of them or to their mother and a very tiny right boot probably belonging to Martha. With them was a school exercise book for home lessons belonging to Kate Elsworth, a small leather purse, a small triangular tin and an election handbill from 1892. The suggested ownership of the boots is based on the girls' ages at the census of 1891.

The Trent family lived in this cottage in the 1930s and 1940s. Walter Trent worked as a groom at Kingston Maurward then Stinsford House and is remembered as always being smartly dressed and with a perfect garden. His son Eric was one of the four men from the parish killed during the Second World War when his ship HMS *Holcombe* was torpedoed in December 1943 by a German submarine.

The cottage was purchased by Fred Parsons with Higher and Lower Bockhampton Farms in 1938 and was sold again in 1950 for £250 and since that time it has remained in private ownership.

Knapwater

The first tenants of the eight Knapwater bungalows moved in during December 1972. They all had connections with Stinsford parish, some being retired staff of the Dorset College of Agriculture, while others had lived in the parish for some years. The first tenants were Mr and Mrs Bill Dunford, Mr and Mrs Gerald Stockley, Mr and Mrs Stan Clark, Mr and Mrs J. Jeans, Mr and Mrs Harry Fost, Mrs Amelia Farr who had lived at Stinsford rectory, Mrs G. Taylor, a native of the parish who returned from Mere, and Mr and Mrs Fred Kellaway.

There had been a long campaign for local authority retirement homes in the parish going back to the end of the First World War. Eventually the bungalows were built on land belonging to the College of Agriculture just to the west of the Old School House in Lower Bockhampton. The name Knapwater was chosen because in his novel *Desperate Remedies*

The official ceremony to mark the completion of the Knapwater retirement bungalows on the day the tenants took possession, December 1972. Left to right: Harry Fost, Amelia Farr, Elsie Fost, Mrs Jeanes, Ethel Dunford, Mr Clark, Mr J. Jeanes, Mrs Clark, Bill Dunford, ?, Colonel Payne (Chairman of the Housing Committee), George Wakely (Chairman Stinsford Parish Council), Henry Hayward (Chairman, Dorchester Rural District Council).

Friends of Bill and Ethel Dunford from Knapwater, joining the celebration of their fiftieth wedding anniversary, March 1982. From left: Kate Wyatt, Clare Carey, Evelyn 'Dolly' Kellaway, Elsie Fost, Ethel Dunford, Harry Fost, Bill Dunford, Fred Kellaway.

Miss Alice Bartlett the postmistress, standing outside her cottage, 1960s. The Post Office and small shop was just inside the front door on the left. The letter-box was next to the porch but has since been moved across the road.

The bungalows at Knapwater, Lower Bockhampton, 2007.

Bill Dunford and Ethel Parker on their wedding day, March 1932. Bill worked as dairyman at Stinsford for Joseph Wyndham Hull and then for the Dorset Farm Institute when it took over the farm in 1947.

A 'Bockhampton' postcard presumably sold by Mrs Bartlett at the Post Office, 1920s.

Cyclists visiting the Post Office on the right, c.1911. The lady in the porch may be Mrs Mary Bartlett who ran the Post Office then. Beyond is a pair of thatched cottages usually occupied by the 'drowners' who worked in the water-meadows just south of the hamlet. In the centre is the enormous horse chestnut tree so many people remember and on the left are two brick cottages with slate roofs. The wall of the school and schoolhouse with the railings of the playground are also on the left. Mr Dare the headmaster seems to have a good crop of runner beans in his garden. The lady cyclist on the left is standing near the Bockhampton gates to the Kingston estate. The lane through the village was not surfaced until the 1930s.

Left: *The same view in 2007. The Old Post Office has been a private house since 1970. Standing next to the porch are Kate Webb and Markus Stickelberger, standing in the lane are Pat Cosgrove with the bicycles and Kay Kearsey with grand-daughter Christa. Beyond is Yalbury Cottage hotel and restaurant, once the drowners' cottages. The horse chestnut tree has gone. A cats cradle of cables and telephone wires hang above the lane.*

Thomas Hardy used nearby Kingston Maurward House as the model for the 'big house' but named it Knapwater House.

Two benches were provided for the tenants, one paid for by a collection in the parish and the other was given by Mrs Paddy Illingworth who lived at Fishing Cottage, now Bockhampton House, in memory of her husband.

The Post Office

The Old Post Office and the garden to the north was the site of a cottage with agricultural buildings around it in 1774, Thomas Brooks being the tenant. By 1825 the farm buildings had disappeared and there was a pair of cottages on the site which by 1839 were occupied by farm labourers.

Some 50 years later Mrs Mary Bartlett of Lower Bockhampton helped her neighbours by getting stamps, cottons and various other small items for them when she pushed her pram into Dorchester. By 1894 she had opened a Post Office, using the larder in her cottage as a tiny shop. Her husband worked as a farm labourer on the Kingston estate and the additional income must have helped support their family of four sons and a daughter, Alice.

In 1896 the Post Office cottage and the adjoining

one were extended at the back with a room downstairs and bedroom above. The building work was carried out by Henry Hardy (Thomas's brother) of Higher Bockhampton and included plastering the shop, letting in a new stone step next to the front door and giving the new bedroom three coats of plaster and whitewashing throughout. The cottage probably got its cast iron windows at this time and is the only cottage which still has a complete set.

When Mrs Bartlett retired her daughter Alice took over. Many people remember Miss Bartlett as she ran the Post Office for more than 30 years until it closed in 1970. She was quite a character who loved to chat with all her customers getting hopelessly behind with her cooking and housework so that customers were often greeted with the words 'oh dear, oh dear, oh dear' when she appeared from behind the curtain which hung between the shop and her kitchen at the back of the cottage.

John Herring of Dorchester recalled many visits to Miss Bartlett in the 1930s with his parents and brother Stephen.

The village Post Office was quite unusual. The entrance had a porch just like the other cottages in the village except that by the wall was a post box. Inside, the passage had a stone-flagged floor with a plaster-clad wall on one side and a wooden partition on the other. When open the postmistress would slide back the hatch to reveal a rosy round-faced lady by the name of Miss Bartlett. She was surrounded by post equipment, scales, date stamps and you could also purchase sherbert dabs, Corona soft drinks, sweets and there were also shelves lined with a large variety of groceries.

In those days it was scene of much activity. A herdsman would pop in on his way to fetch the cows (which would soon amble by to be milked). The game keeper slipped in for some stamps and the estate carpenter had to pick up some groceries for his wife. Soon the village children would come skipping in just out of school with the request for sherbert dabs and two bull's eyes for a penny. The schoolmistress might pop in for a stamp and post a letter.

There was often a panic, because the time had flown by and the postman would soon arrive to collect forms, parcels and other official papers to be stamped with the official stamp. There would be the slamming of the van doors and a rattle of keys as the post box was opened, followed by the cheery greeting of the postman. Parcels were put in mail bags and, with an exchange of documents and official mail, he would be off with the clank of the security bar on the back of the old-style post van.

My brother Stephen, Mum, Dad and I always found plenty of jobs to do. We would go up to the village pump, a meeting-place for all ages, an opportunity to get to know the village people and exchange news while waiting your turn to pump up water. Then back to the scullery to fill the salt glazed urn with water and replace the wooden lid. This room had an aroma of paraffin as the cooking was accomplished on an oil stove when the range was not in use.

The next job was with the milk can down to the other end of the village and up the track to the farmyard and into the dairy, all spotlessly scrubbed out. It was pleasant to hear the rattle of churns and the milk cooler in action and smell the sweet milk.

Father, meanwhile, had found a spade by the outhouse and gone down the garden to dig a hole and empty the bucket from the privy.

These jobs being done and the Post Office and shop closed, we would sit down to a real village tea, and if it was winter, the oil-lamp would be lit and the family gathered round the range in the dining-room for a chat before wandering back home up through the village by way of Dark Hill and Light Hill. It was here my father introduced us boys to the plough and other celestial bodies; on some occasions the sky seemed full of shooting stars.

It was a real treat to be invited out to stay with Miss Bartlett in the village with its strange sounds for a town boy. The cock crowing, the owls hooting at night and the cows lowing as they went off to be milked early in the morning with the drover encouraging them on. You went to bed with a candle up the small twisting stairs to a room under a thatched roof where the swallows nested, and into a feather bed. The mattress had to be shaken up every morning so that you sank into it at night – a pleasant experience not to be forgotten.

So much about village life, what about the postmistress? She was born in the village where her parents kept the Post Office and store. Thomas Hardy was a customer. She left the village in her youth and worked for the large department store in Bournemouth called Beales. She returned when her parents were elderly, to run the family business. We knew her because of our church connections. We affectionately called her Auntie Baa Baa.

One little memory of her will always stick in my mind. For years she would ride her bicycle into town along the footpath past Stinsford church path. During the war years the American soldiers put in water to Kingston Maurward House and the pipe crossed the footpath. One dark night and the black out lights evident, our dear lady did not see the hole in the path and she and her bicycle ended up getting a ducking in the stream by the path. She would have been quite elderly by then, but she did not make a fuss.

In 1851, long before Mrs Bartlett opened her Post Office, the village had a post woman and letter carrier called Mrs Sarah Critchell who was a widow with two grown-up sons working as farm labourers and two daughters at school. A decade later Mrs Christiana Coward was the 'Post Office Keeper' when the 1861 census was taken. She was born in the village in about 1794 and married Robert Coward, a gardener, in 1814. Their son Frederick was a sailor. Thomas Hardy, who would have known the Coward family well, wrote a charming poem about Christiana called 'Geographical Knowledge – A memory of Christiana C--'. He was intrigued that she knew so much more about the different countries in the world from the map on the wall of her cottage than she did about the local area. The final two verses are:

My son's a sailor, and he knows
All seas and many lands,
And when he's home he points and shows
Each country where it stands.

The Old Post Office in early summer 1977 with Margaret Webb who bought the cottage standing outside with the clematis in full bloom.

He's now just there – by Gib's high rock –
And when he gets, you see,
To Portsmouth here, behind the clock,
Then he'll come back to me!

Christiana was widowed in January 1875 and died at the Dorchester Union Workhouse the following year aged 82. It seems sad that she was not able to stay in Lower Bockhampton but like so many widows of those times without pensions she would have been in difficulty. Presumably her son Frederick was away in the Navy and unable to help.

Almost a century later in 1970 the Post Office closed following Miss Bartlett's death and by then Lower Bockhampton had changed. The school which had provided customers for sweets had closed in 1961, most people had their own transport and were able to shop in Dorchester. The Post Office authorities were unable to find anyone willing to take over the business. The cottage had been sold to Fred Parsons in 1939 was sold again in 1950 for £300 with Miss Bartlett remaining as tenant. In 1970 the cottage was purchased as a private residence which it remains today.

The Terrace

The Terrace appears on the 1774 map of Bockhampton Manor but at that time it extended further south to include a cottage immediately next to the lane to the farm that is now a garden. The four cottages were occupied by John Squibb, William Lister, William Frost and Sarah Simmonds. The cottage now called Hillcrest was then the site of an agricultural building. The cottages were usually occupied by estate farm workers or gardeners.

Recent discoveries made when replacing broken flagstones in the two centre cottages included a series of three floors and evidence of a wattle and daub partition below the flagstones of one cottage with pottery fragments dated to the middle of the fifteenth century. In the other cottage more pottery was found including the broken neck and shoulders of a jug, which has been reconstructed, dated to about 1450. It is a pity we shall never know which of the tenants broke and then threw away the jug!

Left: *A reconstructed Verwood pottery jug, probably nineteenth century, found in pieces beneath the garden path of a cottage in the Terrace.*

Below: *May Christopher with grandparents Sarah and Charles Christopher who lived in the Terrace, Lower Bockhampton, c.1914.*

The Atkins family in the garden of their Terrace cottage, c.1937. Left to right: Cyril, Reg, father Charles Atkins, mother Ada, Maurice and George. Charles was a gardener for the Hanburys. When he and Ada first moved to Bockhampton they lived for a while at Pump Cottage where Cyril and George were born, before moving to a 'cottage' in the Elizabethan Manor House and then to the Terrace.

The Terrace at Lower Bockhampton with the 'sentry box' porches, 2007.

By 1839 there were no changes in the plan of the cottages but on the 1886 ordnance survey map the southern cottage had gone and a northern cottage had replaced the agricultural building. The cottages were thatched, the walls of stone, not rendered and with sentry box porches. The cottages were just one room deep, probably with a cat slide roof making a covered area at the back. By 1904 the thatch on the cottages had been replaced with slate and the roof raised to give the upper rooms higher ceilings. At the same time extensions of Broadmayne brick were added to the rear of each cottage providing an additional room downstairs and a third bedroom above. It is almost certain that the work was undertaken by Henry Hardy of Higher Bockhampton who did most of the building work on the estate.

In 1938 the northern cottage was sold by Lady Hanbury to Mr Fred Parsons with Higher and Lower Bockhampton farms and from then it was occupied by his farm labourers including the drowner or waterman who worked the water-meadows. Drowners spent nine months of each year working in the water-meadows, maintaining the ditches and hatches. The name 'drowner' comes from the flooding, or drowning, of the meadows from Christmas each year to encourage the growth of grass in the early spring for sheep and then dairy cows before haymaking. Until about 1960 there were many acres of actively worked water-meadows in the river valley from Frome Whitfield in the west to Bhompston Farm in the east.

When Kingston Maurward estate was sold in 1947 the remaining three cottages became the property of Dorset County Council but during the 1950s and 1960s two were sold to tenants and one to Mrs Illingworth of Fishing Cottage (Bockhampton House) as a cottage for her gardener. The northernmost

cottage belonging Mr Parsons was sold in 1966. All four cottages are now private houses.

Yalbury Cottage

On the Kingston estate map dated between 1800 and 1825 an unidentified building is shown on the same site as the hotel. On the estate map of 1825 two buildings on the site are shown as cottages and on the tithe map of 1839 they are described as 'two cottages and gardens'. Unfortunately the tenants' names are not included on the schedule to the tithe map but they would have been farm workers employed by the tenant farmer Theophilus Pope. There is a gap in the records until 1906 when a schedule was drawn up for the sale of the estate by Herbert Benyon to Major Kenneth Balfour. The tenants then were Christopher Corbin, a waterman, born at Maiden Newton and Joseph Trent, a farm labourer born at Winfrith and both worked for James Hull of Higher Kingston Farm who also had the dairy at Lower Bockhampton.

In the 1940s and 1950s the cottages were still occupied by drowners. George Critchell lived in the northern cottage and Charlie Matthews in the southern, remembered for his very successful mole catching. He stretched the moleskins out to dry on the door of the cottage fuel house and they were eventually sold. It was George Critchell who always walked, with a yoke and two buckets, to fetch his water from the dipping pool on the way to the dairy as he much preferred it to the water from the village pump nearer his home.

In 1967 the cottages were sold by Mr Fred Parsons to a Mrs Lamb of Bere Regis who opened tearooms for visiting tourists and Hardy enthusiasts. Various additions have been made since then to create the present hotel and restaurant.

Left: Mrs Flora Rimmer with her father-in-law Thomas Rimmer, 1950s. Behind them is the northern cottage of the pair which were later sold and converted to tearooms in 1967. It later became Yalbury Cottage hotel and restaurant.

Yalbury Cottage with a snow drift to ceiling height, 1978.

Betty Payne outside her home, the southern half of the pair of cottages which now make up Yalbury Cottage hotel and restaurant, c.1951. The motorbike belonged to her future husband Denis Jenkins who was the first herdsman at the Dorset Farm Institute and whose grandfather had been head gardener to the Hanburys at Kingston Maurward between 1919 and 1929.

Left: *On the left The Cottage and on the right Morello at Lower Bockhampton during the winter of 1978. The 'catslide' roof was a feature of many cottages before two-storey extensions were built at the back. This pair of cottages was built on a plot which Thomas Hardy, builder of Higher Bockhampton and grandfather of the writer, leased by copyhold in 1822. He was intending to build a cottage there but it seems that his plan was abandoned as on the 1839 tithe map there is no cottage on the site and he had died in 1837.*

Right: *The Cottage and Morello now with an extension to the side and back, 2007.*

A group of people from Lower Bockhampton outside the Crabbe family's cottage (now called Morello), c.1940. Left to right: Vic Crabbe, Reg Atkins, Sam Bridle, Tom Rimmer, Eric Trent, Bert Crabbe, Mr James, Lorna and Peggy James.

Above: *This bungalow, Sunnyholme, in Lower Bockhampton was built by the Hanburys after the First World War, originally as two semi-detached homes for estate workers. It was later converted to a single dwelling and was home to Fred Kellaway and his wife Dolly and then the Pinnow family. It was sold by the College and is now a private residence, photographed here in 1998.*

Below: *Diana Rimmer's christening, 1953, with members of the Rimmer family standing under the horse chestnut tree which grew opposite Pump Cottage until c.1970. The granite pillars are the gateway into a field which always had a hayrick inside the gate which is just visible.* Included in the photograph are: *Tom and Maureen Rimmer and baby Diana, Thomas Rimmer, Bill and Flora Rimmer and daughter Jane, as well as Bill, Kate, Joan and Steve Steadman. Margaret Thorne and her daughters Shirley and Carol from Park Cottage, Kingston Maurward and Mrs Elsie Fost from Stinsford are also present.*

Above: *Pump Cottage and Bockton, photographed in 2007. This pair of cottages on the west of the lane through Lower Bockhampton date from about the middle of the nineteenth century. In 1906 Pump Cottage was occupied by the Tizzards and Bockton by the Applins. The Stockley family lived in Pump Cottage in the 1940s. Gerald Stockley worked in the gardens of Kingston Maurward for most of his life, eventually becoming head gardener. He was a keen cricketer who later umpired local matches. Acting as Master of Ceremonies at whist drives and social events was his other forte. The Rimmer family have lived in Pump Cottage and now Rimstead, built behind the cottage.*

Chapter 9

Stinsford and Bockhampton School

The school, c.1920s. It was built in 1847 with the teacher's accommodation on the right. Also on the right is the enormous beech tree which was often called the Greenwood Tree. In the novel Under the Greenwood Tree *by Thomas Hardy the teacher Fancy Day marries Dick Dewey and on their wedding day dancing took place under the tree, which people assumed was next to the school. In fact it seems almost certain that Thomas Hardy had in mind a large beech tree in Yellowham Wood near Keeper's Cottage where, in the novel, Fancy's father Geoffrey lived.*

Opening of the School

Until the school at Lower Bockhampton opened there had been two 'Dame' schools in the parish, so called because they were often run by elderly ladies who charged a few pence a week to teach the children to read and write at a fairly basic level.

The idea of a school for Stinsford seems to have come from the Revd Arthur Shirley, the vicar and Mrs Julia Martin whose husband had purchased the Kingston estate in 1845. The opening of a school at West Stafford in 1846 may also have had something to do with it but there was also a campaign to improve the education of children, particularly in rural areas. In 1847 Revd Shirley wrote to the National Society for Promoting the Education of the Poor in the Teachings of the Established Church so that the school would become part of the National School movement linking it to the Church of England. Revd Shirley, the Martins and the church-wardens were the founding trustees.

The school was built during 1847 on a quarter of an acre of land in Lower Bockhampton, given by the

Martins, which had been the gardens of two cottages occupied by William Dart and Widow Oliver. The building was to accommodate 90 boys and girls in the main schoolroom with a smaller classroom, wash-house, privies and a residence for the school-master. The building costs of £480 were met by grants, contributions from the Earl of Ilchester, the vicar and the parishioners and the deficit of £250 was met by Mr Martin.

The school was converted into a house in 1961 with first floor accommodation added above the old schoolroom. The school bell still hangs in the porch, seen here in 2007.

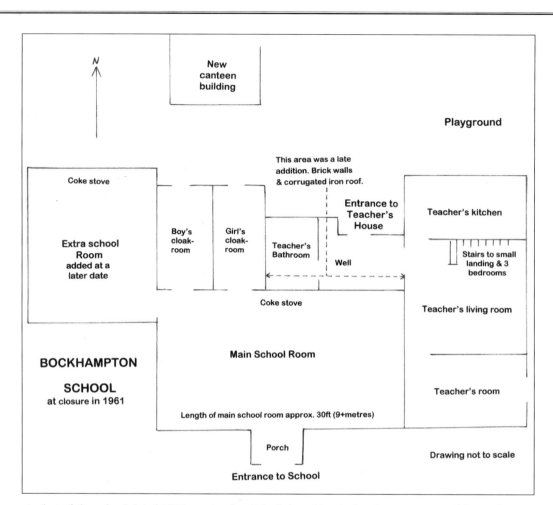

BOCKHAMPTON
SCHOOL
at closure in 1961

New canteen building

Playground

Coke stove

This area was a late addition. Brick walls & corrugated iron roof.

Entrance to Teacher's House

Teacher's kitchen

Extra school Room added at a later date

Boy's cloakroom

Girl's cloakroom

Teacher's Bathroom

Well

Stairs to small landing & 3 bedrooms

Coke stove

Teacher's living room

Main School Room

Teacher's room

Length of main school room approx. 30ft (9+metres)

Drawing not to scale

Porch

Entrance to School

A plan of the school dated 1961, made after it had closed but before it was converted into a house.

Below: *The River Frome in flood, 1999. The road south from Lower Bockhampton to West Stafford has often flooded during wet winters.*

Above: *A view of the school from the north, showing the teacher's house and back of the schoolroom, with the playground in front of the school. Cabbages grow where the bungalow called Copplestones now stands and the Greenwood Tree is still standing so this picture must date from before 1932.*

Notes from the files of the National Society for Promoting the Education of the Poor in the Teachings of the Established Church indicate that the building was 'completed and in operation' by November 1847, which seems to imply that children were attending the school by that time although 1848 is the year most often quoted for its opening. Thomas Hardy is always said to have been one of the first pupils. The series of school log-books kept by headmasters and headmistresses to record the children's progress, visits to the school, the school curriculum, sickness in the school and punishments begin in 1862, long after Thomas Hardy was a pupil.

In these early years schoolchildren paid 2d. a week (less than one pence in modern money) towards the running costs of the school and were often sent home for their 'pence' if they forgot to bring the money. A penny does not seem a large sum but wages for an agricultural labourer in Dorset were very low at this time at about 7s.6d. a week (37p). Parents had to pay for their children to attend the school until 1890.

The school-leaving age was set at 11 years in 1893, 12 years in 1899, 14 years in 1902 and from 1944 children were expected to stay at school until they reached the age of 15.

Teaching at Stinsford and Bockhampton School

It seems that running the school must have been hard and frustrating, particularly in the early years. The schoolmistress in the 1860s seems to have been on duty continuously during the school term. She lived in the schoolhouse, literally part of the school building, taught from Monday to Friday and on Sunday took the children to Sunday Service and Sunday school. During term time the children were also taken to all the church festivals and special services on many saints days. The school was regularly visited by the vicar and by ladies from Stinsford House and Kingston House who often took their daughters, friends and guests to see the children, hear them read and examine the girls' needlework. There were also annual visits from school inspectors to assess the success or otherwise of the teachers' efforts. Funding was dependent on the success of the children in annual examinations in reading, writing, arithmetic and satisfactory attendance. This put the headmaster or headmistress under great pressure particularly when the population of children in the school was always in a state of flux.

The head teacher and the infants' teacher were usually helped by a monitor chosen from the best of the oldest children. Until the 1920s being a monitor was often the first step towards becoming a pupil-teacher and eventually a teacher. However, the log-book is full of complaints from the head teachers about monitors who were lazy, late or 'slack' in keeping order.

Comings and Goings of Pupils

Perhaps the most difficult obstacle to improving the education of the children was the practice of employing agricultural labourers for one year only from Lady Day on 25 March, a practice which continued until the early years of the twentieth century. Almost every year, in April, the school log-book refers to the very many children who left to be replaced by as many new children.

April 1862: Commenced school again. Found fifteen children had left the place almost all these comprising Standard I. Part of the labour of the winter thrown away. Eight new children entered, only two know the alphabet and not one can write at all.
April 1872: Annual migration of farm labourers this year has greatly reduced the attendance this week. Fifteen children removed from the register having left the parish or completed their learning at Standard V. Admitted eleven children on Monday, found some most backward in their school work.

Sickness and Absence

The log-books show how frequently children were ill, particularly in the winter months. Whooping cough was common and spread very quickly amongst the children, as did mumps and measles. Scarlet fever was particularly dangerous and two schoolchildren, Thomas and Job Osmond, died after contracting scarlet fever in 1864.

In the 1920s whooping cough was still common, influenza struck in 1924 and mumps too. As late as 1958 whooping cough kept half the children away from school for weeks at a time.

There were regular visits from the school dentist who used the headmistress's sitting-room when filling children's teeth! In 1953 there were only 22 children on the school roll but even so the dentist spent three days at the school and on the final day a doctor attended in the morning for 'the gas'. The log-book states that one boy ran away – lots of us will remember how he felt!

As the school served a large rural area children were often absent in winter because the lanes from the more distant parts such as Higher Kingston, Higher Bockhampton or Bhompston were so muddy. Children from Higher Bockhampton were sometimes brought to school in a pony and trap in the 1930s and Farmer Snow brought children from Higher Kingston to school in a sort of covered milk float. In the 1950s the road between West Stafford and the school frequently flooded just below Bockhampton Bridge and children had to be taken home via Tincleton and Woodsford or Dorchester on a number of days.

Head teachers often found it an uphill struggle to deal with the frequent absence for all sorts of other reasons too. In the early years parents often kept children at home to look after younger brothers and sisters, probably with good reason considering the large number of children in some families. In May 1864 and again in May 1867 the log-book records some children being kept at home 'bee minding or attending to babies'. Beekeeping was very common and presumably the children were watching for any swarms that might need collecting particularly in early summer. There is a country saying, 'A swarm of bees in May is worth a load of hay, a swarm of bees in June is worth a silver spoon, a swarm of bees in July isn't worth a fly' because they would have no time to make honey before the end of summer.

Children were also absent when special events took place in Dorchester, such as the wild bear show in 1867. There was an annual Dorchester Fair and Candlemas Fair was celebrated in February each year. A Freemason's Procession in Dorchester also left the schoolrooms rather empty.

In the early years the Harvest Holiday was literally taken for harvesting so that the children finished school in the third week of August returning a month later. If the harvest was late the holiday was also postponed.

The headmistress singled out dairymen's children for a special mention in 1872:

Dairymen's children generally attending this school are more irregular than any of the others and give more trouble and as a rule are the most difficult to teach.

The explanation may be that the children were needed to help at home; girls with the dairy work, milking, cheese- and butter-making and the boys bringing in the cows for milking and returning them to the meadows. The dairies at Bhompston and Stinsford were also quite a distance from the school though the dairyman's children at Lower Bockhampton can have had no excuse!

Parents' Attitudes to School

The log-books record some comments on parents' attitudes to school. On the whole parents living in Stinsford seem to have taken the side of their children rather than the teacher. An entry for 1864 notes, 'Could do very well in Stinsford School if the parents were compelled to send their children regularly…'.

In 1866 Miss Reynolds, the head teacher, wrote:

Parents interfering, keeping their children away, or leading their children on to be impertinent, is quite a common occurrence in Bockhampton when any punishment of any kind is inflicted. If parents would only leave the school affairs alone as regards the punishment of the children it would be much better for themselves, the schoolmistress and scholars, for there would be no occasion for nearly so much punishment and the children would make more progress than they

do. The Bockhampton people consider the mistress punishes for her own pleasure instead of the children's good and never think that their boys or girls are kept in or caned for being naughty.

Attendance at school was still not compulsory in the 1860s so there was little she could do except record her frustrations.

There are a number of entries in the log-books to do with homework. Parents were not always in favour of their children being given homework – some claimed their children were 'too busy' while others just did not accept the idea of children taking work home.

Special Days and Holidays

A visit to Kingston House to receive 'Pence and Buns' from Mrs Fellowes, whose husband James owned the Kingston estate, was an annual treat. She took a great interest in the school, was a school manager for many years and provided the poorest girls with cloaks in the 1860s and 1870s. As these were children of men employed by her husband or her neighbour the Earl of Ilchester, perhaps wages needed to be increased to improve the conditions the children lived in, particularly after the findings of the Commission on the Employment of Children, Young Persons and Women of 1857 which found wages to be very low and the condition of cottages in Dorset the worst in the country with the exception of Shropshire. Other ladies in the parish at Stinsford House, Kingston Maurward and Birkin House gave tea parties for the children in the summer and at Christmas.

In the period before the First World War the schoolchildren were often given a half-day holiday on May Day to dance around a maypole which they made themselves.

There were special awards each year for 'regularity of attendance, diligence and good conduct' and amongst the school records are lists of children who were awarded money from the Pitt and Strangways Charity, originally set up in the eighteenth century by Lora Pitt of Kingston House and Mary Strangways of Stinsford House. These awards continued to be made until the school closed.

In the 1920s annual school trips, usually to Weymouth, were organised and funded through the Parochial Church Council. Everyone, mothers and children, travelled in an open-top charabanc bus and lunch was eaten in St Mary's School, not far from the beach. One pupil remembers that tea included bowls of golden dessert gooseberries and other fruit from the kitchen gardens at Kingston Maurward House. As the children rarely travelled beyond Dorchester a trip to Weymouth was very special and exciting.

There must have been great excitement on Empire Day in May 1928 when the children assembled in the playground for the arrival of HRH The Prince of Wales, later Edward VIII, who was passing through

A school and Sunday school outing to Weymouth, c.1926. Adult passengers include: Miss Askew (head teacher) and Miss Willmott, Mrs Atkins, Mrs Critchell, Mrs Kellaway; children include: Maurice, Cyril, George and Reg Atkins, Clifford Wyatt, Hilda and Stella Kellaway, Willie Blackaller and Sam Corbin.

the village on his way to lunch at Max Gate near Dorchester with that 'old boy' of the school Thomas Hardy. When Princess Elizabeth and Lt Philip Mountbatten were married on 29 November 1947 the school closed for a holiday.

A visit to the cinema in Dorchester to see the film *Where No Vultures Fly* had been planned for February 1952 but was cancelled following the death of King George VI. On the day of his funeral the children observed two minutes' silence and listened to the radio broadcast of the service from St George's Chapel, Windsor.

When the Queen visited Dorchester on 3 July 1952 the children had a day's holiday and there was a combined Whitsun holiday and Coronation Day holiday in June 1953 when many of the children took part in competitions held as part of the celebrations at Bockhampton House.

Christmas preparations were a painful process for the infant classes at the school in the 1920s and 1930s. Marian Marsh remembers that boughs of holly were brought to the schoolroom and the infant children's contribution was to strip the leaves from the branches and thread them onto lengths of string using a sacking needle. It was impossible not to end up with pricked fingers and sore knees from sitting on the hard floor. The resulting festoons were taken to the church and wound around the pillars in the nave. Things at Christmas had improved by the 1950s when the children were entertained with a puppet show or a conjuror and a ventriloquist.

Extracts From the Log-Books and Managers' Minute Books

1900–14

In 1905 following a visit from inspectors, the school managers received their report which said that 'the diamond shaped window panes exclude necessary light and are injurious to the eyesight of the children.' This was greeted with 'surprise and indignation'. They took no action and the windows were still in place when the school closed in 1961.

Mrs Tizzard from Lower Bockhampton was offered a fixed monthly payment of 7s.6d. in 1906 for all cleaning in the school. For her fee she had to scrub the rooms at least three times a year.

In the minute book for 1909 the school managers were angry that the Medical Officer of Health had not visited the school during an outbreak of whooping cough. As a result children with whooping cough continued to attend school and passed the infection on to others.

1914–18

During the First World War the children were involved with the war effort in various ways. In 1915 some of the children took part in a Navy League competition for the best essay on 'The Work of the British Navy in the Great War'. Two children gained certificates of merit and another was commended by the judges.

In 1915 Mr Dare the headmaster resigned after 33 years due to his increasing deafness. The school correspondent was instructed to ask the successful candidate the following questions:

What was her husband's profession?
Would he accompany her?
Was she prepared to remain for any length of time?

How times change!

In November 1916, Fred Bartlett, an old boy of the school on active service in France but home on leave, came to the school and gave an 'interesting account of an ordinary soldier's life on active service, his

Above: *Postmarked February 1911, this postcard of Lower Bockhampton shows the Post Office cottage on the right and beyond the pair of cottages which are now Yalbury Cottage hotel and restaurant. A huge horse chestnut tree spanned the road where Spring Glen is now located. On the left is Pump Cottage, children are in the playground high above the lane while other children have gathered to have their photograph taken with the postman.*

Above: *This photograph from shortly before the First World War was taken in the lane in front of the school. The gate from the village of Bockhampton into the grounds of Kingston House can just be seen to the left of the girls. Ann Dare is on the left and another teacher is on the right.*

Right: *Taken on the same occasion as the picture above, most of the boys are holding baskets they are making. Withies for basket making were grown in withy beds near the river.*

Elijah and Ann Dare photographed in the porch of the school. Mr Dare was headmaster from 1882 until 1915 and his wife was also a teacher. The girl standing on the left may be their daughter Hilda who was a pupil at the school.

Children of Stinsford and Bockhampton School, c.1925. Left to right, back row: *?, ?, ?, Sam Corbin, Ron Trevett, ?, ?, Nell Corbin, Ethel Parker, Nell Kirby, Mabel Symes, ?, ?, ?, Margaret Burgess, Miss Trevett;* third row, standing: *Miss Stella Jenkins, ?, ?, ?, ?, May Symes, ?, ?, ?, ?;* second row, seated: *Miss Morgan (infant teacher), ?, ?, Cyril Atkins, George Atkins, other children unknown, Miss Askew (headmistress);* front row: *Unknown.*

work and duties.' The headmaster reported that 'the scholars were intensely interested'. Fred, who was killed later in the war, was the son of William Bartlett and his wife Mary who ran the Post Office and shop opposite the school.

Boys were allowed to gather acorns for a part of each afternoon during a week in November 1917 which were sent to a factory at Holton Heath near Poole where they were processed to make cordite for ammunition.

1919–38
In 1924 the school was visited by a Professor Mikani from Japan who was studying educational methods. He took a special interest in some of the activities of the children including:

... cardboard modelling, Indian Basketry, needlework, nature charts and the apparatus made by Infant Teachers for children's work in Reading, Writing and Arithmetic.

The log-book does not record how the children reacted to the sight of this Japanese gentleman – surely a first for all of them.

An innovation at this time was a woodwork course for the boys at Dorchester Boys' School on Friday afternoons. Some of them have recalled how they dreaded going to these classes with the rough boys of Dorchester and having to walk through Mill Street, Fordington, which was also quite a rough area. Some of the older girls went to the Dorchester Centre for classes on domestic subjects.

Mrs Pride, then Miss Coombs, who taught at the school in the 1930s with Miss Askew, recalled that the school salaries were paid every month but only one cheque was sent and from this Miss Askew had to pay the school cleaner, two teachers and herself. This meant a visit to Lloyds Bank in Dorchester to cash the cheque. If it arrived on a Saturday Miss Askew went to the bank but otherwise Miss Coombs set out for the bank on her bicycle:

The bank clerk always called me 'Fancy Day' because I came from Bockhampton School where Fancy Day was supposed to have lived in Under the Greenwood Tree.

When the school at West Stafford closed in 1934 the children were transferred to Bockhampton and representatives from there joined the school managers.

In 1935 Mr Wyndham Hull, chairman of the managers and farmer of Stinsford Farm, spoke about Dorset County Council's demand that a mains water-supply should be available at the school. The minutes record that he 'felt strongly that the demand for a special supply of water was needless and unreasonable.' He pointed out that water for washing purposes was supplied by the schoolhouse rainwater butts and excellent drinking-water was carried by school monitors from the village well, only 50 yards from the school, a practice that had served many generations of children for the past 100 years. No complaints had been raised by parents, teachers or children. It was the identical supply of water they used and drank in their own homes. Piped water only arrived in 1947 thanks to a link with the new

Above: *Stinsford and Bockhampton School c.1926.* Left to right, back row: *?, Dick Parker, ?, George Chaffey, George Bowles, Raymond Crabbe, ?;* fourth row: *Alan Humber, ? Bridle, Hilda Kellaway, Gladys Blackaller, Stella Kellaway, ?, Laura Morey, ? Hardy, ? Bridle, Roy Kingman;* third row standing: *?, Mary Wallis, ?, Cyril Atkins, George Atkins, Len Grace, Charlie Chaffey, ?, ?;* second row, seated: *Marian Marsh, Cynthia Turner, ?, Norah Bowles, Freda Kellaway, Olive Symes, ?, Betty Fowler, ? (standing);* front row: *Magnus 'Nussy' Kimber, John Bowles, Reg Atkins, Geoffrey Kellaway, Mervyn Turner, ? Bridle, ?.*

Below: *Children of Stinsford and Bockhampton School c.1928.* Left to right, back row: *George Chaffey, Leonard Grace, Charlie Chaffey, Roy Kingman, Ernest Bridle, ? Burton, Raymond Crabbe;* fourth row: *? Bridle, Norah Bowles, ?, Hilda Kellaway, ?, Stella Kellaway, ?, ? Morey from Talbothayes, Alan Humber;* third row: *?, Geoffrey Kellaway, ? Stone, ? Stone from Tincleton, Bill Kimber, ? Taylor, Cyril Atkins, George Atkins, Fred Bowles, George Atkins, Olive Symes;* second row: *Dick Kimber (standing), Mary Wallis (seated), Marian Marsh, Brenda Taylor, ?, Dorothy Lush, Betty Fowler, Cynthia Turner, Trixie Wallis, ? Taylor (standing), ? Bridle, Freda Kellaway;* front row: *Mervyn Kimber, Archie Wallis, Magnus 'Nussy' Kimber, Reg Atkins.*

on the land would be retiring in the near future who she thought would be replaced by younger men and probably with children. There were also strong rumours of a new estate at West Stafford.

As Mrs Nobes retired in December 1959 Mrs L.H. Wakely from Bhompston Farm was appointed as temporary headmistress. The parents continued to be against the school's closure but on 3 June 1960 notices were posted up confirming this would take place at the end of term, although some children were still at the school in the autumn term and when the school opened in January 1961 there were three pupils left who were transferred to Tincleton or Broadmayne School. In March the furniture was removed and the final entry in this long series of log-books stretching back almost 100 years reads 'All stock and furniture removed to Tincleton, Broadmayne and County Hall. School closed and keys handed to Revd Medway.'

The school buildings were sold by auction on 1 November 1961 at The Antelope Hotel, Dorchester, and were converted to a house.

What Happened Next for Two Schoolboys from Stinsford and Bockhampton School

George Russell

George Russell was born at Lower Bockhampton in November 1853, the son of Levi and Jane Russell. His name first appears in the log-book in January 1866 when he must have been one of the oldest boys in the school at 12. A new schoolmistress, Miss Reynolds, came to the school then who must have been more strict than her predecessor judging by the entries in the log-book in the following years. George was punished in January 1866 with Charles Symonds for jumping out of a schoolroom window. In February he was punished again for being stubborn and in March for bad behaviour on the way to church and at the end of that month 'he gave a great deal of trouble' so that the next day he was told to stay away from school until Revd Shirley decided what his punishment should be. However, what this was is not recorded in the log-book. In August he stayed away from school with many other children to watch the Freemasons' Procession in Dorchester. In January 1867 he 'exhibited his temper because his arithmetic had to be corrected' and in February he was punished severely for disobedience. Surprisingly in April he was made a monitor though the head-mistress was 'unsure whether he would go far in the post'. He was still a monitor in June but probably left school that summer as he was 13 years old.

What he did after leaving school is unknown until May 1881 when he married Mary Pitfield at West Fordington and by the time their first child was born, in the following year, they were living in Portsmouth. George had joined the London & SW Railway and became an engine driver. He is shown in a cutting from the *Portsmouth News* of 1962 with his locomotive called 'Eclipse' with its tall chimney and brass dome. The article says that he was given the responsibility of driving the train carrying many of the crowned heads of Europe and Queen Victoria's coffin from Portsmouth to London for her state funeral in 1901. Presumably nobody knew what a troublesome boy he had been to Miss Reynolds the headmistress of Stinsford and Bockhampton School!

William Charles Symonds

Known as Charles to avoid confusion with his father William, William Charles Symonds was born in July 1854, the eldest son of William Symonds and Anne (née Hurst) of Lower Bockhampton. Charles was one of ten children who all seem to have been a great trial to Miss Reynolds. Charles was eventually expelled from school with his sister Elizabeth. He worked as a page in Dorchester but found he disliked indoor work so got a job with James and then Thomas Hardy as a mason's boy. In May 1870 he joined the Navy with another Bockhampton boy, George Squibb, and both joined a training ship for boys at Portland, HMS *Boscawen*.

Charles wrote an account of his life in a small note-book, full of interesting details of his travels and adventures in the Navy. After completing his training in 1871 he joined the crew of the Royal Yacht and was on board when Queen Victoria was a passenger during the summer. By December 1872 he was aged 18 and joined HMS *Aurora* sailing to the West Indies. When he returned to England he went on a gunnery course qualifying as 'Seaman gunner'. He must have done very well because three years later he was promoted to 2nd Class Petty Officer, and at the end of his time on HMS *Minotaur* he qualified as Gunnery Instructor.

He joined HMS *Champion*, a very modern ship for the time, made of steel, as Senior Gunnery Instructor in 1881. On this posting he visited Africa, the Ascension Islands, Montevideo, the Straits of Magelan and Valparaiso. He was able to explore Peru with other members of the crew during some leave before sailing for China, Honolulu, Japan, Russia and Hong Kong. In the vicinity of Java and Sumatra he witnessed the aftermath of an earthquake which caused a tsunami. After three years away the crew were 'paid off' and left the ship to return home via Ceylon, Zanzibar, the Suez Canal and Malta. Charles bettered himself yet again by qualifying to teach officers during the final years of his time in the Navy.

When he left the Navy he returned to Dorchester, his wife and family and opened a greengrocer's shop. After six years he became an agent for the Prudential, a post he held for the next 20 years. So Charles Symonds was another boy who would have surprised his schoolteacher. The Navy had channelled his spirit and energy, which gave him a life he could never have imagined as a boy in Lower Bockhampton.

Above: *The Old Manor House between 1919 and 1929.*

Above: *View across a field in 1947, now planted with mature trees, just east of the Old Manor House showing the square pigeon loft and the large barn where Mr and Mrs Martin held the Harvest Supper, attended by a young Thomas Hardy between 1845 and 1853. Both buildings were demolished after Dorset County Council purchased the estate.*

Right: *The ground floor plan of the Old Manor House when it was divided into four 'cottages'. It is thought that the 'cottages' were created by James Fellowes soon after he bought the estate in 1853. The last tenants left in 1951 and the house was empty and derelict for some years.*

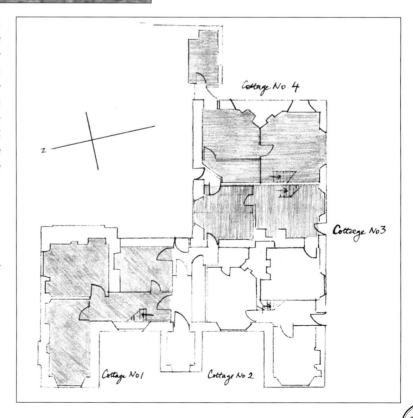

Chapter 10
The Old Manor House

The house was built for Christopher Grey in about 1597 long after the Grey family connection with the manor of Kingston began. In a document of 1406 a Robert Grey was referred to as being 'of Kingston Maurward'. He married Joan, daughter and heiress of Thomas Maurward, whose family had been linked with the manor of Kingston since about 1280.

The plan of the house is an 'E' shape, facing west on rising ground above the valley of the River Frome, near the eastern boundary of the manor of Kingston. Grand houses were usually built facing south and there is a story that the Greys chose not to face south for fear of winds from that direction bringing the plague. Perhaps they were remembering that the Black Death had first come to this country at Melcombe Regis, part of Weymouth, which is due south! Angel Grey, Christopher's grandson, extended the house in the first half of the seventeenth century by adding a wing to the back of the south side, removing windows from the inner walls of the wings at the front for the extension. The windows were not replaced for 300 years.

Angel Grey was named after his maternal grandfather, Angel Smith. Thomas Hardy used the name for his character Angel Clare in the novel *Tess of the d'Urbervilles* and could remember sitting in church as a boy looking up at the Grey family memorial, which includes Angel Grey's name and has a skull carved at the base. Angel Grey married Katherine Stawell in 1630 and they had five children. The coat of arms carved above the entrance porch of the house includes elements from the Grey and Stawell coats of arms and was probably added at the time of their marriage. Following his wife's death in 1663 he was married again to Grace Fullwood but had no more children.

A description of the estate in 1657 comes from a family settlement document. There were 1350 acres of land with barns, stables, a warren, dovecotes, ponds and watercourses, as well as the mansion house and gardens. The size of the estate seems larger than expected as Kingston Maurward College, whose land holding includes the manor of Kingston has 750 acres but this includes the land of Stinsford Farm which was not owned by the Greys in 1657. Without maps from the time it is not possible to explain this.

During the Civil War, which began in 1642 Angel Grey supported the royalists and as a consequence his estate at Kingston was confiscated. Even so he was luckier than Sir John Strangways, owner of the Stinsford estate, who spent years in the Tower of London. In 1646 Mrs Grey agreed to pay arrears of rent to parliament and to provide 40 bushels of wheat and barley to the parliamentary forces. She was allowed £32 from her rent for quartering parliamentary soldiers, presumably somewhere on the estate. During the war the armies of both the King and parliament moved through the area and the position of Kingston Maurward just south of a road between London and the west must have made it a convenient spot for quartering soldiers and holding supplies. Angel Grey later paid £918 for the release Kingston Maurward and his other estates.

In 1660 following the restoration of King Charles II, Angel Grey petitioned by an Act of General Pardon for the return of £3,000 given to him by his mother-in-law Lady Elizabeth Griffin which had been invested in a bond that on her death was intended for Angel's younger children. During the course of the Civil War the bond was forfeited and given to a Sir John Danvers. Angel Grey's petition was eventually successful and following Sir John's death the money was recovered from his estate and returned.

When Angel died in 1670 he was a wealthy man who was able to leave his wife Grace £50 in gold and the same in silver as well as rings, jewels and necklaces, a coach and horses. She was also left all the silver plate, furniture and goods in the house for her lifetime. The Kingston estate was left to Angel's oldest son George and his second son Audelay received £400 as well as a farm in Nether Stowey, Somerset, where Angel was living when he made his will.

Grace Grey died two years after her husband and made bequests to her step-children and step-grandchildren and left £5 for the poor of Stinsford parish. Many of her servants received bequests varying from 20s. to £20, though just 20s. was a large sum of money for a servant in 1670. As often happened at the time two of her female servants were left all her clothes. The most expensive items would probably be sold.

Angel and Katherine's eldest son George Grey married three times and had eight daughters but with no son the estate would pass to Angel's younger brother Audelay who had married Margaret Trevilian. They had three sons George, Henry and Audelay. Henry died in July 1672, before his father who died in 1675. Young Audelay died aged nine in September 1682 and the oldest boy George was buried at Stinsford church eight days after his brother Audelay. As a result it was their seven-year-old sister Lora who inherited the family estates and fortunes in 1682.

How or where she spent her childhood is

unknown. Her mother was left a mansion at Culverhayes, Stratton and Grimstone and they may both have moved there, or as Lora was heiress to the estate, they may have remained at Kingston Maurward. She married a widower George Pitt in about 1699 and lived at the Pitt family's estate at Stratfield Saye in Hampshire where their nine children were born. Their first son named Grey died as a baby in 1700. In about 1717, the Pitts built the new brick house on the Kingston Maurward estate, which they called Kingston House, within sight of the old Elizabethan Manor House. Between then and 1841, when the census records begin, there is no information about the old house.

In 1841 the house was a farmhouse for Theophilus Pope, his wife, four children, a manservant and three other farm servants. A decade later George Singer, the farm bailiff, his wife Helen, three children and a general servant Martha Hurden were living there. George Singer was a Scot and might just have been the model for Farfrae in The Mayor of Casterbridge by Thomas Hardy who was a schoolboy when the Singers lived in the house. The Singer family shared the house with Elizabeth Plowman, a widowed schoolmistress, her daughter Sarah and son Harry. Martha the servant was a local girl and a sister of Fanny who was at school with Thomas Hardy and who was included as Fanny Hurd in his poem 'Voices From Things Growing in a Churchyard'.

James Fellowes purchased the Old Manor House with the estate in 1853 and then made many changes to the house to create a number of 'cottages' for his estate workers. By 1861 Elizabeth Plowman and her daughter were still there and Charles Toms one of the gardeners and his family lived in another of the 'cottages'. A decade later, two more widows, Jane Bishop and Mary Bishop occupied the house with Elizabeth Plowman and her daughter Sarah.

William Purseglove who was butler to the Fellowes family lived in a house with his wife Alvina and children Henry, Ada and Alice from 1884 at a rent of 6d. per quarter, presumably a nominal sum as he was in effect 'living in'. He stayed on as butler when the estate was sold to Major Balfour in 1906 and appears in the group photograph of the Balfour family with their servants. Mrs Gertrude Fellowes left him £100 in her will.

By 1891 Thomas Way was dairyman on the estate having come from Toller in West Dorset. He lived in the Old Manor House with his wife Anne and three grown-up daughters, Susan, Annie and Augusta. Thomas Hardy in Tess of the d'Urbervilles apparently used Thomas Way and his daughter Augusta as models for Crick the dairyman and Tess Durbeyfield. In a Hardyesque twist it was Augusta's daughter Gertrude who later played the part of Tess in the 1920s with the Hardy Players, a group of amateur actors from Dorchester.

When the estate was purchased by Cecil Hanbury in 1914 the Old Manor House was occupied by his staff, including the gardener Joseph Benbow who had been brought to Kingston Maurward to help create the Italian gardens, having already worked in the gardens of La Mortola, the Hanburys' house in Italy. Like many Italians Joseph Benbow was very fond of children and when he sat out in front of the Old Manor House in the summer in his velvet jacket and smoking cap he called out to any 'bambinos' who passed by on their way home from school.

Gertrude Adelie Bugler as 'Tess' was a member of the Hardy Players, a Dorchester group of amateur actors who performed a number of Thomas Hardy's plays adapted from his novels. Thomas Hardy was very appreciative of her interpretation of the character.

In October 1896 Henry Moule created this watercolour from the hill above the Elizabethan Manor House, which can be seen in the distance. In the foreground are the thatched farm buildings of the time. The Kingston Maurward College stables are on the site. Beyond the farm buildings is the back of the coachman's cottage and hay loft.

The Old Manor House soon after the completion of the Armistice Walk east of Kingston Maurward House in 1919, with grand balustrades and steps to the elaborate gateway. Now the stonework, steps and gated entrance are gone.

The entrance to the park from the Old Manor House. Here, between 1919 and 1929, are Mrs Jenkins junr, Stella Jenkins and Mrs Jenkins senr setting out to walk to church through the park.

The Jenkins family in the garden behind the Old Manor House, 1919–29, showing the farm building which is now the Animal Care department of the College. Alfred and Emma had a daughter Stella who was a monitor at Stinsford and Bockhampton School and went on to become a headmistress in a Dorset school. Left to right, back row: ?, Iva Jenkins, ?, Alfred Jenkins, Emma Jenkins; seated: Stella and her brother Denis.

Right: *In 1920 Charles and Ada Atkins lived in one of the Old Manor House 'cottages'. Here their twin sons George and Cyril sit outside their front door with their older brother Maurice.*

Alfred Jenkins, head gardener in the 1920s, came to Kingston Maurward from Castle Freke in Ireland with his wife Emma and daughter Stella in 1919. The family lived in the Manor House conveniently near the glasshouses and kitchen gardens. As head gardener he was involved in the creation of the Armistice Walk between the Temple and house, which commemorated the end of the First World War. Alfred and Emma's son Victor was away in the Merchant Navy so his wife Iva lived with her parents-in-law at the Old Manor House with her baby son Denis. In 1947 Denis would return to work at Kingston Maurward as the first herdsman of the newly created Dorset Farm Institute.

Mr Wallbridge, who looked after the small herd of six Jersey cows that supplied milk to Kingston House lived in the Old Manor House too. The cows were a familiar sight in the park where they were allowed to roam but never seemed to stray out of the park gates as they could have done.

From the late 1930s there was more accommodation in the house than was needed for the estate staff and so the surplus 'cottages' were rented out. Mr and Mrs Meech who had a draper's shop in North Square, Dorchester, were tenants and when Eli Read retired as shepherd at Duddle Farm he and his wife Beatrice rented a part of the house. Eli's sons Eddie and Bill were also tenants. Eddie was in the Army and Bill worked for the County Council before transferring to work for the Dorset Farm Institute when it opened in 1947. The Webb, Donohue and Fox families lived in other parts of the house. It must have been bursting at the seams as one or two of these families were large. The facilities were minimal with no electricity, only outside privies and water had to be pumped from a well outside until a standpipe was provided later. Even so, the house is a place of happy memories for very many of the children who lived there and have spoken about those times.

Dorset County Council purchased the estate from Lady Hanbury in 1947 to set up the Dorset Farm Institute and a number of plans were made for the Old Manor House. One of the earliest was to use it as residential accommodation for women students. The existing tenants were to be given notice to quit and it was suggested by the management committee of the Institute that the tenants could be found alternative accommodation in a disused Army camp at Bradford Down but eventually they were found other accommodation, some moving to Broadmayne.

By 1955 the house was empty and in a very poor state with the roof falling in and windows broken by vandals. The top floor had been abandoned many years before. A plan was suggested to convert it into

Fancy dress in the 1940s at the Old Manor House, probably in 1947 when Princess Elizabeth married Philip Mountbatten. Shirley Thorne, who lived just across from the Old Manor in Park Cottage, is the bride and Sheila Read from the Old Manor is the bridegroom.

Cousins Veronica and Michael Read playing outside the Old Manor, 1949/50. Behind them is Park Cottage, now Green Pastures, with the old stable and barn still attached to it. On the left is one of the piles of dead trees cleared from the park in the aftermath of the occupation by American troops during the war.

Bill Read, originally employed by the Roads and Bridges Department of the County Council, transferred to the Farm Institute in 1948. He was already living in the Old Manor House with his wife and family. He was employed as a general labourer and mole catcher. He also built fences and worked with the cows, c.1950.

Eli and Beatrice Read at Christmas in the 1940s. They lived in the Old Manor House during the Second World War. Eli had been shepherd at Duddle Farm before he retired and two of his sons, Bill and Eddie, also lived in the house with their families.

Eddie Read who was in the Dorset Regiment during the war, looking the part for the time with his Fair Isle pullover and cigarette, 1940s. Behind and to his left is the gate across the lane to Manor Dairy, long since taken away.

Right: *Lona, daughter of Bill and Violet Read and sister of Sheila, achieved her ambition to join the Sea Cadets whilst the family lived at the Old Manor. She is pictured here in the late 1940s.*

flats or for storage but the cost of repairs just to the shell of the building was estimated at £12,300. Discussions took place to see if a grant could be made under the Ancient Monuments Act of 1953 to restore the house and let it to a private individual but the governors of the Institute were not in favour of this idea. Three years later in 1957 the County Council decided that there was no alternative to demolition at a cost of £457 with the materials from the house becoming the property of the contractor.

There were one or two people who tried very hard to prevent the destruction of the house. Miss Violet Cross of Hazelbury Bryan said that although hers was a voice in the wilderness she, like many others, would like to see the building preserved. A year after the County Council's decision to opt for demolition a preservation order was placed on the house to allow more time for a new use to be found for it. The poet John Betjeman, champion of the country's heritage, wrote an article in the *Daily Telegraph* in June 1961 drawing attention to the demolition of buildings by County Councils using the Old Manor House as an example.

In the end the house was saved, but only by chance, as the result of a conversation at a cocktail party between the secretary of the Society for the Protection of Ancient Buildings and Rohan Sturdy who had family connections with Dorset but lived in Bedfordshire. In 1962 a lease of the house was negotiated with Dorset County Council, for a peppercorn rent, providing it was restored at his own expense. The work took six years. He replaced the windows that had been removed by Angel Grey in the seventeenth century and a stair tower was built at the back

using stone removed when the windows were replaced. More stone came from a Tudor house being demolished at North Quay in Weymouth. Windows and a doorway from this house were also incorporated and a wooden staircase which came from Little Haddon Hall, Suffolk, was added at the front of the house. During the restoration, when the cellars were cleared, no evidence was found of an earlier house on the site.

On 26 June 1968 another cocktail party took place, this time at the house to celebrate the completion of the restoration. At a council meeting in August Miss Cross congratulated Mr Sturdy on his achievement in restoring the house entirely at his own expense and so preserving it for the future. She in turn was applauded for her almost single-handed fight over 11 years to stop the house being pulled down. Dorset County Council eventually granted the freehold of the property to Rohan Sturdy. The restoration was completed in time for the house to be used as the venue for events associated with the first Thomas Hardy Festival in 1968.

Rohan Sturdy and his wife never lived in the house and in 1977 it was sold to John and Annabel Evans. In 1998 Andrew and Mulu Thomson acquired it and have embellished the interior with period furnishings which make it a special place to stay for their bed and breakfast guests. They also allowed the Stinsford and Bockhampton Village History Group to hold a two-week exhibition of parish local history in the house during the summer of 2005. Very many of the visitors were attracted by the house as well as the exhibition, not least those who had lived there in its previous incarnations during the 1920s, 1930s and 1940s.

Chapter 11

Kingston Maurward House

George and Lora Pitt 1717–50

Kingston House was built between 1717 and 1720 for George Pitt and his wife Lora and superseded the Elizabethan manor house nearby which had been built by Lora's great-great-grandfather Christopher Grey in about 1591. The house was renamed Kingston Maurward House in 1914.

The new house was described as 'an elegant and stately pile' in Hutchins' *History of the County of Dorset*. It was built at the top of a south-facing slope above the valley of the River Frome and made of brick with stone facings. There are differing opinions about the architect – some suggest it was Thomas Archer, who built Chettle House, but John James of Greenwich, London, is known to have referred to George Pitt as his patron.

Lora Grey was George Pitt's second wife and until Kingston House was built they lived at Stratfield Saye in Hampshire, the Pitt family home. George Pitt was MP for Wareham and for Hampshire between 1698 and 1715 and was a distant cousin of William Pitt the Elder, politician and Prime Minister. Both the Grey and Pitt families were wealthy and owned numerous estates and farms. A coal mine in Durham and a house in Arlington Street, near Green Park, London, were among the properties Lora Pitt had inherited from her family as a child.

After her husband's death in 1734 Lora Pitt appears to have settled at Kingston House, probably sharing it with her son William who had inherited the estate from his father. She purchased a number of additional farms including Frome Whitfield and Coker's Frome. She also bought back the manor of Askerswell, which had been sold by Christopher Grey in 1612. She was known locally for her kindness and generosity and in a footnote in the second edition of Hutchins' *History of the County of Dorset* she is described as:

> ... a lady of great virtue, piety, prudence and affability... doing good was the business and pleasure of her life. She was a public blessing to the poor of the adjacent parish and town of Dorchester...

An example of Lora Pitt's 'doing good' was the building, at her expense, of Grey's Bridge across the River Frome on the outskirts of Dorchester in 1748.

The bust of George Pitt on his memorial in St Michael's Church, Stinsford. He married Lora Grey, heiress of the Grey family fortune and estates. They built Kingston House in about 1717.

'Ladey Pitts bell', with the date 1739 cast into it, is now in the fireplace of the Old Coach House café of the College and pictured here in 2007. There is no clue as to its original position but bells were often used on large estates to announce the beginning and end of the working day to everyone working near or far in the days when fewer would have worn a watch. In the 1940s the bell was fixed up on the pediment of the Coach House.

New approach roads were made across the low-lying land on either side of the river which greatly improved the route into Dorchester. The bridge was made wide enough for carriages and coaches to allow the Pitts, as well as their family and friends, to travel more easily between Kingston House and Dorchester. The old road had crossed Fordington Fields to a narrow bridge over the River Frome somewhere near the bottom of Mill Street, Fordington.

Lora Pitt and Mary Strangways of Stinsford House left bequests for a Pitt-Strangways Charity which provided for the education of five boys from Stinsford parish at Trinity School in Dorchester so that they would learn reading, writing and accounts. The charity paid for their school books and when they left school each boy was given a copy of *The Whole Duty of Man*, a book that explained the moral and religious duties of man. From 1868 the charity provided £12 a year in prize money to reward pupils at Stinsford and Bockhampton School for regular attendance, diligence and good behaviour.

However, things did not always run smoothly between the owners of the Kingston and Stinsford estates. In 1732 a John Stevens was called in by Mrs Strangways Horner, owner of the Stinsford estate, to settle a dispute with her neighbour Mrs Pitt about the way water from the River Frome was used by both estates. The water-supply needed for the 'water engine' at Kingston House, to water the gardens, was sometimes interrupted when the hatches in the fields of Stinsford to the west were closed and Mrs Pitt's taking water from the river sometimes interfered with water-supplies to the fields of Stinsford Farm. John Stevens suggested removing some hatches and constructing an elaborate two-level channel which allowed water to flow to Kingston House and to Stinsford without inconvenience to either estate.

Lora Pitt's last years were spent convalescing in Bath and she died there in 1750 and was buried at Stratfield Saye with her husband. Her will made in 1746 was witnessed by George Lacey, the vicar of Stinsford, which suggests she was living at Kingston House then. Her son William had already inherited the Kingston estate from his father and she left him her house in Arlington Street and three other farms. She left £10,000 to be used to purchase land for her son John. Her daughters, daughters-in-law and granddaughter received £1,000 each, jewellery and £100 for mourning clothes and jewellery. She bequeathed £100 to the minister, churchwardens and overseers of Stinsford church to be used for the benefit of the poor. A further £1,000 was left in trust to build Grey's Bridge, in case this was not completed in her lifetime and for its repair for 30 years. However, the bridge had been built two years before she died, although she may not have seen it herself if she was in Bath by the time it was built in 1748.

Tantalisingly she refers to a number of family portraits in her will. Those of her children were to be taken from Arlington House, London, to Kingston House 'to be heirlooms', whilst others of her husband were bequeathed to her sons William and John. Another portrait of Abigail, Lady Stawell, set in diamonds, was left to that lady's granddaughter Mary. Lora's grandmother was Katherine Stawell and the Rt Hon. Edward Lord Stawell, Baron of Somerton, was left a large brilliant diamond ring. It is disappointing that none of these portraits can be traced.

Lora Pitt was wealthy enough to be able to make bequests in money alone amounting to over £20,000. Her servants were not forgotten, they all received a year's wages and some also received individual bequests.

William and Elizabeth Pitt 1734–74

William inherited the estate in 1734 and owned it for 40 years but no records for these years have been traced. When he made his will in 1770 he was living at Binfield House in Berkshire, the country retreat of his relative William Pitt the Elder, later Earl of Chatham. It is possible William left Kingston when his wife died in 1769. He left bequests to his brother's children: £500 and a gold watch to William Morton Pitt and all the jewels he possessed were left to Marcia Pitt. Mary Johnson of Bockhampton was left an annuity of five guineas 'being the sum my mother desired'. A Mary Johnson, aged 89, appears in other documents of 1774 as occupier of a house and garden in Lower Bockhampton. Born in about 1685 she was ten years older than Lora Pitt so that it is possible that they had known each other for most of their lives. A further £100 was left for the poor of the parish of Stinsford except those already receiving payments from the overseers of the poor.

William's wife Elizabeth, who died in 1769, bequeathed £1,000 to her husband and the diamond necklace and girdle buckle left to her by her mother-in-law Lora Pitt. She wrote:

... the best and most valued thing I can leave him except my hearty and sincere wishes that he may have a second wife who loves and values him as truly as I do.

This is an unusually personal sentiment in a will, which are often very formal. William did not remarry and they both are buried at Stinsford church.

John and Marcia Pitt 1774–87

As William and his wife Elizabeth Pitt had no children the Kingston estate passed to his brother John Pitt of Encombe in the Isle of Purbeck. He had married Marcia Morgan in 1752 and their surviving children were William Morton and Marcia, three other sons having died in childhood. John Pitt was MP for Wareham and Dorchester for 34 years. He was appointed a Commissioner for Trades and

Left: Portrait of John Pitt 1704–87 as a young man. He was the son of George Pitt and Lora (née Grey) and following his brother William's death in 1774 he inherited the Kingston estate when he was 70 years old. He already owned Encombe House and estate on the Isle of Purbeck.

An engraving from the 1774 first edition of Hutchins' History of the County of Dorset *showing Kingston House as a brick building. The gardens are landscaped in the 'Picturesque' style. The artist's viewpoint must have been close to the Tincleton Road looking south across the park. With some artistic licence the Elizabethan Manor House appears immediately to the left of the house and there is a folly partially hidden by trees in the grounds.*

Plantations and between 1756 and 1787 was Surveyor-General of his Majesty's Woods and Forests to George III. His papers include records of the vast quantities of timber felled in the New Forest, Forest of Dean and other areas that were sold to the Navy for shipbuilding during the war with France.

John Pitt made alterations and additions to the gardens of Kingston House and the lake on the south side of the house was made by joining a number of canals. The Grecian Temple was built beside the lake. He seems to have enjoyed designing buildings for his estates having designed the new house and grounds at Encombe when he first acquired it. Accounts for the years 1781 and 1783 include a number of bills for work at Kingston from stonemasons, plasterers, painters to a plumber. Quantities of timber were bought for fencing plantations, for railings and fencing single trees. In 1778 John Pitt was given permission by Justices of the Peace to divert the road from Stinsford Cross to Bockhampton village, as it is today along Light and Dark Hill, and to make the footpath along the river from Grey's Bridge to Bockhampton. Like many gentlemen of his time he wanted to make the park around the house a private place, not one used by 'locals' walking or riding between Stinsford and Bockhampton.

It is not clear how much time John and Marcia Pitt spent at Kingston House compared with Encombe their home for many years. William Pitt, the Prime Minister visited them there a number of times and some have speculated that he may also have come to Kingston to see the improvements.

John Pitt died in 1787 and was buried at Stinsford. His widow Marcia was left an estate at Sunninghill in Berkshire for her lifetime, though she was living with her son William Morton Pitt and daughter-in-law Margaret at Kingston House in 1811 and she died there in 1818.

The Temple to the southeast of the house overlooking the lake is thought to have been built for John Pitt who landscaped the gardens and created the lake when he inherited the estate. The building is brick faced with Portland stone. This photograph from the 1930s shows the statue of Mercury in the centre of the lily pond which was lost during the Second World War occupation by the military.

William Morton Pitt 1787–1836

As a young man William Morton Pitt went to Queen's College, Oxford and the Inner Temple before spending a number of years travelling on the continent, including a visit to Sweden to inspect some mines. Perhaps he was hoping to acquire knowledge to help in running the family's coal mines in Durham, which provided him with as much income as all the estates and farms together. A letter of 1778 implies that he had also visited Russia.

His Family Life

In 1782 William Morton Pitt married Margaret Gambier, daughter of John Gambier, once a governor of the Bahamas. She was described as a 'beautiful and arresting personality'. After their marriage the couple travelled to Italy and France where they danced at the French Court and saw Marie Antoinette.

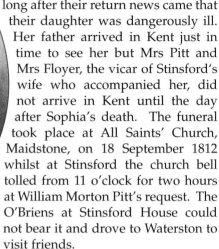

William Morton Pitt 1752–1836.

In 1787 William Morton Pitt inherited the Kingston House estate, Encombe House and its estate, an enormous number of farms, the coal mines in Durham and a house in the best area of London, all at the age of 32.

In September 1806 the Pitts' only daughter Sophia married Charles Marsham, Earl of Romney at Stinsford church. The report of their wedding appeared in the Annual Register which mentioned that she had a fortune of £60,000.

As neighbours and friends of the Pitts, William and Lady Susan O'Brien from Stinsford House attended the wedding and Lady Susan described the events of the day in her journal:

> *... the ceremony was attended by all the servants and the principal people of the parish in the church and great numbers of persons from Dorchester and other places in the neighbourhood. After the ceremony all returned to Kingston in carriages where was a breakfast prepared and as soon as the day cleared up and it could be got ready the dinner on the green before the house for the poor people of the parish began, upwards of two hundred partook of it and after all were satisfied, the remains were collected on a table and the spectators from Dorchester had a scramble for it.*
>
> *Miss Pitt's school of sixteen girls dressed in white stuff gowns with baskets of flowers looked very pretty... About three o'clock the bride and bridegroom set out for Encombe with the cheers and blessing of the happy parish... When they were all gone we came home and met again at dinner which poor Mr Pitt struggled hard to go through cheerfully. Mrs Pitt could not without tears which frequently would steal from her eyes in spite of all her efforts to suppress them...*

Sophia and her husband lived in Kent but visited Kingston House from time to time. On 30 July 1808 their son, named Charles, was born in Kent. In 1811 the Pitts went to visit their daughter at Wateringbury, Kent. Not long after their return news came that their daughter was dangerously ill. Her father arrived in Kent just in time to see her but Mrs Pitt and Mrs Floyer, the vicar of Stinsford's wife who accompanied her, did not arrive in Kent until the day after Sophia's death. The funeral took place at All Saints' Church, Maidstone, on 18 September 1812 whilst at Stinsford the church bell tolled from 11 o'clock for two hours at William Morton Pitt's request. The O'Briens at Stinsford House could not bear it and drove to Waterston to visit friends.

Though greatly affected by her daughter's death, Mrs Pitt's poor health improved for a few years until 1818 when she was again unwell and went to Geneva with her husband in vain hope of a cure. She died at Lausanne, probably of tuberculosis, but was buried at Stinsford church. Lady Susan O'Brien described her and her mother-in-law Mrs John Pitt who died in the same year as 'both kind friends and pleasing neighbours. In earlier times they made Kingston gay and in later times comfortable...'

A year later William Morton Pitt married again at the age of 65. His bride was Grace Seymer, a second cousin, who was 36 years old. She was described by Lady Susan O'Brien as 'very musical, but not belle' but Lady Susan had no doubt that the marriage would add to his comfort and happiness 'of which he has no great store'. Two years after their marriage a twin daughter and son were born in London in May 1821 and christened Harriett Marcia Margaret and William Grey at Stinsford church on 31 July. Two weeks later a dinner was held for all the people of the parish with dancing on the green to celebrate the birth of an heir. A second daughter, Louisa Lora, was born in 1823.

Public Life

William Morton Pitt was MP for Poole between 1780 and 1790 and then MP for Dorset until 1826. He concentrated his efforts in promoting the county of Dorset, supporting William Wilberforce in his campaign against slavery and improving the conditions of the poor and disadvantaged, often using his own money to set up his schemes. He was an active Justice of the Peace and in his thinking and ideas on the rehabilitation of prisoners he was well ahead of his time. He visited Dorchester Prison frequently and in 1792 took King George III to see the hat making factory he had set up to help rehabilitate prisoners and give them some useful employment. He spent much of his time in charitable works. In 1795 he organised a bleaching, spinning and weaving factory at Fordington, Dorchester, set up a herring curing factory at Swanage and a straw plaiting works at Langton. Having sponsored a survey on poverty and the prevalence of smuggling at Corfe Castle he provided alternative employment at a rope and sailcloth factory that he had opened. He also organised Sunday schools for children living in the Isle of Purbeck.

As a result of the war with France he produced a document in 1796 called 'Thoughts on the Defence of the Kingdom'. He meticulously worked out the number of yeomanry and militia needed, the cost of clothing for soldiers and their pay. In the following year he produced a plan to keep registers of all persons in each parish who might serve in a militia, stressing the need to find out what animals, stock, wagons, fuel and potatoes existed so that if an invasion should threaten the information would already be at hand. Interestingly in 1804 returns of men able to serve were compiled so that it seems his idea was put into effect by the authorities.

The 'Defence of the Coast of Dorset' was the subject of his attention in 1798. He produced a report which described the coast, the guns already available for its defence, together with recommendations for improvements, particularly in more vulnerable areas. It is a meticulous document written in his own hand.

No wonder that when William Morton Pitt was described to King George III as a 'business man' the King replied 'Not a man of business, but a busy man'.

Royalty

George III was very fond of visiting Weymouth with the Queen and his children. He came for the sea bathing and his patronage led to the popularity of Weymouth with other members of the royal family and the aristocracy. When staying at Weymouth the King often drove to Kingston, sometimes without giving any advance notice. On one occasion a large party including the King and Queen arrived at lunchtime and found the Pitts and their friends covered in mud, returning from fishing in the lake. The King was delighted at having surprised them and finding them is such disarray and added to the informality of the occasion by hiding in a closet and jumping out at his wife, Queen Charlotte, with a cry of 'Boo!'

King George is said to have been responsible for the transformation of Kingston House from brick to Portland stone after he made comments about the appearance of the brick-built house during a visit in 1794, which were taken as a criticism. Though William Morton Pitt was a rich man with an income of more than £12,000 a year the expense involved in cladding the house with Portland stone was enormous and his finances never recovered. He was

eventually forced to sell Encombe House and other farms to pay off some of his mortgages which stood at £92,000 by 1807.

William Grey Pitt 1836–45

William Morton Pitt and his wife both died in 1836 and were buried at Stinsford. In his will William Morton Pitt appointed trustees to run the estates until his 15-year-old son reached adulthood. The hotel in Swanage, other property in the town, Coker's Frome and Frome Whitfield Farms were sold in 1838 to repay some of the inherited debts and the Kingston estate was re-mortgaged for £55,000 to provide William Grey Pitt's two sisters with annuities for life. When he reached the age of 21 in 1842 the Court of Chancery instructed him to sell the Kingston estate to repay outstanding debts. On 23 July 1844 an advertisement for the sale of Kingston House appeared in the *Dorset County Chronicle* and soon after a purchaser Mr Francis P.B. Martin was found.

William Grey Pitt married Laura Ryves at Bryanston in June 1845. They lived in Hampshire and then the Channel Islands and by 1851 had three sons, William Morton Grey, George Christopher and John, the two youngest born in France. Laura Pitt died at St Helier, Jersey in 1853 aged 33 and William Grey Pitt died in Norwood, Surrey in 1867 aged 46. The final event which linked the Pitt family and Stinsford was the funeral of William Grey Pitt at Stinsford church where his wife was buried two years before. More than 160 years had elapsed since George Pitt had married Lora Grey.

Francis and Julia Martin 1844–53

Francis Pitney Brouncker Martin and his wife Julia Augusta were both in their mid-thirties when they purchased Kingston House.

Julia Martin appears to have taken a special interest in Thomas, the son of Thomas Hardy the builder of Higher Bockhampton and who did a lot of work on the estate for the Martins. She had no children of her own and was obviously very attached to the boy and he remembered her cuddling and kissing him. She said later that she had 'taught Tom his letters' during his visits to Kingston House and he remembered his early encounters with her for the rest of his life including the 'thrill of hearing her frou-frou silk dress' when she bent over him and when it brushed against the font in the church on Sundays. This would have been in stark contrast to the more practical clothes his mother and aunts would have worn. Likewise the difference between the interior of Kingston House and the cottage at Higher Bockhampton would have been both dramatic and magical for such a dreamy boy of six or seven. Thomas became one of the first pupils at the new school at Lower Bockhampton and attended for a year until his mother took him with her when she visited her sister in Hatfield. They were gone for some time and when they returned Jemima Hardy chose to send Thomas to school in Dorchester. Julia Martin was most upset and as a consequence no more building work on the Kingston estate was offered to his father for some time.

Julia Martin and Thomas Hardy next met a few years later at a Harvest Supper for the estate workers which took place in the big barn that then stood up the hill from the Old Manor House. Young Tom had persuaded some local girls to take him along and when Mrs Martin arrived with her house guests she made a point of speaking to him saying that she thought he had deserted her. He apparently burst into tears and said he would never do such a thing.

The Martins sold the estate and left the parish in 1853. In *The Early Life of Thomas Hardy* ostensibly written by his wife Florence but which was largely the work of Hardy himself, there is a comment that Francis Martin 'had impoverished himself by attempting to farm part of his land with the aid of a (perhaps rascally) bailiff.' By 1871 the Martins were living at New Shoreham, near Worthing and at the time of the census that year they had a visitor with them: Mary Singer, daughter of George Singer, their farm bailiff on the Kingston estate in 1851. It seems that the Martins either disagreed with Thomas Hardy that George Singer had been 'rascally' or, if they did, they valued the friendship of his daughter sufficiently to have her as their guest 18 years after they had left Kingston House.

In one of his notebooks Thomas Hardy also described Francis Martin as 'generous, rash and unconventional'. How he was unconventional is not explained.

James, Gertrude Fellowes and J. Herbert Benyon 1853–1906

Above left: *A portrait of James Fellowes, probably painted in 1851 just two years before he became owner of the Kingston estate.*

Above right: *Gertrude Charlotte Micklethwaite and James Fellowes were married in 1847. This miniature is dated 1851.*

The sale of Kingston House was advertised to take place by auction at 12 o'clock on 5 July 1853. The sale particulars show that the estate then included nearly 1,150 acres, 'a noble and handsome mansion with beautiful park' and the 'picturesque village of Bockhampton, manor, trout fishery, lake, etc'. The house is described as remarkably dry and healthy with a lofty hall, an elegant and highly decorated saloon, a library, morning-room, drawing-room and dining-room all on the ground floor. On the first floor there were three lofty and airy bedrooms, each with a large dressing-room, a water closet and four other best bedrooms. Above on the next floor were ten other bedrooms, nurseries, store rooms, house-maids closet, linen room and a water closet. It is worth remembering that water closets were not available in the homes of the estate workers until a century later!

The 'Domestic Offices' are described as 'very complete'. In the basement there was:

... an excellent lofty kitchen and scullery, house-keeper's and butler's rooms, footman's pantry, servants' hall, still room, store room and superior and capacious cellars.

The stabling for eight horses, harness room and standing for several carriages was to the east of the house with coachman's apartments, surmounted by a turret clock. Added to all this was a wash-house, laundry, complete brewhouse, bakehouse, ice-house and coal sheds.

Its not known if the house was sold at the auction or whether James Fellowes was able to purchase beforehand. Although he came originally from Huntingdon and his wife from Norfolk it seems likely that the Fellowes chose to move to Dorset to be close to his brother Richard whose home was not too far away at Englefield House, Berkshire. The Fellowes also had a house at 6 Bryanston Square, London.

Although there were no portraits to help picture Francis and Julia Martin when they owned the estate, fortunately there are for James and Gertrude Fellowes, painted soon after their marriage in 1847. They look young and confident; their surroundings hint at affluence.

By 1881 the Fellowes family had a large number of servants at Kingston House including a butler, footman, house boy, lady's maid, housekeeper, three housemaids, a kitchen maid, scullery maid and laundry maid who all 'lived in'. The gardeners generally lived in Lower Bockhampton and the coachman in the cottage opposite the Old Manor House.

Although James Fellowes owned the estate from 1853 until his death in 1889 very little information has been found about this period. His widow remained at Kingston House though her son 'Mr Herbert' had inherited it. He had changed his surname to Benyon as a condition of inheriting the

Above left: *A miniature portrait of Mrs Gertrude Fellowes, probably painted in 1883. Thomas Hardy mentions her as 'The Lady Gertrude, proud, high-bred' in his poem 'Voices from Things Growing in a Churchyard'.*

Above right: *James Fellowes, aged 69 in 1883.*

Left: *The splendid Benjamin Campbell, head gardener to the Fellowes family from 1899 until 1906, who lived in the thatched Gardener's Cottage in the grounds of Kingston House with his wife Ellen and children Mary, Isabella, Benjamin, Ellen, Ian and Donald. Benjamin and Ellen were both from Scotland. The family left the area in 1906 probably as a consequence of Mrs Fellowes' death and the sale of the estate.*

Above: *Park Cottage, 1949, once the coachman's cottage with the adjoining hay loft in place. The cottage now stands alone and is called Green Pastures. The Old Manor House is across the lane.*

Two Honiton lace motifs dating from 1870; bird at nest and spider's web, from a beautiful flounce which once belonged to Mrs Gertrude Fellowes of Kingston House, now on display at Allhallows Museum, Honiton.

Park Cottage, c.1950, still with the same windows, home of the Thorne family. Left to right: Caroline Thorne, Mrs Margaret Thorne and Shirley Thorne.

Major Kenneth Balfour and Mrs Balfour, his second wife, with their children and an older boy and girl who were the children of Major Balfour's first wife. Major Balfour is seated near the centre with a white handkerchief in his breast pocket and his wife is on his right. William Purseglove, the butler wearing a dark suit, stands behind the lady on Major Balfour's left. The chauffeur is sitting front left and standing behind him are two splendid elderly be-whiskered men. The men at the back are probably the gardening staff. The photograph was taken to the east of the house with the staff annexe on the right without its additional floor added after the fire of 1928. Nicholas Balfour, one of Major Balfour's sons, has dated the photograph to 1913, the year before the family left the house.

Right: *The south front of Kingston House, later renamed Kingston Maurward House, and the lake, c.1906. There was once a boathouse at the eastern end of the lake.*

The surviving portion of a group photograph of the staff of W.E. Jones of Bournemouth, c.1906, who undertook alterations at Kingston House probably when Major Balfour bought the estate. The man seated on the extreme left in a bowler hat is Carey Butler, who was the foreman painter for W.E. Jones.

The saloon during the Balfours' time (1914). This room is now called the Pengelly Room and still has its beautiful painted decoration.

Englefield estate from his uncle Richard. He made frequent visits to Dorset from there to supervise the Kingston estate.

Mrs Fellowes frequently called at the school to see the children's work, particularly the girls' sewing, often taking her daughter Georgiana and visiting ladies with her. She gave the poorest girls clothing from time to time. When Stinsford Parish Council was formed in 1894 Mrs Fellowes was elected a member and served until her death in 1906. When she was buried at Stinsford, her coffin was wheeled on a hand bier through the gardens to the church. Because of her kindness to the schoolchildren the headmaster, Mr Dare and his wife took about 60 of them to the funeral to line the churchyard path. Each carried a bunch of spring flowers that they later dropped into the open grave as they filed past, which must have been a daunting experience for such young children. Ben Campbell, the head gardener, and the other gardeners had lined the grave with moss and bunches of primroses.

Several of the servants were beneficiaries of Mrs Fellowes' will among them the butler, William Purseglove who received £100. Mrs Gamble, caretaker of 6 Bryanston Square, was left £40. She was the widow of George Gamble the Fellowes' coachman until his death in 1886 aged 46. It seems he caught pneumonia whilst waiting on the coach during a cold January night to take Mr and Mrs Fellowes home after a ball. Mrs Gamble was then employed as caretaker at Kingston House when the family were at Bryanston Square and vice versa so that she always had somewhere to live and a small income to bring up her five daughters.

The contents of Kingston House were sold by Dukes at a four-day auction held between 18 and 21 September 1906. Presumably Mrs Fellowes's children had already selected the things they wished to keep but even so hundreds of items appear in the catalogue from elaborate French furniture to flower pots. Major Kenneth Balfour, who had purchased the estate, made successful bids for furniture, a manual fire-engine and a roan gelding called Peter with his mowing harness. Other local people, some of them servants, who made successful bids included Purseglove, Trent, Udall, Voss, Tizzard, Bartlett, Campbell and Matthews. It must have been quite something for employees and tenants to take home to their cottages items that had once graced the mansion of their wealthy employer. Perhaps some of them are treasured still!

Major Kenneth Balfour 1906–14

Major Balfour purchased the Kingston estate for £32,500 in 1906, three years after his second marriage to May Broadwood and in the year he was defeated defending his seat as MP for Christchurch. Three children from his second marriage were baptised at

St Michael's: Kenneth George in 1909, Andrew David Arthur in 1911 and Violet Rosemary in June 1913.

About half of a group photograph has survived showing a team of men who worked for W.E. Jones of Seamore Road, Westbourne, Bournemouth which has a caption that reads: 'Alterations at Kingston House, Dorchester by W.E. Jones, Contractor, Bournemouth.' Some 28 men, including Carey Butler, the foreman painter, appear in the surviving portion so that there must have been at least 50 in all. It seems very likely that after the elderly Mrs Fellowes's long occupation of the house Major Balfour and his wife, who were in their forties would have wanted changes to the house, particularly perhaps to its decoration.

Major Balfour decided to part with Kingston House after eight years and sold it to Cecil Hanbury in 1914. However, he kept Higher Kingston, the northern part of the estate where he planned to build a new house for himself. He planted an avenue of

Above: *The entrance hall in 1914, just before the house was sold by Major Balfour. The pillars are decorated to imitate black marble and the fireplaces are smaller than those the Hanburys installed later. The library can be glimpsed through the open doors on the right.*

Below: *The sitting-room at the southwest corner of the house as it was when the Balfours lived at Kingston House, 1914. The Hanburys altered the room by unblocking windows on the west wall and changing the ceiling shape. It is now the Whatmoor Room, a conference and meeting room.*

trees to line the driveway, which can still be seen to the east of Higher Kingston. Major Balfour served in France during the First World War and his name appears on the Roll of Honour at St Michael's. After the war he decided to sell Higher Kingston, abandoning his plans for the new house and moved to Winterbourne Steepleton Manor.

The Hanburys 1914–47

Cecil Hanbury purchased Kingston House soon after his marriage to Dorothy Symons-Jeune and from 1914 the house was called Kingston Maurward House rather than the plainer Kingston House.

Cecil Hanbury had previously worked in China where his family had business interests but his ambition was to become a member of parliament and after unsuccessful attempts in 1922 and 1923 he was elected MP for North Dorset in 1924. He was knighted in the Jubilee Honours List of 1935. Lady Dorothy had already been honoured with an OBE, probably for her work with the Red Cross in Dorset.

The Hanbury and Symons-Jeune families had a great enthusiasm for plants and gardens. Cecil's father Thomas and uncle Daniel had purchased La Mortola, a villa on the border of France and Italy, in 1868 where they developed the gardens visited by many, including Queen Victoria. In 1903 Thomas Hanbury gave the Wisley estate to the Royal Horticultural Society, now the organisation's headquarters. Dorothy's father was a landscape designer and her brother Bertie had a special interest in rock plants and phlox, winning gold medals at Chelsea. When Cecil and Dorothy purchased Kingston Maurward they must have been attracted by the prospect of developing the gardens. Cecil Hanbury eventually inherited La Mortola and they always had a house in London.

The Hanburys had three children who were all christened at Stinsford: Thomas born in 1914, Peter in 1916 and Caroline in 1920, who was usually known as 'Sammy' or 'Sam' – it is said because her mother

wanted another boy! Thomas Hardy was one of Caroline's godparents and on her christening day he presented a poem, specially written for the occasion. Cecil Hanbury also informally adopted Harry Nowell, a boy who was living on the estate in poor circumstances. He was supported financially as a child and young man. He was buried in the Hanbury family cemetery at Stinsford in 1999.

The Hanburys were very wealthy and employed about 30 people including a butler, lady's maid, a cook, footmen, housemaids, a boot boy, a head gardener, two other senior gardeners in charge of the pleasure and vegetable gardens and a number of general gardeners. When their children were young a nanny and children's nurse were also employed.

With their family connections to Italy Cecil and Dorothy Hanbury both supported Mussolini and the Italian Fascist Party in the 1920s and 1930s. Sometime before 1931 the King of Italy, on the recommendation of Mussolini, conferred the Grand Cordon of the Crown of Italy on Cecil Hanbury for his charitable work there while Dorothy Hanbury was the first English woman to become enrolled as a member of the British Italian Party and with other like-minded women gave her wedding ring to the party to be melted down and sold to raise funds. Cecil Hanbury's support for the Italians in 1935, after they had invaded Abyssinia, was opposed by his North Dorset constituency party and as a result he decided not to seek re-election.

The Hanburys were known for their weekend and shooting parties. They had a wide circle of friends from the world of politics, the arts and society generally. Amongst their guests at Kingston Maurward were the Prince of Wales, later Edward VIII; his sister Princess Mary, the Princess Royal; the Home Secretary William Joyson Hicks, Sir James Barrie, Augustus John and Thomas Hardy. Rosita Forbes who wrote about her travels in the Middle East was another guest. It is said that some guests flew in by private plane, while many arrived in chauffeur-driven limousines. Christmas parties were held for guests and for

Kingston Maurward House, c.1930. The Hanburys added the summerhouse in front of the staff annexe on the right of this photograph. They also made the Italian garden to the left of the house and built the Temple of the Four Winds seen on the far left.

Tommy and Peter Hanbury in the grounds of Kingston Maurward in the 1920s accompanied by Charles Atkins who worked for the Hanburys as a gardener for many years.

Above: *Tommy and Peter Hanbury on a trip to the seaside with Enid Houghton Brown who worked in the nursery until 1919.*

Left: *A game of haymaking in the park at Kingston Maurward, c.1919. Left to right: Peter Hanbury, Tommy Hanbury with Enid Houghton Brown and ?, nursery staff.*

Above: *The summerhouse added to the eastern side of the house by the Hanburys between 1914 and 1937 to allow meals to be taken 'al fresco'. The building has since lost it's decorative ironwork and is now incorporated into the Conference Hall.*

Below: *The drawing-room at the southwest corner of the house, now used as a conference and meeting room, 1930s.*

The entrance hall of Kingston Maurward in the 1930s. The earlier fireplaces were replaced by the Hanburys with the large yellow marble ones seen in this photograph which are still in place. The beautiful colour scheme and decorative painting was restored in 1987, the painter was Frederick Tyrell.

Above: *A rally of guides and brownies was held in honour of the visit by Princess Mary, the Princess Royal. They organised a march past the Princess, Lady Digby and other dignitaries. Mr and Mrs Hanbury were amongst the party.*

Left: *The Princess Royal visited Kingston Maurward to present new standards to the North, South and West Dorset divisions of the Girl Guides, 31 May 1930. She was the only daughter of King George V and Queen Mary and was President of the Girl Guides Association.*

TO-DAY (THURSDAY)

KINGSTON PARK

DORCHESTER.

JULY 24th and 25th, 1929

Magnificent

MILITARY DISPLAY

A Musical Ride by the 1st King's Dragoon Guards

In Pre-War Full Dress Uniform. DAILY at 3.30 p.m.

TENT PEGGING, &c., each Evening at **6.45 p.m.**
DANCING each Evening from **7.30 p.m.**

AT THE

Dorset Horticultural Society's

ANNUAL SHOW

OF

FLOWERS, FRUIT, VEGETABLES, AND HONEY.

By kind permission of CECIL HANBURY. Esq., M.P.

The Beautiful Gardens of Kingston Maurward

Including the sunken Italian and Japanese Gardens
Will be open to the public

The Full Band of the 1st King's Dragoon Guards will play during the Show

Ask your nearest Motor Coach Owners for particulars of Cheap Excursions.
CHEAP FARES from many stations on the Southern & Great Western Railways.

Admission : Wednesday, July 24th, 2 p.m. to 5 p.m., **2**/- ; 5 to 10 p.m., **1**/-
Thursday, July 25th, 11 a.m. to 2 p.m., **2**/- ; 2 to 5 p.m., **1/6**
5 p.m. to 10 p.m., **6d.** (Children Half Price.)

Car Park, **1/-**. Round the Ring, **2/**. Motor Cycle, **6d.** Bicycle, **3d.**

For full particulars apply to the Hon. Secretary,
R. WALLIS, KINGSTON MAURWARD, DORCHESTER.

Above: *The wedding of Tommy Hanbury and Joan Eve in July 1934 at St Margaret's, Westminster. Caroline Hanbury, sister of the bridegroom, is the first brides-maid behind the bride and groom.*

Right: *The grounds of Kingston Maurward House were often made available for public events by the Hanburys such as this military display by the King's Dragoon Guards which was combined with the Dorset Horticultural Society Annual Show, July 1929.*

The Hanburys gathered at Kingston Maurward to celebrate Tommy Hanbury's coming of age, October 1935. Left to right: Joan Hanbury (Tommy's wife), Tommy, Lady Dorothy with her grandchild, Peter Hanbury, ?, Sir Cecil with Kiki the Pekinese dog, Caroline 'Sam' Hanbury.

staff too. There was always an enormous Christmas tree in the hall decorated with candles, the butler standing close by with a wet sponge on a long pole to snuff out any candles likely to cause a fire.

When the Hanburys entertained life was particularly hectic for the staff. Fires had to be lit in all the rooms, including bedrooms. Extra staff came with some of the guests but if a lady arrived without a maid the housemaids were expected to look after her, as well as keep up with all their other duties. The staff discretely watched from the top landing as the guests went down to dinner in their finery. All reminiscent of the film *Gosford Park*! Special arrangements were put in hand to ensure that the generator which supplied electricity on these occasions did not fail. Jewell and Norcombe, a firm of electricians in Dorchester, were asked to send a man who stayed on duty overnight to make sure that if it did, it was quickly restored.

In 1916 during the First World War a group of local amateur actors and actresses, known as The Hardy Players gave a performance at Kingston Maurward of *The Dynasts* by Thomas Hardy in aid of the Red Cross Hospital Supply Depot. Dorothy Hanbury was then Vice President of the Red Cross in Dorset. The grounds were made available for other public events too; a Girl Guide Rally in May 1930 and in June 1937 a county-wide 'Keep-Fit Rally' was staged in the Park. In 1928 the Blues Regiment came to Kingston Maurward and paraded on the site of the present cricket pitch complete with the drum horses like those seen at the Trooping of the Colour. The gardens were always open to the public on Thursday afternoons, when shops in Dorchester closed for a half day. The entrance to the gardens was just off Church Lane and an admission fee of 6d. was collected by Mrs Bowles, whose husband worked at Stinsford Farm. The proceeds were given to charities.

Dorothy Hanbury travelled across Europe by car to Italy quite frequently taking her lady's maid, Miss Hassan with her. Miss Hassan and Mrs Marsh, wife

of the head gardener at Stinsford House, were great friends and Mrs Marsh's young daughter Marian wished she could travel abroad too but as she couldn't she asked Miss Hassan if her doll 'Zinga' could go to Italy instead. Miss Hassan agreed and quite soon postcards came from 'Zinga' to Gardener's Cottage at Stinsford from the leaning tower of Pisa amongst other places. After a while Marian missed her doll so much she wished she would come home, then one day there was a knock at the door and sitting outside was 'Zinga' holding a little basket with an orange, some sweets and a pretty mosaic brooch all the way from Italy. Marian Marsh still has the brooch and revealed that she was a teenager before she discovered that 'Zinga' actually spent the whole time in her Granny's cupboard!

In March 1932 the Hanburys had some unwelcome publicity in the national and local press, when their 17-year-old son Thomas, who had just left Eton, eloped with Joan Eve aged 16. The couple got to Gretna Green but the blacksmith was unable to marry them because they had not lived in the area for the necessary three weeks, so they left for Glasgow. Thomas had left a note telling his parents what he planned and so they set off in pursuit, chartering a plane at Croydon to take them to Scotland. After a forced landing due to bad weather at Blackpool they continued their journey by car. Arriving in Glasgow at about the same time as Thomas and Joan the four had dinner together before returning to London. Soon after Thomas was sent to Canada but a year later the engagement was announced and he and Joan married in July 1934 at St Margaret's, Westminster, a very grand affair.

Life For the Staff in the House

Mabel Symes worked for the Hanburys in the 1930s. She was the daughter of Charlie and Jane Symes from Stinsford. He was a hedger and relief shepherd for Joseph Wyndham Hull at Stinsford Farm. Mabel was second housemaid and was paid 3s.0d. a week. During her first days there she worried that she would never find her way around, but she soon knew every room. She discovered in her first week that Lady Hanbury could be very particular. When she went to Lady Hanbury's bedroom to close the curtains a few minutes after four o'clock Lady Hanbury said, 'I like my curtains drawn at four o'clock and it's now two minutes past.' She said she thought 'What have I come to?', but found that Lady Hanbury was not always so sharp and looking back found the whole thing funny.

On another occasion whilst working in the basement early one morning Lady Hanbury's bell rang and as she was on her own, Mabel thought she had better respond. Lady Hanbury wanted the fire lit and a tray of tea and toast so Gilbert Parker, the butler, got the tray ready while Mabel lit the fire.

Above: *On the roof of Kingston Maurward in April 1931 taking a break from their duties. Left to right: Mabel Baker (kitchen maid), Laura Way (scullery maid), Gordon Watts (under chauffeur), Cyril 'Charlie' Treasure and Bob Holt (menservants), accompanied by a pet dog. In the evenings when off duty the girls collected rose petals in the gardens for the pot pourri vases in the house.*

Right: *Servants who travelled from Kingston Maurward to Arndilly House, Cragellachie, Scotland in 1931. The Hanburys went to Scotland every year for grouse shooting and salmon fishing. The staff travelled by bus in advance of the family which took two days. Left to right: Cyril 'Charlie' Treasure, Gordon Watts the under chauffeur, Gilbert Parker the butler.*

Left: *House and kitchen maids at Arndilly House in 1931. Left to right: Mabel Symes (housemaid), Laura Way (scullery maid), Mabel Baker (kitchen maid) and Smutty the dog who travelled with the staff from Kingston Maurward, jumped into bed with the girls and left paw marks all over the sheets at the hotel during an overnight stay during the journey north. 'Good thing we were leaving' Mabel Goldsworthy (née Symes) recalled.*

Right: *On 11 November 1928 fire broke out in the roof of the annexe. The fire brigade used water from the lake to put out the fire but the upper floor and roof were entirely destroyed.*

Left: *The ewer presented by Cecil Hanbury of Kingston Maurward House to William Painter who drove the fire-engine to Kingston Maurward on 11 November 1928. Similar ewers were presented to other members of the crew. The inscription reads 'From Cecil Hanbury Esq. MP as an appreciation of good work at Kingston Maurward Fire, 11 November 1928'.*

The housemaids made the polish they used from beeswax and so Mabel quickly pushed the sticks into the polish tin so that when the fire was lit it blazed up really quickly. Lady Hanbury thought this was marvellous, 'but of course she didn't know the secret!'.

The indoor staff in the 1930s were Gilbert Parker the butler; Cyril 'Charlie' Treasure, second butler; Miss Parry, the housekeeper; Patricia Cahill, head housemaid; Mabel Symes, second housemaid; Ethel Parker, another Stinsford girl daughter of 'Shep' Parker, was third housemaid. The housemaids' work must have been extremely hard without modern equipment. The Portland stone stairs from the hall to the upper floors were washed with cold water and rubbed over with hessian sacking whatever the time of year. In the kitchen Mrs Bugler was the cook; Mabel Baker, kitchen maid and Laura Way, scullery maid. Mrs Bugler, who was quite a large lady, rode a motorcycle to get about. She must have been quite a strong character because when she heard that Mr Hanbury wanted to install Esse cookers in her kitchen she went to Thurmans, a shop in Dorchester, to have a look at them. She asked the shop assistant if it was possible to bake an ice cream in such an oven – she was told, probably not. In that case, she said, she didn't want one but would keep her range which she could get red hot and make a baked Alaska with no trouble. 'You can't do them in an Esse' she reported back to her employer.

Bob Bolter was head chauffeur and Gordon Watts under chauffeur; Bob Holt did jobs in the house and was 'boots'. All these people 'lived in', the female staff in the annexe and the men in the basement of the main house whilst some of the married staff lived in the Old Manor House.

Mabel spent a lot of time with Caroline Hanbury, who was ten years old in 1930. Her room was on the top floor of the house near the nurseries. When the Hanburys bought 41 Smith Square, London, Mabel was sent there with Caroline. She accompanied her to school every morning, in the chauffeur-driven Rolls Royce. Mabel and Caroline sat in the back but could hardly see out as the seat had been lowered to suit Lady Hanbury who was quite tall. After school the two explored the gardens next to the Houses of Parliament close to Smith Square.

Flowers from the glasshouses and gardens at Kingston Maurward were taken by car to the London house every fortnight – and sent back again if not exactly right! Charles Atkins, one of the gardeners, travelled with the flowers in the chauffeur-driven Rolls Royce, making the round trip in a day.

In the summer each year the Hanburys travelled to Scotland for the grouse shooting and salmon fishing. The staff were sent ahead, taking two days to make the journey. Even Smutty the dog who belonged to one of the staff, went with them.

The staff annexe was partially destroyed by a fire which broke out in the early hours of 11 November 1928. Bob Bolter, the chauffeur and his wife, were woken by the noise of the fire in the roof above their bedroom and raised the alarm. The Hanburys were hosting a weekend house party and the guests had to evacuate the house as a precaution. As the fire brigade could not be raised by telephone Bob Bolter drove to Dorchester to call them out and within five minutes the crew were at their headquarters, then in Trinity Street, and hurried towards Kingston Maurward. The motorised fire-engine was driven at great speed along the London Road and through the then narrow gateway to the park. Water had to be pumped from the lake and the staff were helped to escape from the building before the ceilings and chimneys fell in and the roof collapsed. Cars belonging to the Hanburys and their guests were moved from the garage. Furniture from the lower rooms and the estate office were moved by the staff, guests and Cecil Hanbury.

An account of the event in the *Dorset County Chronicle* a few days later reported Cecil Hanbury's praise for the fire brigade. As the fire occurred on Armistice Day, once the fire was out, Mrs Hanbury invited the men of the brigade to join the house party to listen to the service broadcast on the wireless from Whitehall. After several hours work the men might have preferred to go home to breakfast and a hot bath! Cecil Hanbury later presented them with engraved silver ewers as a token of his thanks.

The Outdoor Staff

In 1919 Alfred Jenkins came to Kingston Maurward from Castle Freke in Ireland, to be head gardener. The gardeners he supervised were Gerald Stockley, Reg or Ted Wallis, Walt Christopher and Fred Stemp. Gerald Stockley and Walt Christopher were still working at Kingston Maurward after 1947 when the Dorset Farm Institute opened.

The Italian garden was laid out to the west of the house and the Japanese garden made on the slope between the house and the lake. Joseph Benbow,

Alfred Jenkins became head gardener at Kingston Maurward in 1919. Before coming to Dorset he had worked at the Abbey Gardens on Tresco, Isles of Scilly and at Castle Freke in Ireland. There are glasshouses now on this spot to the north of the walled garden at Kingston Maurward.

Housemaids and garden staff taking time off in the gardens around the decorative well head in 1930. Back row, left to right: Ethel Parker (housemaid), Roy Bartlett (gardener), Pat Cahill (head housemaid); front row: Gerald Stockley (gardener), Mabel Symes (housemaid), Wilf White (gardener). Roy Bartlett was the nephew of Miss Bartlett who ran the Post Office, Lower Bockhampton. Ethel Parker was the daughter of John 'Shep' Parker, shepherd at Stinsford. Ethel later married Bill Dunford, dairyman at Stinsford Farm.

Hamner Cecil Hanbury, always known as 'Peter', aged 23, with his bride Prunella Kathleen Charlotte Higgins, 1939. Many of the staff from Kingston Maurward were invited to London to join in with the celebrations.

Mabel Symes holding Mrs Hanbury's Pekinese dog Kiki, 1930s. Bobby Bolter, young son of the chauffeur Bob Bolter is with her in his pedal car. They are standing on the steps of the Temple of the Four Winds in the gardens of Kingston Maurward, built on the sighting mound used when the house was built c.1720. When Lady Hanbury sold the estate in 1947 she had the temple removed to La Mortola, her house in Italy. In 1995 a new Temple of the Four Winds, constructed from original drawings, was built on the same site in memory of Ralph Fitzau, sponsored by his widow Jenny.

Above centre: Mr Walt Christopher, in charge of the fruit and vegetable gardens, working in the hot house. He worked at Kingston Maurward for 39 years and won many prizes for his employers at the South of England and Chelsea Flower Shows. He stayed on to work in the gardens when the Farm Institute took over the house and grounds. He lived in the thatched cottage next to the fruit and vegetable gardens.

The Italian garden as it was in July 1941 which seems little changed from the period before the war. Although the pool is empty the lawn edges are still being kept trim by a gardener, seen at bottom left.

An undated postcard, possibly from the 1930s, shows the bridge that once linked the walk around the lake with the largest of the six islands. When the lake was dredged in 1983 it was reduced in size and now has fewer islands.

head gardener at La Mortola, was brought to Kingston Maurward to assist with the creation of the Italian garden.

Following Alfred Jenkins's death in 1929, Mr Jarratt was appointed head gardener, Fred Stemp was in charge of the pleasure gardens, while Mr Wallis and then Walt Christopher ran the kitchen gardens. The general gardeners were Gerald Stockley, Wilf White and Roy Bartlett, grandson of Mrs Bartlett who ran the Post Office in Lower Bockhampton.

In the 1930s and 1940s the gatekeeper at the lodge was Tommy Lush who had lost a leg in the First World War. The lodge was probably built by the Fellowes family in the second half of the nineteenth century.

Ernie Thorne, who was a young gardener at Kingston Maurward just before the Second World War, described working in the gardens then. He was paid about £1.10s.0d. a week like Jimmy Tribe, another young gardener. He remembered that a team of gardeners hoed the gravel paths three abreast. As the most recently employed gardener, Ernie was left to look after the gardens whilst the other staff went to London in 1939 for the wedding of Peter Hanbury and Prunella Higgins. He described how he received his instructions:

The day before they went I had to go up to where they grew all the flowers and vegetables in the greenhouses and see the head gardener up there. First time I met him and he showed me what to do. I was to tap the flower pots with a long stick with a knob. 'If he's dull he don't need any water and if he do ring give him a drop of water.' It was wonderful up there, they had a big house full of carnations, all buds and coming out and there were peaches up there too. All sorts of stuff they had in them greenhouses – for them days 'twas a near miracle.

One afternoon in 1940 Mr Stemp came to see Ernie and the other gardeners to say that all territorials had to report to the barracks.

We were hoeing then, so we picked up our hoes, washed them off and put them away. We didn't see the gardens or Mr Stemp again. He didn't give us our pay then but sent it on. It was as quick as that, in the middle of gardening.

As territorials the men knew that they would be called up but so sudden a change from gardener to soldier must have been hard to believe and quite bewildering.

'That Was the End of it All'

Following Sir Cecil's death in June 1937 Lady Hanbury put the estate on the market in the following year but no buyer was found although she did sell Higher and Lower Bockhampton Farms to the tenant Mr Fred Parsons. During the war she lived in a flat on the first floor of the house on the west side overlooking the Italian garden, whilst the remainder of the house was used by the Royal Army Medical Corps after their evacuation from Dunkirk in 1940 and later by soldiers of the 1st Division of the US Army. In 1946 Dorset County Council purchased the house and estate of 131 acres for £23,000. In 1943 Lady Hanbury married the Revd Ruthven Forbes and afterwards lived at La Mortola in Italy, which she eventually gave to the Italian state in 1960.

'That was the end of it all' is a telling remark made by someone reminiscing. The estate was the workplace for almost everyone living in Lower Bockhampton, the largest of the hamlets. The cottages were almost exclusively owned by the estate, and whilst they were very basic, the rents were modest and rates were paid by the Hanburys. The Mellstock Hut had been provided for the parish by the Hanburys with no charges for its use. Down the years the estate owners had taken an interest in the school and the welfare of their staff, though wages were often low. Perhaps most significant is the sense of belonging that so many people mention when they look back. Everyone not only knew everyone but their extended families too. It really was the end of a very long era.

The grave of Sir Cecil Hanbury, who died in June 1937, in the Hanbury family plot opposite the churchyard. The sculptures of the deer have long since gone and the area has become rather dark now that the trees have grown taller.

Men working to remove the large areas of concrete, once the stands for oil and petrol cans, and the roads linking each one, 1947/48. Some of the workers were men from Eastern Europe, displaced as a result of the Second World War.

'Shep' Parker on the left lending a hand with setting up the 'stooks' or 'stiches', bundles of wheat or oats stacked together in a pyramid shape to dry before being taken from the fields, 1949.

Gerald Stockley, who worked in the formal gardens for the Hanburys and for the Farm Institute, was appointed groundsman in 1948. He was a keen cricketer so must have found relaying the cricket pitch in the park very satisfying.

Charlie Symes hedge laying along the A35 in about 1950 before the traffic became as heavy as it is today.

John Bowles thatching a rick, 1949. He was born at Stinsford and worked all his life on Stinsford and the College farms until he retired in 1988.

Alfred Pride working on the yew hedges in the formal gardens, using an early powered hedge trimmer. He could remember the hedges as they had been before the Second World War and offered to restore them. He was the first caretaker of the Farm Institute, from 1948.

Left: Charlie Symes at lambing time, 1964, sheltering in the shepherd's hut which has found a new use in the Visitors' Centre at Kingston Maurward. His special skill was hedging but he also helped 'Shep' Parker. He worked for Joseph Wyndham Hull before Stinsford Farm became part of the Farm Institute and retired in 1960. Charlie and his wife Jane lived at 2 Stinsford Cottages next door to the Parkers at number 1.

Left to right: Fred Kellaway (brick-layer), Tom Tetsill, from Dorchester and Bernie Marsh from Dewlish (carpenters), the first members of the estate building team, 1948. Fred and Tom worked together for 28 years.

Chapter 12

The Dorset Farm Institute

Between the purchase of the estate in 1947 and the arrival of the first students in 1949 the house and estate were prepared for their new function. This chapter concentrates on that period as very many of the staff lived in the immediate vicinity and most were already employed on the estate or at Stinsford Farm.

Towards the end of the Second World War the 1944 Education Act introduced new ideas including opportunities for further education in agriculture. The farm institute at Cannington in Somerset was the first to open in the South West and the Education Committee of Dorset County Council looked for a suitable site for an institute for Dorset. They chose the Kingston Maurward estate, which was being sold by Mrs Hanbury Forbes, as it was close to the centre of the county with suitable buildings to adapt as classrooms and living accommodation. Kingston Maurward House, the Elizabethan Manor House, the walled garden with its greenhouses, 20 acres of formal gardens including the 8-acre lake, 74 acres of land, farm buildings and 11 cottages were all for sale at the bargain purchase price of £23,000. The only drawback was the small area of farm land available but this problem was solved by a 99-year lease from the Earl of Ilchester for Stinsford Farm, which had 378 acres, immediately to the west of Kingston Maurward. The tenant Joseph Wyndham Hull, who was nearing retirement, kept the tenancy of the farmhouse and 5 acres of land for his life and that of his wife but gave up the farm in October 1948.

Kingston Maurward House had suffered from its occupation by the Royal Army Medical Corps and the US Army during the war. Having been the home of a wealthy family, the house was stripped of its furniture and sparsely equipped for offices and accommodation for servicemen. Even so it was found to be quite sound, apart from death watch beetle in the roof timbers. Conversion of the house to provide classrooms, accommodation for students and offices cost £19,744, partly offset by the sale of lead from the roof, which was sold for £3,520!

Plans were drawn up to establish how the main house, annexe and Old Manor House could be used. The basement of Kingston Maurward House was designated for laboratories, store rooms, a cloakroom, drying room and shower baths. The ground floor would provide a lecture room, library, dining-hall, kitchen and servery, staff cloakroom, general office and students' common room. The Principal would have a sitting-room, kitchen and dining-room on this floor and a flat and office on the first floor. Matron, the warden and a lecturer would be accommodated on the first floor with a staff room. The second floor would provide residential accommodation for 30 male students. Married accommodation for the caretaker and nine domestic staff would be provided in the annexe. The Old Manor House was destined to be a boarding-house for female students with a resident kitchen maid, chambermaid and part-time cleaners but this never came about due to the very poor condition of the house and the cost of repairs.

In the year leading up to D-Day in June 1944 the grounds had been used to store five million gallons of fuel and oil on 40 concrete platforms. Four Nissen huts with concrete bases and temporary concrete roads remained in the park when the estate was purchased in 1947. A claim was eventually made to the War Department to cover the cost of removing the concrete and restoring the park to some sort of order. The fencing had been broken and many of the trees felled whilst the formal gardens had suffered with few gardeners left to care for them. The lake was eventually reduced from 8 acres to 3½ acres and the cost of restoration of the gardens and lake, apart from wages, was more than covered by the sale of the estate fishing rights.

It was suggested that large areas of the gardens should be bulldozed as uneconomic, but fortunately this idea was not taken up and by 1962 the gardens were well on the way to recovery.

In 1949 the Farm Institute considered, but rejected, a request that a training centre for TB (tuberculosis) convalescent patients be set up at the Institute to teach rural crafts such as thatching, hurdle making, basket making, horticulture, as well as bee and poultry keeping. The patients would be partially cured but needing an open air life rather than returning to industrial occupations. It is perhaps surprising that 300 patients would have benefited from this scheme, although whether these patients were from Dorset or a wider area is not known.

Staff

All Mr Hull's staff at Stinsford Farm were re-employed by the Farm Institute when he retired. They were shepherds John Parker, known as 'Shep' Parker and his son John; Bert Crabb, head tractor driver; Fred Bowles, tractor driver; George Bowles, labourer; Bill Dunford, cowman; John Bowles, thatcher; Charlie Symes, labourer and hedger; Fred 'Benny' Atkins, carter, and an un-named waterman probably George Hansheen. Most earned £4.15s. or £4.10s. a week plus overtime and the shepherds were also paid a lambing bonus.

In December 1947 Walter Christopher, who had worked in the gardens for many years, was made head gardener. Alfred Pride, who lived in Lower Bockhampton and worked at County Hall, was appointed caretaker in April 1948. Bill Read, who already lived at the Old Manor House transferred from the Roads and Bridges Department of the County Council to the Farm Institute as a labourer.

Other early appointments were two carpenter/ handymen, Tom Tetsill and Bernie Marsh. Many years later in 1982 Tom Tetsill wrote down his memories of these early years:

After being demobbed from the services after the war I returned to my trade as a carpenter... I espied a vacancy for a carpenter/handyman at Kingston Maurward... As I had worked for many years building parts of this estate for my late employer, this would be just the work I would enjoy.

Eventually I was called for an interview to County Hall, and set off dressed in my new demob suit and shoes, and after being warned by the caretaker that the boardroom floor was highly polished, finished my entry on my back in front of the Committee. After a while I had notification from County Hall that myself and Mr B. Marsh from Dewlish had been accepted... and were to meet Mr Bennett from the Committee and the County Architect Mr E. Rickets at the main entrance to Kingston Maurward House on 22 March 1948 at 9a.m.

I arrived at the entrance lodge on my bike, complete with tools, etc., but on cycling down the drive a sorry sight met my eyes. What was once an immaculate park now consisted of rows of rusty Nissen huts, concrete bases, concrete roads, dead trees and rusty barbed wire everywhere. After a tour round the estate with Mr Ricketts and Mr Bennett I had the impression it would take about ten years to get the place anywhere near shipshape... As the alterations to the main house were to be done by contractors it was Mr Bennett's wish for Mr Marsh and myself to restore the peach-houses, vineries and an assortment of other green-houses which at the moment consisted of as much galvanised iron and sacks of glass, but proudly cared for by a wonderful old gardener, Mr W. Christopher.

After inspecting many old buildings, we decided on the old stables as a workshop, along with a friendly crowd of rats, and as all materials such as timber were on ration after the war we set about making benches, stools and steps from any timber we could salvage, along with two rick ladders. Our next worry was transport, until we found a two-wheeled Army hand-cart which served us well for many weeks to come.

Two men were lent from the County Council to help with the estate work. One, the late Bill Read, was an all round countryman – hedging, fencing, rabbiting – and his job was to cut his own piles and rails wherever

they could be found. I can remember him striding off across the park carrying six piles and a sledgehammer on his shoulder and, as always, a quart bottle of cider in his jacket pocket.

Things now began to move fast, as one morning we were informed that Mr Kenney (the Principal) had bought four in-milk cows at Reading market, and we had to repair and whitewash the estate cowstall. Mr Marsh was given the job of making a milking stool for Bill Read to do the milking. Also at this time the only water available at the Manor building was a hand pump attached to a well which often ran dry; also no electricity, the only lighting by hurricane lamp.

As I look back I remember things which seem impossible at Kingston Maurward today. The arrival of the first tractor left in charge of the late Harry Richards, who was so proud of it that he wanted to spend Saturday mornings on cleaning and maintaining it (in those days we worked till one o'clock on Saturdays). I remember the building of a bull pen for Bill Dunford from trees cut on the estate and old doors from Manor stables; it answered the purpose and made the bull look a dwarf in size.

The engineers' workshop during those days was the garage and stables at the main house, and I remember helping to repair threshing machines, elevators and grass cutters under the watchful eye of Charlie Symes, Benny Atkins and Bert Crabb, who knew these machines inside out. All wonderful craftsmen of the land. Mr Marsh was a great help in all this work, as he came from a village family of wheelwrights and often had a day off to make a coffin when one of the villagers passed away.

On looking back I could write about many events that made life happy and contented. The arrival of a horse and cart – one for use at Stinsford and one for the Manor's use – which (if we could catch it) we could use for hauling our building materials around, and often when the water well ran dry at the Manor Farm, it would bolt with the rattle of milk churns bringing water from Stinsford Farm. [There was a] coal-fired boiler in the old dairy at Stinsford for washing purposes and another one which Ron Maple, the pigman, boiled swill in, with the help of a heavy ploughshare weighing down the safety valve to get extra steam!

In these early days there were no teaching staff, the main house being in the hands of the builders. In June a mate in the trade as bricklayer was appointed to work with me, by name Fred Kellaway and for 28 years we worked together happily and contentedly.

Early Years Recorded in the Farm Diary

The diary is a record of each day's work by farm employees and a few sample days give an idea of the work required to restore and set up the estate for the future. On Monday 4 October 1948 Fred Atkins and Bert Crabb were ploughing the field Mile Tree for

How milk used to be collected from the Farm Institute dairies, 1950s. Bill Dunford (left) worked for Joseph Wyndham Hull at Stinsford Farm and became an employee of the Farm Institute in1947. Jack Buckerell (right) of Stalbridge was appointed bailiff for the Institute in October 1948 and stayed until he retired in 1960.

Left: *The Ferguson tractor, bought for the Farm Institute in 1948, being used for haymaking. Jackets, waistcoats and caps or hats were normal working clothes for the men then – no covered cab or ear protectors and no radio!*

Below: *A 1951 picture of Denis Jenkins with Bonny who was supposed to provide transport in the early days of the Farm Institute, but only if she could be caught! Behind is the front of the old barn where as a boy Thomas Hardy attended a Harvest Supper organised by the Martins who owned the estate at the time. Just the footings of the barn are left now.*

winter wheat and both saw a demonstration of the new Fordson tractor while Fred Bowles had a demonstration on the Ferguson tractor recently purchased for £827 complete with 'a set of appliances'. Shepherds John Parker and his son John were hurdling the flock of Dorset Horn ewes in Exhibition Field. George Bowles and George Hansheen spent the day cutting and shaping piles for fencing the park. John Richardson took up iron railings and did some hedge trimming helped by John Bowles. Bill Dunford, the dairyman, was working in the dairy.

A week later 'Benny' Atkins and Bert Crabbe were ploughing, Fred Bowles hauled hurdling and wire in the park and spent the rest of the day discing. 'Shep' Parker and his son still had ewes in Exhibition Field and some in the park, while George Hansheen worked in the water-meadows taking out ditches. Charlie Symes and George Bowles were fencing in the park, John Richardson and John Bowles spent the day cleaning up at Stinsford Dairy and Bill Dunford was working in the dairy as usual.

At the end of the year 'Benny' Atkins, the brothers Fred, George and John Bowles, Bill Read and John Richardson were all cleaning Stinsford Barton and the roadway to Butchers Close. The Parkers were tending sheep and Bill Dunford the dairy cows. George Hansheen was taking out ditches in the water-meadows in preparation for the flooding of the meadows in the new year.

Early in 1949, six months before the Institute's first students, arrived Denis Jenkins and Ben Boughton were appointed as herdsmen at Manor Dairy. Denis Jenkins already had connections with Kingston Maurward as his grandfather had been head gardener in the 1920s.

By July 1951 the Institute had been open to students for two years and farming activities had finally taken priority over reclaiming the park and replacing fencing. The farm diary reported that water was hauled for pigs, poultry, heifers and sheep. Bert Crabb, along with George and Fred Bowles were ploughing but Fred was also sent to Dorchester to collect a piano for a dance before going back to harrowing!

In 1999 Kingston Maurward College celebrated the fiftieth anniversary of the first students arriving in 1949. As part of the celebrations the Kingston Maurward Association produced a history of those years, *Celebrating the First Fifty Years*, edited by Jim Wilson.

Domestic staff of the Farm Institute standing in front of the summerhouse, c.1950, built by the Hanburys, now part of the Conference Hall. Left to right, back row: *Doreen Key, Betty Key, Harry Fost, Jane Rimmer, Violet Read;* front row: *Jean Linnington, Brenda Kellaway.*

Chapter 13

The Farms and Farming in the Parish

The tithe map for the parish was made in 1839 and shows all the farms, cottages and fields. With it is a schedule, called the apportionment, which lists the owners, occupiers and the name and acreage of each field.

In the 1830s there was a depression in agriculture and it was also a time of unrest amongst agricultural workers in Dorset and in other counties, because of the very low wages and the introduction of threshing and other machines on farms, which the labourers saw as a threat to their jobs. Wages were notoriously low in Dorset and living conditions were generally extremely poor. George Loveless of Tolpuddle was one of six men who went to his employer to ask for an increase from 9s. to 10s. a week, the same wages as other men in the district but a few months later their wages were reduced to 8s. a week. The men met with William Morton Pitt the owner of Kingston estate who was a Justice of the Peace to explain their grievances. He suggested that they should send three representatives to County Hall to meet with their employers and James Frampton a senior Justice of the Peace, who was also a landowner. Unhappily the men were told they must work for what their employers saw fit to give them and soon after their wages were reduced again.

George Loveless decided to set up a union in Tolpuddle to try to gain bargaining power as a larger group of men. However, landowners and the government were determined to suppress unions and control outbreaks of dissent. The men were charged with administering an unlawful oath, a law which was normally applied to men in the Navy who mutinied. The men from Tolpuddle were sentenced to seven years' transportation to Tasmania and were told by the Judge that this was not for anything they had done, or that he could prove they had intended to do, but as an example to others. The men came to be known as the Tolpuddle Martyrs. After campaigns for their release four of them arrived in London in June 1837 and the fifth returned later. They are celebrated each year at the Tolpuddle Martyrs' Festival.

As late as 1867 the usual wage for an agricultural labourer in Dorset was 10s.0d. a week, or 9s.0d. if a cottage and garden was provided. Some additional money could be earned at harvest time. In Dorset it was quite common for a whole family to be employed, with wives expected to work, often in winter, in the turnip fields like the character of Tess in Thomas Hardy's novel *Tess of the d'Urbervilles*.

Thomas Lock, farmer at Higher Kingston, gave evidence to the Commission on the Employment of Children, Young Persons and Women in 1867. He told the Commissioner that about 11 adult women went to work in the parish of Stinsford.

The only way they can be got to go is by making it a condition of hiring the husband that they should go. They get 6d. a day or 8d. if they don't get 'grist' (corn before being milled). Boys leave school for regular employment at eight or nine years of age. Owing to the turnip cultivation they are wanted more in winter than summer.

Boys were sent to work to supplement family incomes and the report goes on to say that more boys of this age were working in Dorset than any other county. The youngest boys earned 2s.0d. or 2s.6d. a week, whilst a carter's boy or cow boy would earn 3s.0d. Boys, too, could earn a little more at harvest time when girls also worked in the fields.

For labourers who did not have a cottage provided as part of their employment the rent was usually about 1s.0d. a week. Most cottages had large gardens which were used for growing vegetables, keeping chickens and often a pig, all helping to feed the family. The report points out that the condition of the cottages in Dorset was 'more ruinous and contain worse accommodation than those of any other county… except Shropshire'. Cottages were described in some parishes as a disgrace to their owners – Charminster, Fordington, Bere Regis and Winfrith are mentioned but not Stinsford. It would be nice to think that the Earl of Ilchester and James Fellowes of Kingston were more considerate employers.

Stinsford Farm

The Earl of Ilchester's farms in the parish were Stinsford Farm and Bhompston Farm a mile or so to the east. Both had meadows by the River Frome and land rising towards Waterston Ridge in the north.

William Harding leased Stinsford Farm from 1822 and during his tenancy a fire at the farm in 1825 was thought to have been started deliberately. In December 1830 the newspaper, *Bell's Weekly Messenger*, reported that two ricks belonging to William Harding were set on fire, but with the help of local people the fire was prevented from spreading further. This was the time of agitation by farm workers and fires were often assumed to have been started deliberately.

Above: *Stinsford Farm with its full complement of old farm buildings, 1930s. In the foreground is the lane to the church, beyond the farm is the lodge to Kingston Maurward House and just visible on the left of the lodge are some of Stinsford Cottages.*

Above: *The thatched cart shed which once stood next to the lane between Stinsford Farm and the church. It was thought to be very old.*

Right: *Eweleaze barn is said to have been built by the first Thomas Hardy who died in 1837, although a map of Stinsford Farm dated 1759 also shows a barn on the same site – possibly the barn was built before Thomas Hardy's time.*

Above: *A treat for all the dollies to sit out in the garden with Daisy and Jo, children of Joseph and 'Daisy' Wyndham Hull, 1920s. Behind them are the two thatched farm workers' cottages on the Tincleton Road with Birkin Cottages to the right.*

Right: *A gathering of hunt followers in the 1930s. In the foreground 'Bubbles' Hull, to the right her father Joseph Wyndham Hull, her mother Margaret 'Daisy' and older sister Jo. The Hulls farmed at Stinsford Farm from 1876 to October 1948, though did not leave the farmhouse until 1968.*

Stinsford farmhouse, home of three generations of the Hull family from 1876 until 1968, pictured in 1930s. There was a dairy house and barn on the same site in 1759.

Seen here in 2007, Stinsford farmhouse converted in the late 1990s to become the centre for Kingston Maurward Training and now as the Stinsford Business Centre, of Kingston Maurward College.

By 1839 William Harding had been succeeded by Stephen Toghill Harding, possibly his nephew. At the census of 1851 he and his wife had ten children, a cook, nurse, housemaid and under-maid all living together, which must have been quite a squash as the farmhouse is not that big.

An isolated cottage is shown on the 1839 tithe map at Slyers Lane, now the B3143, a mile north of the London Road. The census of 1841 confirms that bricks were being made on the site as brick maker John Davis, aged 30, lived there with his wife, children and William Riggs aged 20 who was also a brick maker. Ten years later William Riggs was the brick maker, living at Brick Kiln Cottage. There are no references to brick makers in later census returns and the cottage has disappeared.

Joseph Wyndham Hull succeeded his father Joseph Symes Hull as tenant of Stinsford Farm in 1906. Shortly before he retired himself in 1947 he wrote an account of the way the farm had been run since 1876 when his father first rented it. In his father's time it had been a sheep and corn farm with a small dairy of about 20 cows looked after by a dairyman and his wife who did the milking, made butter and blue vinney cheese. The original flock of sheep on the farm were the Hampshire Down breed but this was soon replaced by a Dorset Horn flock. This breed was popular because it produced lambs well before Christmas, attracting the best prices. This flock, one of the oldest registered in Dorset, was still at the farm in 1947 when it became part of the Dorset Farm Institute. By 1915 the number of cows was increased and milk was sold direct to a milk factory, which gave a better financial return. This change was common on many Dorset farms at that time and ultimately led to a dramatic fall in the production of local

cheeses. Many people will remember churns of milk at farm gates waiting to be collected by the milk factory lorries in the days before milk tankers.

Most of the farm workers' cottages at Stinsford were across the Tincleton Road from the farmhouse. A pair of thatched cottages and several more to the east, were built of brick, with allotment gardens. In the early years of the twentieth century there was one cottage near the farmyard. This was occupied by the Bowles family in the 1930s.

Another fire broke out at Stinsford Farm in November 1911, reported in the style of the time in the *Dorset County Chronicle*:

The Dorchester Fire Brigade had their slumbers disturbed at an early hour yesterday morning... Shortly before two o'clock a messenger cycled to Dorchester bearing the intelligence that a fire had broken out in the granary on Mr J.W. Hull's farm. The fire bell was rung and the brigade messengers went round to the firemen, who, with their chief officer, Captain H. Watts, quickly assembled at the fire station in Princes Street. The steamer and appliances were got in readiness and the horses were about to be brought from Mr W. Hammond's stables, when a second messenger arrived on the scene and countermanded the order for the brigade, the fire having been put out. The firemen thereupon returned home and resumed their slumbers.

More drama was reported in the press in April 1937 when four cows were killed during a gale. A large chestnut tree was brought down bringing with it a telephone wire which became 'live' when it touched electricity cables. The unfortunate cows strayed too near. The article praised the efforts of a young married dairyman, William Dunford, who drove the

Left: *John Foot aged about five on his tricycle near his home at Birkin House Cottages, 1940s. Behind him is the group of cottages for Stinsford Farm workers.*

1 and 2 Stinsford Cottages and Birkin Cottages in the background, 1940s.

John Parker, known as 'Shep' Parker, with splendid whiskers, snowy white shirt, 'weskit' and gaiters, 1930s. The two Dorset Horn sheep from his flock look equally splendid. 'Shep' Parker was shepherd at Stinsford Farm for Joseph Wyndham Hull and the Farm Institute. His son John worked with him and then succeeded him as shepherd when his father retired.

'Shep' Parker's wife Frances outside their cottage at Stinsford, 1930s.

On 24 February 1903 Flora Hull, daughter of Joseph Symes Hull of Stinsford Farm, married Rupert Tory of Winterborne Clenston. The wedding took place at Stinsford church and the wedding breakfast was at the farmhouse where the guests were photographed. Apart from the bride and groom and the bride's parents on her left no others have been identified.

Above: *The Bath and West and Southern Counties Show took place at Dorchester for a number of years. Plans of the showground exist for 1872, 1887, 1908 and 1928. The site was the field appropriately called Exhibition, part of Stinsford Farm, on the corner of the London and Piddlehinton roads. The Dorset County Show now takes place opposite at Coker's Frome.*

Right: *Exhibition field as it might have been with 30 detached houses and 'Nursery Ground'! The plan was drawn up by Crickmays, architects of Weymouth, in 1872 the same year that Thomas Hardy left the firm to become a full-time writer. A surprising 'find' amongst the archives of the Earls of Ilchester.*

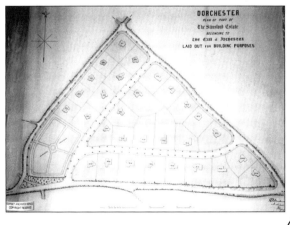

animals to safety, risking his own life and saved hundreds of pounds' worth of stock. Bill Dunford continued to work at Stinsford Farm when it was part of the Farm Institute and he eventually retired to live at Knapwater in Lower Bockhampton with his wife Ethel.

Joseph Wyndham Hull was a churchwarden for 60 years, a manager of Stinsford and Bockhampton School and member of Stinsford Parish Council and his wife Daisy ran the Mothers' Union for many years. Photographs of the Hull family include a splendid photograph of the wedding party when Flora, Joseph Wyndham Hull's sister, married Rupert Tory in 1903. Others from the 1920s and 1930s show the farmhouse as it was. Many people who knew the farmhouse then remember the old railway carriage in the garden used as a children's playhouse. It was also used to house the milk cooler at one time. Mr and Mrs Hull continued to live at Stinsford farm-house, after his retirement, until the late 1960s.

Bhompston Farm

Bhompston Farm, like Stinsford, was owned by the Earls of Ilchester and their predecessors. It is on the eastern side of the parish with the farmhouse and buildings on rising ground above the river and water-meadows. A survey of the farm dated to the eighteenth century includes field names: Ham, a watered meadow; Gossehams, a water mead; Pig's Mead, a water mead; Blot Hams a water mead; Furzzie Close and Marnels for tillage; May Close, an arable and pasture area. The heath was partly enclosed and sown to wheat at the time.

By 1839 Bhompston was farmed by James Cake and his wife Catherine. The farm had 320 acres with 40 acres of heath in 1851. Nine men and four boys were employed by the Cakes to run the farm and dairy. Ten years later James's son, another James, had taken over the farm with his wife Charlotte Augusta.

By 1871 Joseph Kellaway, born in Cerne Abbas, was running the dairy at Bhompston. In Dorset it was common for the dairy on a farm to be leased or rented by a dairyman, the rent based on a price per cow. The dairyman's wife made butter and cheese and cared for the calves often with the help of her daughters working as dairymaids.

By 1881 there were six cottages at Bhompston occu-pied by five agricultural labourers, a cowman and dairyman, as well as the farmhouse. Sparrow Cottage stood on its own in a small triangular plot facing onto the Tincleton Road quite close to Heedless William's Pond. By 1935 it had been aban-doned and was eventually demolished because of the difficulty in getting clean water from the well.

When Thomas Hardy wrote the novel *The Return of the Native* he based his description of the Yeobright's home on Bhompston farmhouse which in the novel is called Blooms End where mummers performed

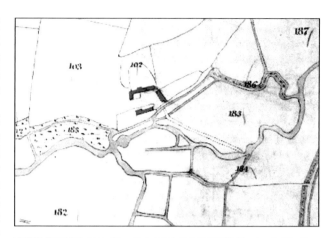

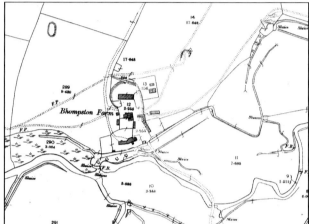

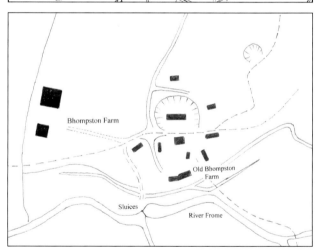

Bhompston maps showing the changes of 170 years. Top: *1839 tithe map;* middle: *1902 Ordnance Survey map;* above: *Bhompston in 2007.*

'St George and the Dragon' at the Christmas revels.

Since 1935 four generations of the Wakely family have farmed at Bhompston as tenants and more recently as owners since Ilchester Estates sold the farm. The original farmhouse is a private house and the farm buildings have been converted into cottages.

Heedless William's Pond, which was once part of Bhompston Farm, is just inside the parish boundary a few hundred yards off the Tincleton Road. The old story of how the pond got its name concerns a coach driver who had the reputation for driving recklessly.

A collection of horseshoes found in the water-meadows of Bhompston Farm. Left to right, top row: *type made between the eleventh and sixteenth centuries, a sixteenth- to seventeenth-century shoe, a seventeenth-to eighteenth-century shoe.* Front row: *nineteenth-to twentieth-century carthorse shoe, a shoe for a hunter of the same period.*

An undated watercolour sketch by Henry Moule (1825–1904) of Headless or Heedless William's Pond, c.1890.

View across the water-meadows to Bhompston Farm showing the old farm buildings now converted to cottages with the 1930s houses up on the hill, seen in 2007.

The south side of the old farmhouse seen from the water-meadows, 2007. The dairy, where butter and blue vinney cheese was made, was attached to the farmhouse and has been incorporated into the present house.

A 2007 view of the north side of the old farmhouse, Blooms End in Thomas Hardy's novel The Return of the Native, *though Hermann Lea, who traced many of the buildings used by Thomas Hardy in his novels, noted that it was much changed by the 1920s.*

The new farmhouse built in 1964, pictured in 2007.

One day driving down Duddle Hill he, his coach, horses and passengers ended up in the pond where they all perished! Sometimes the pond is called Headless William's Pond but 'Headless' is thought to refer to the folk name for the roadside stone, possibly a boundary marker, which stands next to Pond House. Another possibility is that in the Dorset dialect of years gone by 'heedless' could sound like 'headless'.

The land to the north of the Tincleton Road, originally part of Bhompston Farm, has become Pine Lodge Farm and Yellowham Farm. The owners of Pine Lodge Farm have established tearooms which also offer lunches. More recently 'Zorbing' has been introduced, an exciting but possibly hair-raising activity, rolling along and down a sloping field suspended inside an enormous transparent ball! At Yellowham Farm accommodation for visitors is available in attractive surroundings on the very edge of Yellowham Woods.

Kingston Estate Farms

Until about 1800 the estate was probably run as a single unit from Home Farm near the Old Manor House. Sometime between 1800 and 1825 the owner William Morton Pitt divided his estate into three separate farms which were rented to tenant farmers. Greyswood Farm later called Higher Kingston Farm was created on land north of the turnpike road, now the A35. Manor Farm included the land south of the A35 to the Tincleton Road and the water-meadows south of Kingston House. Home Farm was the smallest with land in the park north of Kingston House and fields east of Bockhampton Lane.

Greyswood Farm, Later Higher Kingston Farm
The farmhouse was built by 1800 and by 1825 there were one or two additional farm buildings or cottages nearby. Thomas and Joseph Bedloe have been identified as early tenants. By 1844 Thomas Lock was the tenant farmer living at Higher Kingston

Thomas Lock and his wife Anne (née Pouncy). As a boy Thomas Lock went to sea but then chose to be a farmer sometime before he married in 1834. He was a church-warden for many years, as well as an overseer and guardian of the poor. He died in 1879 at Higher Kingston, his wife having died two years earlier.

with his wife Anne and their family of five sons and three daughters. By 1851 there were six cottages around the farmhouse, occupied by a shepherd, a carter and several agricultural labourers. Some of the men had sons who also worked on the farm as labourers, a shepherd's boy and a carter's boy.

Thomas Lock died in 1879 and he left instructions in his will that the farm should be run by his son Reginald for the benefit of his brothers and sisters until the youngest, Horace, became 21. Reginald appears to have carried out his father's wishes as the farm changed hands soon after Horace Lock became 21 so that by 1883 James Symes Hull was tenant of the

Ploughing at Higher Kingston, c.1910.

Stan Clark combining at Higher Kingston Farm, 1950s.

Higher Kingston House, 2007, which was built in the late-eighteenth century and in the twentieth century was the scene of several incidents during the Second World War.

farm as well as Home Farm and Lower Bockhampton Farm too. His brother Joseph was already tenant of the Earl of Ilchester's Stinsford Farm.

In 1899 the rent for the three farms was dramatically reduced from £1,100 to £750 probably because of the difficult economic times in farming then. It is interesting to see from the accounts of Henry Hardy the builder of Higher Bockhampton, that the tenant farmer and the tenants were treated exactly the same when it came to decorations, whitewash was standard for all, regardless of status!

In 1914 Major Balfour sold the Kingston estate to Cecil Hanbury. Although he kept Higher Kingston House and farm for a few years he eventually sold up in 1920. Directories for the following years list the names of a number of residents of Higher Kingston: 1920 to 1923 Major Richard Partridge and in 1927 Colonel F.W. Scott. General Broad purchased Higher Kingston House and farm in 1938, selling off the farm to the Holland family who still own it as part of Holland Farms. When General Broad sold up in 1947 the house was purchased by Revd Strickland Taylor, headmaster of Cheam School who renamed it Little Cheam. This name still appears on some modern maps though it has not been called that for some time. The house was last sold in 1989 and continues to be a private residence

Higher Bockhampton Farm

The farm buildings are of traditional brick and flint, built in 1849 for Mr Francis Martin who had purchased the Kingston estate two years before. The date and his initials can be seen on the end wall of one of the buildings. There was no farmhouse with this farm which was originally known as Higher Bockhampton Buildings but when the Hanburys acquired the estate in 1914 they had a house built, in the Arts and Crafts style for their farm bailiff, in the nearby hamlet of Higher Bockhampton. Mr Fred Parsons and his family lived at Mellstock House from 1926. In 1966 Mr Parsons retired and the two dairies, most of the land and the farm workers' cottages were sold. The chicken units remained for some years and were not sold with the rest of the farm. Higher Bockhampton Farm was purchased by the Dorset Farm Institute in 1966 but the land north of the Tincleton Road was sold again and is now Thorncombe Farm.

Binding hay on Higher Bockhampton Farm. Unfortunately the two men have not been identified, c.1940.

Four farm workers at Higher Bockhampton Farm, c.1940. Left to right: ?, Johnny 'Jack' Richardson, Walter Hyde, ?.

Doreen Ferris had been evacuated from Southampton to Higher Bockhampton during the war and had lived with the Hydes at 4 Higher Bockhampton. She often made visits in later years. Here she is presumably at Higher Bockhampton Dairy, c.1950s, lending a hand or just trying her hand!

Higher Bockhampton Farm Dairy House at the time it was sold by Fred Parsons and bought by the Dorset College of Agriculture, 1966. Its name is confusing as although it was the dairy attached to Higher Bockhampton Farm it is closer to Lower Bockhampton and just north of the Old Manor House. The farmhouse was built at the very end of the nineteenth century by Henry Hardy of Higher Bockhampton during the Fellowes' ownership of the estate. The house is now used as offices by College staff.

Harvest time at Higher Bockhampton. The threshing-machine is being driven by power from the tractor. In the more distant past a steam engine would have been used. Several ricks can be seen in the background, c.1940.

Walter Hyde thatching a rick with at least two more to do, c.1940. Their size can be judged by comparison with his bicycle propped against the rick.

Kingston Dairy or Lower Dairy – Now Lower Farm, Lower Bockhampton

For many years Kingston or Lower Dairy was attached to Higher Kingston Farm, presumably to provide a dairy for a farm that was some distance from the river and water-meadows, so essential for dairy cows. Before the arrival of piped water to the troughs in the fields, dairy farming was not possible at Higher Kingston. The water-meadows at Lower Bockhampton also provided early spring grazing for sheep and hay in summer.

Between 1841 and 1861 the dairy was run by John Vine and his son. Hand milking meant that most dairy herds were relatively small and would proba-

bly have included about 20 or so cows. By 1864 David Strong and his wife had taken over the dairy but tragically he was drowned in the River Frome in April 1876 at the age of 45. Information given at the inquest explains what happened and provides a glimpse into the start of a dairyman's day. It seems he got up at about 4a.m. and when Robert Cable who helped look after the cows called at the farmhouse at 5.30a.m. Mr Strong was enjoying a pipe by the kitchen fire and fastening up his boots to go out to the dairy. He said that it was a nice morning and poured Mr Cable a glass of porter. He seemed well and in good spirits. When Mr Cable returned from looking after the cows he was surprised that the milk had not been skimmed so he called on Mrs Strong to

Left: *The farmhouse at Lower Farm, Lower Bockhampton, built in Broadmayne brick in the 1890s by Henry Hardy, pictured in 2007.*

The original farmhouse at Lower Farm, Lower Bockhampton, which was replaced by the Broadmayne brick house, soon after this painting was made by Henry Moule, December 1894. The house was later converted into a cart shed and stable. The large stone at the corner of the house is still in place. The cottage next to the bridge in Bockhampton Lane, now Bridge Cottage, is in the background.

George Atkins from Lower Bockhampton with one of the Treasure brothers who ran the dairy at Lower Bockhampton, 1940s.

Left to right: Roy, Reg, Marion and Jo Kellaway at Frome Farm, West Stafford, c.1950. In 1966 their father Frank bought Lower Bockhampton Farm.

Some of the hatches still in place at the 'swimming hole', Lower Farm, on the southern edge of the parish, 1967.

The yard behind the farmhouse at Lower Bockhampton Dairy, c.1960. Cows kept their horns then.

Roy and Eve Kellaway at Lower Farm, Lower Bockhampton, 2007.

The brickwork is still in place but the hatches, apparently made with timber from Yellowham Wood, have gone.

The picturesque dairy cottages at Coker's Frome with children in pinafores and a fine example of a farm wagon, c.1891. In the background is All Saints' Church spire on the left and St Peter's Church tower in the centre.

Coker's Frome farmhouse on the left with its farm buildings, early 1900s. The house was destroyed by fire in 1948.

The drowners' cottages at Coker's Frome Farm, c.1904. In the 1930s the cottage on the left was occupied by Arthur Richardson and on the right by Jim and Mildred White. The two cottages are now one and are no longer part of the farm.

Pigeon House Cottages in August 1889 on what seems to be wash day with clothes hung in the garden to dry. The cottages are some way north of Coker's Frome Farm buildings but were part of that farm. Painting by Henry Moule.

see if her husband was in the house but he was not there. A search was made and Mr Strong was found at 7a.m. lying in the river in about 3 feet of water. A surgeon was called from Dorchester who arrived at 8a.m. but unsurprisingly he could not be revived. A verdict of 'found drowned' was returned. Thomas Lock, the tenant of both Higher Kingston Farm and the dairy was foreman of the jury. David Strong's widow Ann (aged 35) and four children aged between five and 12 were living in Durngate Street, Dorchester, five years later in 1881.

John Udall followed David Strong as dairyman at Lower Bockhampton. He and his wife Annie had eight daughters and two sons. By 1891 the daughters Emma aged 19, Bessie aged 18, Caroline 17 and Amelia 16 were all working as dairymaids which always brings to mind images of the dairymaids in the film *Tess* based on Thomas Hardy's novel *Tess of the d'Urbervilles*.

In about 1894 a new Broadmayne brick dairy house with cheese room and milk house was built by Henry Hardy at Lower Dairy. Stone for the chimney pieces in the kitchen, parlour and three bedrooms were supplied by Mr W.J.B. Hounsell of Broadway. The Hounsell family connection with Bockhampton has been maintained as at the time of writing Mr Hounsell's grandson lives in Lower Bockhampton. The old farmhouse was made into a stable, cart-house and wash-house.

In 1915 Frank and George Bissell rented the dairy with Higher Bockhampton Farm from the Hanburys for £870 a year. Fred Parsons, who followed as tenant then purchased both farms from Lady Hanbury in 1938 for £13,000. Jack Treasure and his brother Harold ran the dairy for him. In those days the cows went over the bridge to the meadows during spring and summer and apparently left the lane in quite a mess. There was a ford across the river at the side of Bockhampton Bridge in what is now part of the garden of Bridge Cottage.

When Fred Parsons retired in 1966 Lower Bockhampton Farm was bought by Frank Kellaway who ran the farm until he retired to Spring Glen, Lower Bockhampton, when his sons Roy and Joe took over. Children of the 1930s can remember fetching milk from the dairy in Lower Bockhampton in small cans, something that happened again in the big freeze of 1978 when it was impossible to get to the shops in Dorchester.

Coker's Frome and Frome Whitfield Farms

Coker's Frome and Frome Whitfield became part of Stinsford parish in a reorganisation of parish boundaries in 1894. Like other farms the land rises from the River Frome up towards Waterston Ridge. By 1894 Coker's Frome Farm had been owned by the Mayo family for over 50 years.

In 1894 John Mayo was farming at Coker's Frome having been at an Upwey farm for many years. He was one of the first members of Stinsford Parish Council in 1894 and was a manager of Stinsford and Bockhampton School. His son George, who had been farming at Troytown near Puddletown, took over the farm in 1912. George's wife Louisa was the daughter of James Symes Hull of neighbouring Higher Kingston Farm. George and Louisa Mayo lived in the original farmhouse which burnt down in 1948. Like his father George Mayo was also a manager of the school in Lower Bockhampton.

Algy Mayo was the next generation of the family to farm at Coker's Frome. In the 1950s land towards the north of the farm was sold and became Home Farm and bungalows were built along the ridge itself. Algy Mayo's son John and his wife farm at Coker's Frome at the time of writing. In 2000 the fields in the southeast corner of the farm were made the permanent home of the Dorchester Agricultural Show, which has since been renamed the Dorset County Show. The new showground was officially opened by HRH Prince Charles, Prince of Wales.

In 1894 Frome Whitfield Farm was part of the estate of Lieutenant General Shurlock Henning who owned Frome Whitfield House. In 1891 Joseph Studley lived at Frome Whitfield Farm. He and George Studley of Litton Cheney leased the farm and dairy from Lieutenant General Shurlock Henning. In later years it was farmed together with Coker's Frome by the Mayo family.

Now a mixed farm of 170 acres the present owners, like those of most other farms in the parish, have diversified the business to offer holiday accommodation to visitors.

Ben Fowler outside his cottage, sitting on the sink under the water pump playing his accordion on a summer evening, 1930s. His audience are his granddaughter Irene Willis, and Nipper the Jack Russell dog. Ben saved the life of his employer Algy Mayo when he was being attacked by a bull.

Above: *Ben Fowler's wife Mary 'Bessie' cooking up outside the cottage, 1930s.*

Right: *Ben Fowler with his daughter Blanche, 1930s. When Ben was interviewed for the job of carpenter at Coker's Frome the Mayos wanted a man with a son to who could look after the sheep. Ben's sons were working elsewhere so Blanche took on the job of shepherd.*

A pause in haymaking for a bit of bread and cheese at Coker's Frome Farm, 1930s. Left to right: Arthur Richardson, Algy Mayo, Ben Fowler, George? Horlock, Charlie Larkham. The little boy is John 'Jack' Richardson.

A break from building a rick at Coker's Frome, 1940s. Left to right: *Algy Mayo, ?, ?, John 'Jack' Richardson, Arthur Richardson, ?, Ben Fowler, ?.*

Snow clearing party at Coker's Frome, 1950s. Left to right: *Arthur Richardson, Charlie Larkham and Raymond Brown.*

Stacking bales at Coker's Frome, c.1960. Left to right: *Arthur Richardson and John Mayo.*

Higher Bockhampton Maps Showing the Changes of 170 years

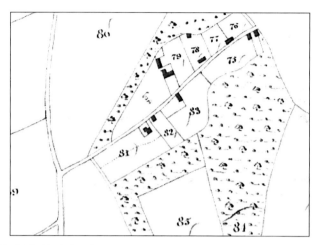

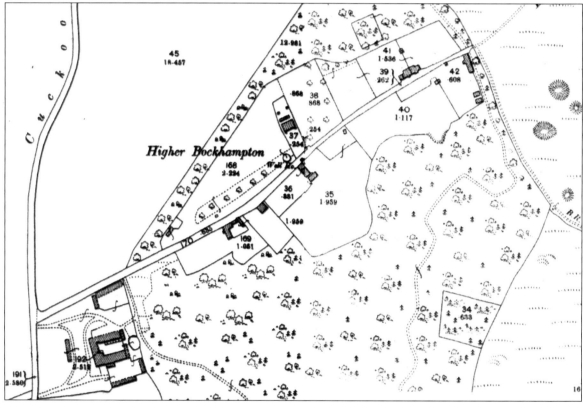

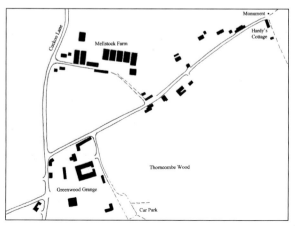

Top: *1839 tithe map;* centre: *1902 Ordnance Survey map;* bottom: *Higher Bockhampton in 2007.*

Chapter 14

Higher Bockhampton and the Hardys

The hamlet of Higher Bockhampton, in the north-east of the parish, is in a secluded and wooded area with Puddletown heath to the east and Bhompston heath to the south. The Roman road from Dorchester to Badbury passes through Thorncombe Wood nature reserve to the south of the hamlet and nearby are the prehistoric barrows 'Rainbarrows', one the site of a beacon during the Napoleonic Wars.

On a plan of the Kingston estate made between 1800 and 1811 a lane, off what is now called Cuckoo Lane, is marked as 'The new street' and one cottage labelled 'Hardy's Cottage' is the only building at the very end of the lane. The area was particularly isolated, on the very edge of the heath which then stretched away east to the edges of Poole. The heath was once the source of furze and turf, used as fuel. It was always a favourite spot for picnics until 1946 when thousands of conifers were planted by the Forestry Commission. Fortunately in the past few years a considerable area has been cleared and is being returned to heathland again. At first the hamlet was called New Bockhampton but this changed later to either Upper or Higher Bockhampton, both names appearing in different records in the nineteenth century. However, Higher Bockhampton has been used for many years.

The road to Higher Bockhampton leads to a turning to the car park and Greenwood Grange. Beyond the unsurfaced lane to the hamlet is just one car's width and the surface is mostly covered with sand. As cars are not allowed along this portion of the lane it is still a quiet walk with just the crunch of footsteps as you make your way.

An undated watercolour by Henry Moule of 'Tinkleton Heath' which gives some idea of the appearance and size of the heathland around Higher Bockhampton in the nineteenth century. It must have looked very similar for many years before.

Some Early Residents

The lane through the hamlet to the forest edge was once known as Veterans Alley because several retired military men lived along it including Captain Percival Meggs, Lieutenant Thomas Drane a retired naval officer who had taken part in the Battle of Trafalgar and Captain Robert Gambier.

Captain Robert Gambier of the Navy was the nephew of William Morton Pitt's wife Margaret, a connection that probably led to his stay at Higher Bockhampton, which was part of the Pitts' estate. He arrived with his wife Caroline and their young daughter in 1818 but exactly where they lived is not known. Captain Gambier was on half pay, probably because there were not enough ships in the Navy to give employment to every man qualified to be a captain. Lady Susan O'Brien of Stinsford House commented at the time that the family were 'living on love and bread and butter and what happier thing? None in the world!' She was sympathetic because she had married for love herself and had been short of money too. In 1821 Captain Gambier and his family left for Bridport when he joined the Preventive service in an effort to stop smuggling, which was widespread along the coast of Dorset. He eventually became an Admiral and commanded the Mediterranean fleet.

Henry Kentfield, was a mail coach guard who must have found it very convenient to live so close to the turnpike road between Dorchester and London. Wearing his red uniform, he used a pony and gig to travel into Dorchester where he joined the mail coach. He armed himself with two pistols, a cutlass and blunderbuss in case of trouble during the journey. Apparently he also surreptitiously took the opportunity to carry goods of his own to sell in London, including butter, eggs and game bought from local poachers. These were packed in a hamper and taken down the path called Snail Creep from Higher Bockhampton to the turnpike road by John Downton, a young man who lived in the hamlet with his parents George and Olive Downton. The coach would halt momentarily opposite Snail Creep and the hamper would be hidden in a box under Henry Kentfield's seat until the coach reached London.

By 1839 when the tithe map was drawn up, the hamlet had grown to about ten dwellings. A pair of cottages had been built at the top of the lane near Hardy's Cottage, one of them occupied by William and Mary Keats. He was a carrier, or tranter, who worked for the builder and stonemason Thomas Hardy, hauling building materials. The story of William and Mary Keats's romance is told *In The Life of Thomas Hardy* by Florence Hardy, but which was almost entirely written by her husband Thomas Hardy for her to publish in her name after his death:

Mary L. a handsome wench had come to Bockhampton, leaving a lover at Askerswell, her native parish. William Keats fell in love with her at the new place. The old lover, who was a shoemaker, smelling a rat, came anxiously to see her, with a present of a dainty pair of shoes he had made. He met her by chance at the pathway stile, but alas on the arm of the other lover. In the rage of love the two men fought for her till they were out of breath, she looking on and holding both their hats the while, till William, wiping his face, said, 'Now Polly which of we two do you love best? Say it out straight!' She would not but said she would consider. The young man to whom she had been fickle left her indignantly, throwing the shoes at her and her new love as he went. She never saw or heard of him again and accepted the other. But she kept the shoes, and was married in them.

The marriage of William Keats and Mary Lovell of Askerswell, took place at Stinsford church on 23 April 1821.

The Keats's neighbours in the other cottage of the pair were James Hardy and his wife Jane (née Coward). James was a brother of Thomas at Hardy's Cottage and like him was a stonemason. James Hardy's daughter Teresa was born in 1844 and having spent her entire life in Higher Bockhampton, was the last member of the Hardy family to live there. She moved not far away to Lower Bockhampton in 1919 to share the cottage next to the bridge with two other spinsters, Emily Whitaker and Jane Plowman.

The Hardys and Their Cottage

Hardy's Cottage was the first to be built in about 1800 on a plot leased by John Hardy of Puddletown from

Hardy's Cottage at Higher Bockhampton, where Thomas Hardy the poet and novelist was born in 1840, photographed in the 1950s.

William Morton Pitt, the landowner, as a home for his recently married son Thomas. Such an isolated spot must have had disadvantages but it was reasonably close to Puddletown where John Hardy worked as a builder but was far enough away to offer new opportunities to Thomas without taking work away from his father. Thomas's wife Mary Hardy described their cottage, as it was when she first lived there, to her grandson Thomas, the future writer. He wrote the poem 'Domicilium' based on what she told him, the final lines below describe the surroundings:

*Our house stood quite alone, and those tall firs
And beeches were not planted. Snakes and efts
Swarmed in the summer days, and nightly bats
Would fly about our bedrooms.
Heathcroppers
Lived on the hills, and were our only friends;
So wild it was when first we settled here.*

'Efts' is a Dorset dialect word for lizards and 'heathcroppers' the ponies that once roamed the heath.

In a notebook Thomas Hardy mentions his grandfather's involvement in smuggling when he and his wife Mary first lived at New Bockhampton. Tubs of brandy were brought inland from the coast on horseback at night:

A whiplash across the window pane would awake my grandfather at two or three in the morning, and he would dress and go down. Not a soul was there, but a heap of tubs loomed up in front of the door. He would set to work to stow them away in the dark closet and

This cottage at Upper or Higher Bockhampton was painted by Henry Moule and dated 2 November but without a year. A note under the painting explains that the elms had been destroyed since and a well house had been built. The cottage appears on the 1839 tithe map when it was occupied by Charles Keates but the cottage itself has gone. The site is the garden of 'Greenwood'.

nothing would happen till dusk the following evening, when groups of dark long-bearded fellows would arrive and carry off the tubs.

By 1811 the Hardys had neighbours in three other cottages and a growing family of their own of three boys and three girls. Their youngest son, the second Thomas, eventually joined his father and brother James in the family building business. As a family of builders and masons the Hardys were much better off than people in the parish employed as labourers on the local farms. Hardy's Cottage was leased from the estate and was not a 'tied' cottage, occupied only as long as a man was employed by the estate, which was often for just a year. Many labourers were forced to find new jobs every year but the Hardys knew they would have their cottage and plot of land for at least two generations. Their income would have been much greater than the 7s.6d. or 10s.0d. a week paid to labourers in Dorset in the nineteenth century. In time these advantages would enable Thomas and Jemima Hardy to apprentice their son Thomas to an architect and send their daughters Mary and Kate to college to train as teachers.

The Hardy family had been members of the church band of musicians since they first moved to the parish and their musical skills were also put to good use at entertainments around the parish when the group were known as the Bockhampton Band. On Christmas Eve 1827 members of the band were involved in two incidents in Dorchester. John Hardy, son of the first Thomas Hardy, was in the kitchen of the Phoenix Inn in High East Street with other members of the band when a group of Fordington Mummers came to the door and one of them knocked the drumstick from John Hardy's hand. As he stooped down to pick it up he was knocked over by one of the mummers and when he went out into the street he was knocked down again several times and was 'much bruised'. The case was eventually considered by the Justices at the Borough Quarter Sessions when Thomas Amey denied he had struck John Hardy. The Justices took into account Amey's previous good character but still sentenced him to two weeks' imprisonment.

There was a second incident later that night between the Bockhampton Band and the Fordington Mummers. Rivalry between the groups had broken out because the band had been playing on the mummers' 'patch' in Dorchester and taking their earnings in the process. The report of the ensuing court case, this time before the County Assize, in January 1828 described a 'battle royal' which took place late on Christmas Eve. James Keats told the court that at about 10 o'clock he and the band were passing between Swan Bridge and Grey's Bridge quietly making their way home when they were followed by the Fordington Mummers and a dozen others. He and John Hardy were carrying the drum

when John Lock came up and said he would break the drum and pulled off his coat, wanting a fight and George Burt also wanted to fight with John Hardy. James Keats and John Hardy attempted to get away but were followed by all the mummers and others who then surrounded the band. James Keats received a severe blow on the body, another on the back of his head and a gash on the forehead with a sword, presumably the wooden one which featured at the Phoenix! James Keats's statement was corroborated by William and Charles Keats and John Hardy, perhaps not surprising as they were all neighbours! Some of the mummers were found guilty of riot and assault on James and William Keats and received harsh punishments. James Burt was sentenced to six months of hard labour, while George Burt, John Lock and Joseph Lucas were each sentenced to three months of the same.

Thomas Hardy, Novelist and Poet

In 1839 the second Thomas Hardy married Jemima Hand a cook at Stinsford House. When their son the third Thomas Hardy was born on 2 June 1840, the Hardy family were well established at Higher Bockhampton having lived in the cottage at the end of the lane for 40 years. On that early summer day there was a moment of doubt that the baby would survive and it is said that it was thanks to Mrs Elizabeth Downton, their neighbour who was a midwife, that he survived. At home the boy was called Tom or Tommy and in 1841 a sister Mary was born, followed by Henry in 1851 and Katharine (Kate) in 1856.

Tom was apparently too weak to go to school until he was seven years old but this may have had something to do with the distance from home to school which was over a mile. His mother encouraged him to enjoy reading, as she did, from an early age. The extra years at home would have given him plenty of opportunities to explore the countryside around the cottage and begin his lifelong interest in nature and people. He was also regaled with stories of the past by his widowed grandmother Mary who lived with them and by his mother.

Mrs Julia Martin, wife of the owner of the Kingston estate knew Tom before he went to school. It seems likely she would have come to know of him through the work his father did on the estate. Aged seven he did go to school and was one of the first pupils at Stinsford and Bockhampton School when it opened in 1847. By then he was fit enough to walk the mile or so to Lower Bockhampton and back each day. Unfortunately there are no surviving records from the early years of the school that might tell us about his first days at school. After a year his mother took him with her on a prolonged visit to Hertfordshire to care for her sister and on their return to Higher Bockhampton in 1850 Tom was sent to school in Dorchester.

121

Thomas Hardy aged 16, the year that he left school and began his apprenticeship with John Hicks the architect, at the office in South Street, Dorchester, 1856. He walked from Higher Bockhampton into Dorchester and home again, a good five miles each day.

Above, below left and below: *September 2003 at Hardy's Cottage. Members of the Thomas Hardy Society with musicians from 'The Madding Crowd' group re-enacting 'Going the Rounds' as described in* Under the Greenwood Tree *for a BBC Radio 4 programme broadcast on 18 December. 'Going the Rounds' is normally performed in early December every other year.*

Right: *Thomas Hardy with family and friends at a picnic on Black Heath, behind Hardy's Cottage, 1917. In her diary his sister Kate Hardy mentions who was at the picnic. Thomas Hardy is on the left wearing a boater hat.   The others she names are: Florence Hardy and her sister Eva Dugdale, Mr and Mrs Constance Pocock, Colonel Inglis and his wife Ethel who was a friend of Florence Hardy's, their son and daughter, Hermann Lea (author and photographer), Miss Kitty Cressy, another young lady and Kate Hardy herself who is seated behind Thomas Hardy. In the foreground is Wessex the Hardys' renowned dog.*

A copy of the *Boy's Own Book* in a Dorchester bookseller's window caught Tom Hardy's eye when he was aged 12. In it were articles on sports, chemistry, card tricks, chess, bird watching and gardening. One night Tom went with his father and other musicians to play at a wedding feast and although he was told not to accept any money the guests 'put enough pennies in his cup' to allow him to buy the book soon after. It is possible that the bookshop was owned by Mr Foster whose son recalled Tom Hardy reading books there and bringing in some particularly good eating apples, a variety known as Bockington, or Bockhampton Sweet, which was once a popular local variety.

Lots of Stinsford girls from Tom Hardy's youth are mentioned in his poems and notebooks. Emily Dart, probably a relation of his Uncle John Hardy's wife Sarah; Rachel Hurst two years older than himself, daughter of William and Ann Hurst of Higher Bockhampton, 'with her rich colour, vanity, frailty and clever artificial dimple-making'; Elizabeth Bishop was also two years older than himself, a gamekeeper's red-haired daughter. He recalled her smile, her singing and her beautiful outdoor complexion. With some artist's licence in changing her name, he later celebrated her in the poem 'To Lizbie Browne'. Louisa Harding, two years younger than Tom, was a daughter of the farmer at Stinsford who went to boarding-school at Weymouth where Tom Hardy searched for her on Sundays to try and see her again. He discovered the church she attended, but when he saw her she 'volunteered a sly smile of recognition the sole reward for his time-consuming lovelorn efforts.'

Tom Hardy was at school with Fanny Hurden. Her parents were John Hurden, a waterman and his wife Charlotte and Fanny's maternal grandfather was Henry Coward the village tailor. Late in his life Tom Hardy still remembered and regretted how she had been burnt when he had pushed her against the hot stove in the schoolroom. As 'Fanny Hurd' she is mentioned in his poem 'Voices From Things Growing in a Churchyard'. She was working as a servant in Dorchester in the spring of 1861 but died aged only 20 in October that year. The headstone on her grave in Stinsford churchyard was restored in 1999 thanks to the late Dr James Gibson, a Hardy scholar.

In July 1856 Tom Hardy left school and began his career in architecture, walking across the fields each day from Higher Bockhampton to the office of John Hicks, a Dorchester architect. At about this time he also developed his sketching and watercolour painting skills helped by Henry Moule, son of the vicar of St George's Church, Fordington, who sketched and painted hundreds of local scenes, some included in this book.

Tom Hardy left Dorset to work for a London architect in April 1862 returning home in 1867 to work again for John Hicks. He also began his first but unpublished novel *The Poor Man and the Lady*. He moved to Weymouth in 1869 for a while, joining Crickmays, the firm of Weymouth architects and began his novel *Desperate Remedies* which is set partly in Weymouth, which he called 'Budmouth'. In this novel Knapwater House is modelled on Kingston House, complete with a temple in the grounds and an Elizabethan manor house. He then spent several periods in London before returning to Crickmays when he was sent to Cornwall to begin work for the restoration of St Juliot's Church in North Cornwall. It was there that he met his future wife, Miss Emma Gifford.

In 1871 he began the novel which would be called *Under the Greenwood Tree*, which has more connections with the parish of Stinsford, which he called 'Mellstock', than any other. It is possible to walk around the parish following the story although characters' names are just slightly changed and some features of the landscape repositioned. The church musicians, the Mellstock Quire, who feature in the story are obviously modelled on the Hardy family's experiences as Stinsford church musicians who, like the Mellstock Quire, were displaced by a barrel organ.

Thomas Hardy and Emma Gifford married in 1874 and eventually settled at Max Gate in 1885 the house he designed and his brother built on the outskirts of Dorchester but with Stinsford in sight to the north. He was a regular visitor to Higher Bockhampton until his family left in 1913 and to Stinsford church. Following the death of his wife Emma in 1910 he married Florence Dugdale in 1914. His last visit to the cottage at Higher Bockhampton in November 1926 was with Cecil Hanbury of Kingston Maurward House, who owned the cottage.

Thomas Hardy died in January 1928 and in recognition of his importance as a poet and writer his ashes were interred in Westminster Abbey. In a twist worthy of one of his own novels it was decided that his heart should be removed and buried at Stinsford where he had said he wished to be buried. Henry and Kate Hardy were unhappy about the arrangement and Teresa Hardy, their 84-year-old cousin, who was interviewed by a reporter from the *Daily Mail*, made her feelings quite plain. She said she was:

... grieved that they are going to take poor Tom away to London. He wanted, I know, to lie with his own folk in the churchyard yonder. Poor Tom he was a clever boy, but I never thought he would take to writing and I did not like it when he did. Writing, I think, is not a respectable way of earning a living. I am quite sure that he did not find all his queer characters hereabouts. He must have discovered a good many of them when he went to London.

Of course having lived her whole life in the parish she saw all the local people as familiar neighbours certainly not as 'queer characters'.

Two funerals took place simultaneously one at

Westminster Abbey, attended by Florence, his sister Kate and the great and the good. At Stinsford Thomas's brother Henry Hardy was chief mourner and the service was led by the Revd Cowley. Thomas Hardy's heart was buried in the grave of his first wife Emma who died in 1912. There were huge crowds at both events; there were queues to get into Westminster Abbey and the churchyard at Stinsford was packed, some people causing outrage by standing on the old table tombs for a better view. The weather in London was dismal but Kate Hardy noted in her diary that the sun shone at Stinsford.

The Portland stone tomb had been made by Hounsell's of Broadwey, Weymouth in 1912 and in 1928 the firm prepared the grave and attended the funeral, later adding the new inscription.

A granite obelisk was erected near Hardy's Cottage by a group of Thomas Hardy's American admirers. It was unveiled in April 1931 by Professor J. Livingston Lowes of Harvard and Oxford Universities.

Hardy's Cottage After the Hardys

Henry, Mary and Kate Hardy left the cottage in 1912 for Talbothayes, a house built by Henry near West Stafford. From then until 1921 Hermann Lea, author, photographer and friend of Thomas Hardy lived at the cottage. Together they wrote *Thomas Hardy's Wessex*, a guide to the places mentioned in Hardy's books and poems. Florence Hardy told a friend in 1914, at the beginning of the First World War, that the people of Bockhampton and Stinsford had declared Hermann Lea, whose mother was German, a spy. Florence Hardy described him as actually one of the most harmless of men.

Other tenants were found for the cottage including the Bearpark family who arrived in 1925. Isabel Bearpark's memories were originally published in *Dorset Life* in 1998. As a child aged six she remembered her bedroom nearest the stairs which had once been Mary and Kate Hardy's. Like Hilda Burnett who lived in Lower Bockhampton in the 1930s, Isabel remembered how primitive everything was, no bathroom or toilet and water for cleaning and washing came from a pump by the scullery sink. Drinking water had to be fetched from the well down the lane. School was a walk of a mile or so away, the afternoon walk home being more fun as they used to play games of 'I spy' and would hold races between children going home to the crossroads to Higher Bockhampton and Tincleton. In winter they played games at home including draughts or Ludo and when it rained there was hopscotch or skipping on the stone-floored scullery.

Isobel Bearpark particularly remembered a journey to Dorchester to buy a zinc bath which meant a walk down Snail Creep to the main road and a wait for the carrier's van which operated one day a week

Terry (left) and Rob Linee, September 2003, custodians of Hardy's Cottage at the time of writing, which is owned by the National Trust. They are pictured with Claire Kendall-Price the narrator for the Radio 4 programme 'Going the Rounds' which was partly recorded in and around the cottage.

between Blandford and Dorchester. Everyone sat on wooden seats along the sides of the van with baskets, sacks, parcels and chickens filling up the floor space. On the way home the zinc bath filled with shopping took up most of the space.

After being set down, we all four perilously manoeuvred the bath over the stile and carried it between us, with many stops to rest, across the meadow, up the hill, down along the edge of the wood through the gate from the heath and finally home.

In 1937 the cottage was purchased by Mr Fred Parsons as part of Higher Bockhampton Farm and was then rented out. That year the *Dorset County Chronicle* reported a case of vandalism that was 'Not funny just ignorant'. The signpost 'To Hardy's Cottage' at the crossroads was altered to read 'To Laurel and Hardy's Cabbage'!

When the cottage was sold many people had suggested that it should be become 'national property' which it did in 1948 when the National Trust bought it for £3,500. Custodians were appointed, who originally lived in the cottage which was opened to the public in a limited way. Miss Evelyn Evans, Jim and Ruth Skilling, Anna Winchcombe who wrote the book *The Wayfarer* about Thomas Hardy's life, Joe and Vee Linee were all custodians. The Linee family connection with the cottage continues with Terry and Rob Linee as custodians at the time of writing.

Woodlands

This cottage, with Hardy's Cottage, is thought to be the only original building to have survived at Higher Bockhampton. As already mentioned, in the early years of the nineteenth century one half was occupied

The approach to Upper or Higher Bockhampton from the heath. On the left is the back of Hardy's Cottage and in the centre further along the lane is the pair of cottages occupied by James and Jane Hardy and William and Mary Keats in 1839. Just beyond is the thatched roof of another cottage which was occupied by one of Joseph Bedloe's farm workers. Henry Moule added October 13 to his water-colour sketch but did not add a year.

by William and Mary Keats and the other by James and Jane Hardy whose daughter Teresa succeeded them as tenant. By the 1940s Mr and Mrs Charlie Miller and their children Alan, Brian and Christopher lived in the cottage nearest Hardy's Cottage. Charlie Miller was one of the Higher Bockhampton men who joined the Home Guard. Willa Eunson and her husband, who came originally from the Shetland Islands, lived in the other cottage. The pair of cottages were sold in the late 1960s and converted to a single residence.

Egdon Cottage

Egdon Cottage appears in the background of a photograph taken by Hermann Lea in the early years

Numbers 1 and 2 Higher Bockhampton when they were sold following Fred Parson's retirement from farming, August 1966. The tenants of the time were Mr W. Legg and Mr R. Fanton. The pair were converted to one house soon after.

of the twentieth century. It was occupied by Mr Davies a gamekeeper and then in the 1940s by Mr and Mrs Farr and their daughters Elsie and Marion. At this time the cottage had a 'tin roof', probably made with corrugated iron. It was sold by Mr Fred Parsons in 1961 to a Mr G. Paull for £600 and has been a private house ever since.

Numbers 1, 2 and 3, 4 Higher Bockhampton

The pair of Broadmayne brick cottages, Numbers 1 and 2 Higher Bockhampton, probably built by the Hardys, are in exactly the same style as Numbers 3 and 4 which were built earlier. In the 1940s Mr Archibald Watts and his wife lived at Number 1 and Cecil Samways, his wife Eva and children Ronald, Len and Dorothy were at Number 2. By the time the cottages were sold in 1966 they each had a bathroom with hot and cold water and a toilet indoors! The tenants were Mr W. Legg at Number 1 and Mr R. Fanton at Number 2. They have since been converted to form one house called 'Greenwood'.

During the Second World War Number 3 was occupied by Mr and Mrs Hargreaves and their daughters Monica and Iris while Mr Walter Hyde and his wife Beatrice lived at Number 4 in the 1940s and 1950s. The cottages were purchased by the Dorset Farm Institute in 1966 but were sold again 1967. These cottages are still a pair.

Mellstock House

Mellstock House was built on the site of an older cottage, in the Arts and Crafts style, by the Hanburys for their farm bailiff soon after they purchased the estate in 1914. In 1938 Mr Fred Parsons who had been a tenant of the Hanburys for some years, purchased the house he lived in with Higher and Lower Bockhampton Farms. The Parsons then moved to Lane House in Cuckoo Lane while their

Numbers 3 and 4 Higher Bockhampton, 2007.

The cottage which once stood on the site of Mellstock House, seen here c.1912. Behind is another small cottage, now called Egdon Cottage, and the roof of the Broadmayne brick pair of cottages, now Greenwood.

Mellstock House today with Egdon Cottage further along the lane on the right, 2007.

The Bridle, Riggs and Crabbe families all related by marriage were photographed at Higher Bockhampton in the 1930s. Left to right, standing: Archie Watts from 1 Higher Bockhampton, ?, ?; middle row: Bert Crabbe who lived in Lower Bockhampton and Edwin Burden of Basingstoke; seated: Dora Crabbe (née Riggs) wife of Bert, Mrs Bridle previously Mrs Riggs, Margaret Burden (née Bridle), wife of Edwin.

Children in Mrs Samways' garden at Higher Bockhampton, 1940. Standing: Doreen Ferris; left to right, seated: Monica Hargreaves, Dorothy Samways, Molly Ferris. Doreen and Molly were evacuated from Southampton and lived with Mr and Mrs Hyde at 4 Higher Bockhampton. The Hargreaves lived next door and the Samways family just across the lane.

Built for Francis Pitney Brouncker Martin in 1849, this building and others on the site were known as Bockhampton Buildings and later became part of Higher Bockhampton Farm. Now it is part of the Greenwood Grange complex of holiday cottages, pictured here in 2007.

The two Woolaway bungalows at the junction of Cuckoo Lane and the lane down to Higher Bockhampton, 1966. They were built for Higher Bockhampton farm workers but were demolished early in the twenty-first century.

The modern but traditional cottages built on the site of the Woolaway bungalows, 2007.

son Alfred and his wife Honoria Parsons lived at Mellstock House. In 1971 Joe and Vee Linee moved to the house.

Greenwood Grange

The Higher Bockhampton Farm buildings next to Thorncombe Wood have been converted into a complex of holiday cottages. The original farm buildings were constructed in 1849 for Francis Pitney

Walter and Beatrice Hyde in their garden on a summer's evening, 1940s.

Brouncker Martin, who had bought the Kingston estate in 1845. His initials and the date 1849 appear on the end wall of one of the buildings.

More Recent Additions to the Hamlet

Both Clare's Cottage and the bungalow Yalbury Wood were built in the 1960s on land that was originally part of Higher Bockhampton Farm.

In Cuckoo Lane the Woolaway bungalows built for farm workers in the 1950s have been replaced by two traditionally built modern cottages and two houses. Lane House was built in the late 1950s for Mr Fred Parsons and his wife.

Two small business parks known as Hampton and Mellstock Business Parks have been created on the site of the chicken farms.

Above: *Fred Parsons who owned the farms at Higher and Lower Bockhampton from 1938 to 1966 with his wife Mabel and son Alfie who ran the chicken farm at Higher Bockhampton, 1950s.*

Right: *Three ladies from Higher Bockhampton, c.1950s. Left to right: Mrs Tizzard, Mrs Hyde and Mrs Eunson photographed near the church.*

Left: *Cecil and Eva Samways in 1979. They lived at 2 Higher Bockhampton in the 1940s and 1950s with their children Ronald, Len and Dorothy.*

Below: *Looking east from Cuckoo Lane, 1950s. Left to right: Puddletown forest behind 3 and 4 Higher Bockhampton and across the lane, with Thorncombe Woods behind are 1 and 2 Higher Bockhampton, Egdon Cottage and Mellstock House.*

Chapter 15

The Second World War

When war was declared in September 1939 there must have been many people in the parish who could clearly remember the First World War, which had ended only 21 years earlier. The Roll of Honour board in the church lists the 75 men from Stinsford who served in that war, of whom five were killed. Their families must have had particular memories and worries at the prospect of another war.

Preparations on the Home Front

Some preparations had already been made locally in case of another war. A newspaper cutting dated 31 March 1938 explained that Lady Hanbury had made arrangements for part of Kingston Maurward House to be converted into a first-aid dressing station as it had been during the First World War. A waiting-room, reception area, washing and first-aid treatment rooms would be available. Every room would be gas proof and the basement equipped with five air locks. Mr C. Skinner of Higher Kingston had been appointed general superintendent and air-raid wardens were Lady Hanbury, Mr J. Wyndham Hull and Messrs Stemp, Snell and Parsons. Dr Graham Jones of Bockhampton House was the medical officer. Lady Hanbury and Mrs Skinner were planning weekly lectures in each hamlet and householders were shown how to make their homes gas proof. Lady Hanbury was reported as believing there would be no question of war or invasion if every man and woman in England was prepared. She thought that the war would be fought as much on the home front, in the cottages, as in battle and so it was every-one's duty to be prepared. She said she had found that some people were not very receptive to her ideas. Her forthright response was to say, 'That may be so, one doesn't mind if they are gassed.'

The minutes of the Parish Council meeting in November 1938 include the appointment of billeting officers in the parish, Mr J. Wyndham Hull for Stinsford and Higher Kingston, Mr F. Stemp of the Old Manor House for Lower Bockhampton and Bhompston, Mr P. Parsons of Mellstock House for Higher Bockhampton and Mrs Rood for Frome Whitfield and Coker's Frome.

At Southampton in June 1939 the staff of the Education Office prepared a leaflet entitled 'The Government Evacuation Scheme' in an effort to address how this would affect Southampton, answer-ing questions people might have about the evacuation. Parents of children at Swaythling School were amongst those who received a copy which would eventually help them prepare for their children's evacuation away from Southampton to other parts of Hampshire and Dorset. One of the questions the leaflet tried to answer was 'How long will it (evacuation) last?' The answer was frank and rather touching:

We cannot say. It may be only for a very short time. If evacuation is ordered before war is declared, and, as we all hope, war never comes, it may only be for a long week-end. Even so, it will be well worth while, if only as a kind of insurance. Please think it over very care-fully.

The War Comes to Stinsford

In his record of services at St Michael's Church the vicar, Revd G. Moule, included some notes about the progress of the war. In May 1940 his entry reads:

The German hordes overrun Holland, Belgium and northern France. Large congregation on the Day of National Prayer, May 26. The 'miracle of Dunkirk' followed with news of the safety of some from this parish. Later in June news was received of the safe return of all ten of our men who were in the BEF [British Expeditionary Force].

The BEF was forced by the German forces to retreat to the northern coast of France where they were rescued by ships of all types and sizes. Boats from ports along the South Coast of England, including Weymouth, crossed the English Channel, facing great danger, to act as ferries taking men from the beaches to larger ships, before returning with their own boats loaded with soldiers.

One of those rescued was Cyril Atkins from Lower Bockhampton, who was in the Royal Army Service Corps. He recalled his experiences immediately before and at Dunkirk:

Well we were carrying these bridge sections in convoy. I was driving when we were halted and given five rounds of ammunition and a rifle each and told to hold this hedge line through the night – well, grown men wept. But nothing happened and in the morning we were ordered back towards the coast. We weren't ever allowed to rest. 'Keep moving' they said 'Keep moving'. We were so tired but we couldn't stop. We got to the beaches, we lined up and waited for a ship. I waded out into the water but the first one was full up so I stood there up to me neck in water until we were taken aboard a destroyer. It was a lovely hot sunny day and I lay down on the deck and fell asleep and when we got to England and I woke up, I was completely dry again!'

In August 1940 Revd Moule wrote:

A severe air battle over part of the parish in the afternoon. Bombs dropped within half a mile of the Church. No harm done. Evening service delayed till 7p.m. but a few came to thank God in church for the safety of our church and the preservation of some of our church members.

The bombs appear to have fallen in the fields nearer Fordington.

Great tension on September 8 and 15. The 'Battle of Britain' fought and won on the Sunday following the 'Day of National Prayer' on 8 September. Many alerts in our neighbourhood during the critical months from August and September onwards but no damage to life or property in this parish.

The minutes of the Parochial Church Council recorded the transfer of the church silver to Salisbury for safe keeping 'for the duration'. Another entry states that railings around Thomas Hardy's grave and another on the south side of the church were removed to be used towards the war effort for making armaments. This is surprising as no photographs have ever come to light which show railings around Thomas Hardy's grave.

When rationing was introduced the people of Stinsford were certainly less affected by food rationing than those living in towns and cities. Most cottages and houses had gardens large enough to grow a good selection of vegetables and many had fruit trees too. Very many people kept chickens for eggs and meat. Rabbits were also kept by some although there was a ready supply in the fields. It seems that quite a few fish were also 'liberated' from the river for a change of menu and eels were also popular.

Crash at Higher Kingston

On 11 October 1940 152 squadron was 'scrambled' from Warmwell airfield and flew over the parish. Meanwhile Higher Kingston's five-year-old Donald Mackenzie and his twin brother were watching the aircraft overhead from the garden of Kingston House as they often did. On this occasion they saw a plane pouring out smoke which seemed to be heading directly for the house. The boys and their mother took shelter in the cellar and soon after heard a loud explosion nearby. As they rushed out to see what had happened they saw a khaki parachute coming over the house with a figure hanging below which

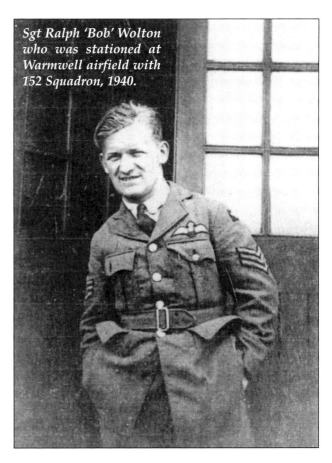

Sgt Ralph 'Bob' Wolton who was stationed at Warmwell airfield with 152 Squadron, 1940.

just cleared the chimney-pots before landing on the lawn. Naturally there was some confusion as to whether the pilot was British or German but the gardener, Mr White, confirmed that he was 'one of ours'.

The pilot Sergeant 'Bob' Wolton later described what happened. He was flying his Spitfire over the parish when, diving away to follow other members of his flight, his aircraft began to vibrate, he was thrown out of the plane so violently that his 'Sutton' harness broke, he damaged his knees and most of his trousers were removed exposing his tattered pyjamas. To speed his take-off he had pulled his uniform on over them. He fell from about 15,000 feet to about 1,000 feet before his parachute opened and on landing was badly winded so cushions and blankets were brought out from the house to make him comfortable. He was then taken by ambulance to Kingston Maurward House where the 150th Field Ambulance of the Royal Army Medical Corps were based. Fortunately he was able to return to Warmwell after a few hours. It was thought that the radiator had been wrongly fitted and the force of his descent caused the bolts holding it in place to fail, which in turn resulted in the starboard wing breaking off. The plane crashed just across the main road from the drive to Kingston House.

A small fragment of an aircraft with a part number on it was found at the edge of Grey's Wood behind Kingston House in 1998. It has been identified as part of a Spitfire, probably Sergeant Wolton's.

In November 1940 Maurice Halna du Fretay escaped from northern occupied France in his two-seater plane and landed near Stinsford Farm.

Escape From France

Another unexpected arrival by air occurred on 15 November 1940 when a two-seater monoplane landed in a field north of Stinsford Farm having flown from German occupied northern France. The plane was piloted by a young man, named Maurice Halna du Fretay, accompanied by another man. He had dismantled the plane and hidden it on his family's estate until he was ready to leave when it was reassembled with the help of friends. Maurice and his passenger took off from the road intending to fly across the Channel to Start Point in Devon but the wind drove them eastwards over Portland Bill and they landed instead at Stinsford Farm. The men were taken to Dorchester Police Station where they told the police that they wished to join General de Gaulle's Free French Air Force based in this country. Douglas Eaves, an evacuee from Southampton, remembers that he went along the river path from Bockhampton to Stinsford with some friends to see the plane but could not get close as it had been cordoned off by the police before it was taken to Warmwell airfield.

Maurice Halna du Fretay did join the Free French Air Force and having completed training was posted to 607 Squadron, flying his first mission in November 1941, a year after his arrival in this country. In the spring of 1942 he was transferred to 174 Squadron, flying Hurricanes, undertaking extremely dangerous tasks, including low-level bombing and attacking ships and convoys in occupied France at Calais, St Omer, le Touque, Boulogne-sur-Mer and Abbeville. In August that year the squadron provided air cover for the unsuccessful attack on Dieppe by the Canadians and on 19 August whilst returning from this operation his Hurricane came down and he was lost at sea. He was 22 years old. Maurice Halna du Fretay was made a Chevalier of the Legion of Honour, having already received the Croix de la Liberation for his escape from France.

A Prisoner of War

Kingston House was the landing place of another pilot. Donald Mackenzie remembers going into the kitchen to find his mother giving a cup of tea to a German airman who had crash landed, walked up the drive and surrendered. Donald's father was home on leave from the Army and complained to his wife that she should not be offering tea to an enemy but she pointed out that he had just given the airman a cigarette! A date for this incident has not been identified.

The Home Guard and Auxiliary Unit

A photograph of the area's Home Guard, taken in 1940 at Plush, includes 39 men from the parish, who were either in reserved occupations, too young or too old to serve in the Armed Forces.

Meetings of men in the Home Guard from Lower Bockhampton sometimes took place in the workshop of the old forge next to Bridge Cottage. In winter, with no heating, this was a very cold and damp place near the river so in desperation a small fire would be lit. This was not all good news as without a chimney smoke soon built up. There was no need for any 'blacking up', so as not to be seen in the dark, as the thick smoke did the trick!

Pillboxes were put in place early in the war when invasion was threatened. These were intended to provide a fall-back line from which to defend the land. A pillbox survives on the southern edge of the parish, to the side of the road to West Stafford. Now covered in a good deal of ivy and hemmed in by trees it is still possible to stand next to it in winter and see the large area of land which could have been watched for possible invaders.

In Thorncombe Wood a rather different relic of the war, a bunker, has been traced which was used by an auxiliary unit. Members of these units were usually selected from the local Home Guard and were men with detailed knowledge of the local area who trained separately to act in the same way as resistance groups in Europe if there was an enemy invasion. Special bunkers were provided, located in remote often wooded areas, designed so that men could go to ground at the time of any invasion. The bunkers contained food and water reserves and were fitted with beds and toilet facilities. They also had

A gathering of the Area Homeguard at Plush, 1940s. Left to right, back row: *Herb Downton, ?, Fred Bowles, George Bowles, ? Russell, ? Sant, ?, John Parker, George or Fred Lovell, Reg Atkins, Charles Atkins, Tom Greening, Bert Foot;* middle row: *Fred Parsons, ? Upshaw, Tom Stroud, Charles Symes, ? Tory or Titch Upshall, ? Lovell, ? Cosh, Cyril Kingman, Albert Lovell, 'Fido' Harrison, Archie Watts, Fred Thorne, Walt Hyde, ? Tyrell;* front row: *Tommy Cosh, ? Gregory, Bert Crabbe, Philip Tory, Fred Atkins, John Chapman, ?, Roy Kingman, ?, Jack Wichard, ? Gregory, Charlie Miller.*

Above: *The Home Guard contingent from Higher Bockhampton, probably before or after an Armistice Day parade, 11 November 1940.* Left to right: *Walt Hyde, Alfie Parsons, Archie Watts, Charlie Miller, ?.*

Above, right: *Alfie, son of Fred and Mabel Parsons outside Mellstock House, Higher Bockhampton, c.1940. He was a member of the Home Guard until he joined the Royal Air Force and became a pilot.*

Right: *A cutting from the* Dorset County Chronicle *of June 1940 referring to the danger of invasion with silhouettes of two troop-carrying German planes, published to help men of the Local Defence Volunteers distinguish them. The Local Defence Volunteers later became the Home Guard.*

Above: *'Bubbles' Hull and Richard Gooch cleaning out the Women's Voluntary Service van used to deliver drinks to troops at Crossways. 'Bubbles' lived at Stinsford Farm and Richard at Stinsford vicarage, 1944.*

Left: *Charles Atkins of Lower Bockhampton joined the Home Guard. His sons all joined up: Maurice was in the Royal Army Medical Corps; Cyril in the Royal Army Service Corps; George in the Royal Artillery and Reg in the Army.*

escape routes, often a concrete tube that exited some distance away from the bunker. The men were to operate in groups of six or seven and carry out campaigns of destruction and harassment of the enemy, usually at night. During the day they would carry on with their daytime jobs whilst gathering information about enemy activity which could be used against them in night-time operations. Although the position of the bunker is known it has not been possible to identify the men who operated from it. Lists of names have survived but they are not linked to any unit or area but to Dorset as a whole. Of course the invasion did not come and it was never necessary for the men to use their special training but, having been sworn to secrecy when they joined, many members of the auxiliary units are said to have kept their activities secret for the rest of their lives. The bunker was scheduled for destruction in 1949 as a possible danger to the public.

The Voluntary Aid Detachments, Red Cross and Women's Voluntary Service

The Dorset group VAD 4 was formed during the First World War and in the Second World War worked closely with its sister organisation the Dorset Red Cross. Mrs Weber of Birkin House was Commandant of VAD 4 whose members helped the war effort by working in hospitals where there was a shortage of staff. They also worked at Air Raid Precautions

(ARP) First Aid posts, ran a maternity home for evacuated mothers, helped in clinics and worked with District Nurses. Mrs Weber went on to become First Aid Commandant for the 54 rural parishes in the county as part of the Rural ARP scheme.

Lady Hanbury was Dame President of the Red Cross in Dorset whose members trained so that they could undertake similar tasks to members of the VAD. Doris Parsons of Higher Bockhampton was a member of the Red Cross and worked at Dorset County Hospital during the war.

The WVS brought the children's school lunches from the central kitchens every day and locally Richard Gooch from the vicarage and 'Bubbles' Hull from Stinsford Farm ran a WVS van to Crossways to provide refreshments to men and women in the Armed Forces.

Children From Southampton

On 1 July 1940 31 children from Swaythling School, Southampton and their teacher Miss Lilian Marsh were evacuated to Dorset. Two other children, Maureen and Doreen Ferris, came from Basset Green School. In the leaflet about the evacuation scheme the authorities in Southampton included a suggested list of clothes the children should take with them when evacuated. For girls: one vest or combinations, one pair of knickers, one bodice, one petticoat, two pairs of stockings, handkerchiefs, slip and blouse, cardigan; for boys: one vest, one shirt and collar, one pair of pants, one pullover or jersey, one pair of knickers, handkerchiefs, two pairs of socks or stockings; for all: night attire and if possible boots or shoes and plimsoles. The children were only allowed to bring one piece of luggage:

Food for the journey should be easy to carry. Bottles should not be taken. The following are suggested as suitable: sandwiches (egg or cheese), packets of nuts and seedless raisins, dry biscuits (with little packets of cheese), barley sugar (rather than chocolate), apple, orange.

Left to right: *Molly, Alan and Doreen Ferris, c.1940. Whilst Molly and Doreen were living at Higher Bockhampton their brother Alan was evacuated to West Stafford. The girls had attended Bassett Green School in Southampton.*

The children were billeted either in the parish of Stinsford or West Stafford and went to school in Lower Bockhampton. Miss Marsh, their teacher, moved into the schoolhouse with the headmistress Miss Jones. At first all the Southampton children were taught in the Mellstock Hut just along the lane from the school but after a short time they were integrated into classes with the local children and the Hut was used as a general classroom.

Evacuee Recollections

Bob Salway and his brother Paul were billeted near West Stafford:

It was during the hay-making season that I found myself with a coach load of others standing tearfully on the village green right in front of The Wise Man at West Stafford. My brother Peter and I were billeted with Mr and Mrs Davis at Talbothayes Cottages. We were sent out to play in the field behind the cottages with Cyril Baggs and John Bartlett who lived in the same row of cottages and we were soon diving into the piles of hay and having a whale of a time. Southampton and the bombing suddenly seemed a long way away. Mr and Mrs Davis immediately became Uncle Tom and Aunty Hilda, who treated us as their own and we absolutely adored them.

We went to school at Bockhampton in the Hut just a little further along the road from the main school, our teacher was Miss Marsh from Southampton. The younger children were taught by Miss Morgan and we soon progressed up to the main school to be taught by Miss Jones, 'Guvvy' we called her. I soon became friendly with Phil Stockley and life was idyllic, a hurried pack lunch and a mad dash down to the bridge to see who could spot the biggest pike.

Some of the classmates I remember are Phil Stockley, Raymond Hayes, Ken Cutler, Sylvia and Nigel Baggs, Reggie Crockford and his brother, John Corbin, Violet Woodsford, Margaret Slade, Peter Crabbe, Dorothy Puckett, Joan Tizzard and the Kellaway brothers. Also the Rowell sisters whose father was gored by a bull in July 1940.

Bob and his brother kept in touch with Mr and Mrs Davis after the war and made a visit from Southampton on a tandem.

Douglas Eaves was also billeted for a few months at Talbothayes Cottages with Mr and Mrs Bartlett:

As for the school it came as a surprise to find you were a member of a school of approximately 48 instead of a class of the same number with a 'cane happy master'. There were two classrooms of five–nine year olds and ten–14 year olds. The field down from the school was used as a sports or play area.

In class we sat two to a desk and during air raids we sat under the desk, there being no shelter in the grounds. During one raid it was my turn in the visiting dentist's chair. His treadle drill took your mind off the raid and I came out minus a couple of teeth and a lot of fillings. What hurt most though was I was unable to eat my lunch of egg sandwiches which I had to take home again. After 63 years I still think of those sandwiches at the mention of Bockhampton.

Bob Clarke was billeted with Mr and Mrs Old, near the Post Office at West Stafford and also remembers working in the fields at harvest time.

Doris Wray, now Green, was originally evacuated to Osmington Mills but after about a year was moved to 'School House' in West Stafford with the Slade family. Like many other evacuees she remembers the long walk to school and packed lunches. On 13 July 1943 Miss Marsh took Doris to the doctor because she had been bitten on her leg by a dog, something she never forgot.

The children from Southampton and Miss Marsh eventually returned home at the end of 1944.

Children From London

June and Shirley Hill were evacuated to Lower Bockhampton and by the time they arrived in the winter of 1941 they had already been evacuated once before to High Wycombe from their home in Battersea in London. They arrived at Bockhampton

School after a journey by train the day before to Poole where they stayed overnight in a hotel before travelling on to Bockhampton by bus. They were the only children from their school to come to the area. Like the children from Southampton they were allowed to bring a small suitcase with essential clothing. The local schoolchildren were outside in the playground as they arrived and some called the girls 'Ginger' as they both had red hair but later they were more affectionately known as the 'Copperknobs'.

Inside the school, ladies from the parish who were expecting to take in an evacuee were sitting around the room and June, who was eight then, remembers insisting that she and her sister had to be kept together and that her mother had said they were not to be separated. Of all the evacuees June and Shirley were almost the last to be found a billet, June thinks this was partly because there were two of them and Shirley, who was only six years old, was upset and cried all the time. Unfortunately they were unhappy in their first billet so when Molly Ferris, a Southampton evacuee, left to return home the Hill sisters asked Mr and Mrs Hyde at 4 Higher Bockhampton if they could take her place. From then on the sisters settled in and were very happy. Mr and Mrs Hyde had no children of their own but were 'a wonderful couple and so good with children'. June and Shirley shared a bedroom with Doreen Ferris, Molly's sister, who had stayed on. The cottage at Higher Bockhampton was very different from home in London as it had a privy in the garden and everyone had to wash in bowls of rainwater.

Uncle Walt built a playhouse in the garden for the girls and Aunty Beat found an old oil stove which no longer worked for pretend cooking. The girls put on little plays to entertain Uncle Walt and Aunty Beat. The children often played in the woods around Higher Bockhampton where a favourite game was drawing the plan of a house on the ground with a stick and playing 'pretend' in each 'room'. The girls went for long walks on the heath with the Hydes who told stories as they walked along. They saw deer coming to drink at the pond and picked wild flowers for school projects. Mrs White who lived at Hardy's Cottage then used to invite them to tea in her beautiful garden. All of this was very new to children from Battersea!

In the summer the girls took lemonade and sandwiches out to men working in the fields and June went potato picking for Mr Parsons at Higher Bockhampton Farm. There was also lots of fruit picking in the garden, especially blackcurrants which were bottled and later made into puddings. The girls had their own patch of garden where they grew lupins and pansies. They also picked blackberries in late summer.

The girls walked to school from Higher Bockhampton with their friends. Dinners were brought to the school every day for the evacuees by the Women's Voluntary Service. June's favourite was on Mondays when they had mash and mince and

Sisters June and Shirley Hill who had been evacuated from Bermondsey in London, pictured in 1941.

rhubarb pudding with pieces of ginger; she often kept a piece of ginger in her mouth all afternoon at school! Her strongest memory is coming home from school to the smell of home baking.

Shirley's best friend, Marion Farr, lived across the lane with her sister Elsie and parents. June's special friend was Veronica Wayman who lived in the bungalow at Lower Bockhampton. She was a big fan of Roy Rogers so her father took Veronica and June to the cinema in Dorchester several times to see Roy Rogers films.

At Christmas a small tree from the woods was decorated with paper lanterns. Mrs Hill sent presents for her daughters to be found on Christmas morning. As travel to Dorset was so very difficult in wartime June and Shirley had just one visit from their mother in their five years at Higher Bockhampton.

Shirley and June went home at the end of the war but Shirley was so unhappy she returned for another year. Like many other evacuees they had come to love their new life in the country:

Aunty Beat and Uncle Walt were like Mum and Dad to us. We have lovely memories and it was the best part of our lives going to live up there at Higher Bockhampton.

On a visit to Stinsford and their old haunts in 1999

Right: *Frank Tapper a clerk with the RAMC who arrived at Kingston Maurward from Beaminster soon after the retreat from Dunkirk in 1940.*

Below: *The Higher Bockhampton Knitting group in the garden of Mellstock House the home of Fred and Mabel Parsons. Left to right, standing: Mrs Mabel Parsons, Mrs Beatrice Hyde; seated: Mrs Amelia Farr, Mrs Miller and son, ?, Mrs Watts, ?, Mrs White; front: Shirley and June Hill (evacuees from London) and Marian Farr.*

Men of the RAMC with Lady Hanbury (seated, fourth from the left), with Kiki her Pekinese, 1941.

Shirley left the following comment in the Visitors' Book at St Michael's:

Evacuee from London in 1941, stayed with Mr and Mrs Hyde until 1945 at Higher Bockhampton where my values and who I am today were formed. Thank you all from the bottom of my heart.

Children's Contributions to the War Effort

During the war children from Bockhampton School were expected to help with potato planting and picking for Mr Wyndham Hull at Stinsford Farm and for Mr George Wakely at Bhompston and Mr Fred Parsons at Higher Bockhampton.

Evacuees and local children from Higher Bockhampton joined Mrs Mabel Parsons' knitting group at Mellstock House on Tuesdays after school. The ladies and girls knitted 'comforts' for the troops sometimes putting their own names inside the articles they knitted. Their work contributed to the Dorset County Comforts Committee and the group was recognised as 'Mrs Parsons Group of Workers'. Children from Stinsford and Lower Bockhampton went to Kingston Maurward House where Mrs Stemp read Dr Dolittle stories whilst they too knitted scarves for the troops.

The Armed Forces Based in the Parish

Royal Army Medical Service

In 1940 the 150th Field Ambulance, Royal Army Medical Corps were based at Kingston Maurward House and in 1941 the 9th Field Ambulance arrived including Private Frank Tapper who was a clerk. Following their escape by motor boat and trawler from Dunkirk in May 1940 his unit was sent to Beaminster before moving to Kingston Maurward House. Frank worked in the Orderly Room which

3 January 1941. Left to right: William ?, Frank Tapper, Pete ? and Brian ?, RAMC ambulance crew, three of them smoking as so many did!

was on the left inside the entrance of the hall. Officers had accommodation on the upper floors whilst the men slept in the basement where they were plagued with midges from the lake. The RAMC kitchens were set up in the courtyard between what is now The Old Coach House Café and classrooms. The cooks used enormous stoves rather like primus stoves, powered with petrol and the food was served in a dining-room in the basement.

Fishing in the lake was a favourite spare time occupation for the men using rods made from the bamboo growing near the lake. The most memorable catch was a 24-pound pike found under the weir at the east end of the lake, which was despatched by a hefty blow and promptly turned into enough fish cakes for everyone. Football was another way to pass the time and visits to Dorchester were made by walking along the river path. Frank cycled to Beaminster several evenings a week to see his future wife who he had met there before being transferred to Kingston Maurward.

The American Army

Several regiments of the 1st Division of the US Army, known as 'Big Red One' from its badge, were based in the parish in the year before D-Day.

In the year leading up to D-Day in June 1944 there were hundreds of American GIs of the 1st Division 'Big Red One' in the parish but very few photographs have come to light. This is Earl Overlock with Lady Hanbury's grandchild, Easter 1944. Lady Hanbury's daughter-in-law and children were staying in the first floor flat in Kingston Maurward House.

Left: *American soldiers from the 1st Division 'Big Red One' were camped in Yellowham Woods in the build-up to D-Day on 6 June 1944 when they left for Normandy and Omaha Beach, pictured here in 1943 or 1944. The GI sitting down is Art Pinnow who was awarded the Purple Heart medal for his actions in saving two injured buddies whilst under fire by carrying them up the beach to the protection of a sea wall.*

Art Pinnow, 1944.

A spectacular mishap! An American M7 self-propelled gun named Le Venger, The Avenger, by the Free French Army, well and truly stuck on Bockhampton Bridge about the time of the invasion of France, summer 1944. The photograph was taken by Alf Pride who lived in the Terrace near the bridge, using a camera hastily borrowed from his neighbour Elsie Fost.

Trying to sort out the problem! The Free French soldiers have painted a map of France on their vehicle, summer 1944.

Above: *Victor Crabbe and Reg Atkins from Lower Bockhampton in their service uniforms during the Second World War.*

Left: *George Atkins at home on leave during the Second World War. He is standing in front of the Atkins family home in the Terrace, now Roller Cottage. George was posted to Dover Harbour where he was in a gun battery before transferring to the Royal Artillery with the Devonshires and then the Welsh Borderers.*

The 18th Infantry Regiment had a base at Kingston Maurward House. The house was used for offices and the park to the north of the house became an enormous fuel and oil storage area with five million gallons stored in cans stacked on 40 concrete platforms, covered with tarpaulins and camouflage, said by some to look rather like haystacks from a distance.

In his booklet 'The D-Day Build-Up' as remembered by Dorchester lad Ivor Strange, a Bofors anti-aircraft gun was positioned on the roof of Kingston Maurward House. Sentry posts were set up at The Lodge and at Park Cottage, now Green Pastures, at the other end of the park near the Old Manor House. Mrs Margaret Thorne who lived at Park Cottage with her husband Charlie and two daughters, Shirley and Caroline, remembers that some of the American soldiers on sentry duty who had grown up in towns and cities, were rather nervous on dark nights. They would suddenly fire their guns when small animals moved around in the undergrowth nearby and it was a miracle no one was shot by mistake.

It seems American soldiers were billeted with local families, for example, a Sergeant Goody stayed with the Pride family in the Terrace at Lower Bockhampton.

Denis Dunford and John Foot, boys from Stinsford, used to visit the GIs in the park through a hole in the hedge where Maurward Close is now located. They were given chocolate, dried soup, which they had never before encountered, and bully beef to chew, another novelty.

Ron Webb who lived at the Old Manor House during the war remembers being invited by the Americans to watch the latest American films long before they were generally released in this country, in the basement of Kingston Maurward House. The GIs always had chewing-gum to give to the children and there was no shortage of sweets or oranges.

There were many black American soldiers who drove the lorries. They made endless journeys between the railway stations in Dorchester and Kingston Maurward carrying stores and supplies. They also laid a water pipe from the London Road near Grey's Bridge along the river path to Kingston Maurward. Many of these men were based in a camp in Yellowham Woods and in the run-up to D-Day bombs were dropped on the heath nearby.

The 20th Engineer Regiment also had men in the parish near Yellowham Woods amongst them Art Pinnow from Syracuse, New York State. He had already served in North Africa, Sicily and Italy and been decorated for bravery. During his time in Dorset he met and became engaged to his future wife Betty Battrick of Bere Regis.

Just after 6.30a.m. on D-Day, 6 June 1944, Art Pinnow was in one of the first waves of soldiers to go ashore on Omaha Beach where most of the soldiers from this area landed having sailed from Weymouth. His unit was to clear mines and obstacles on the beaches but many men were killed as they tried to wade ashore. Once on shore they were pinned down by enemy fire and Art Pinnow was injured with a shrapnel wound to his head. Despite this he managed to drag a wounded 'buddy' up the beach to the shelter of the beach wall, returning to the shoreline to rescue another. He was eventually evacuated to the safety of a military field hospital. By nightfall the beach head was won and his unit joined others to take the village of Coleville-sur-Mer. For his courage under enemy fire he was awarded the Purple Heart. He recovered to fight in France and Germany and when he returned to England on leave he and Betty were married at Bere Regis in June 1945. It is good to be able to link the bravery of a man who we know spent time in this area to the dramatic events of D-Day. Sadly very little can be traced now of the hundreds of other American soldiers who were billeted in the parish in 1943 and 1944.

The American Signal Corps

In 1981 Hubert Meredith returned to Kingston Maurward with his wife and recalled that when he arrived in the summer of 1943 he had no real idea where he was as all the road signs had been removed to confuse any enemy spies. For seven months he worked in a small room on the first floor of the house broadcasting music around the house, grounds and to units elsewhere in the area. In 1944 Deidre Levi stayed at Kingston Maurward House in her school holidays with her step-grandmother Lady Hanbury and heard the music of Glen Miller and other American bands wafting through the house.

The Free French

The Free French soldiers who came to our area in 1944 went across to France in July following the D-Day landings and became part of General Patten's Third Army. In the run-up to their departure one of their M7 self-propelled guns became stuck on Bockhampton Bridge and was photographed for posterity by Alf Pride of Lower Bockhampton.

Men From Stinsford in the Armed Forces

Men from Stinsford who are known to have joined the Armed Forces are the Atkins brothers from Lower Bockhampton: Maurice served with the Royal Army Medical Corps, Cyril joined the Royal Army Service Corps, George joined the Artillery and Reg was also in the Army. Tom Rimmer also from Lower Bockhampton served in India with the Army. Others in the Army were: Harry Fost, Frank? Taylor, Bill Blackaller and Eddie Read. Victor Crabbe, Eric Trent and Walter Symes joined the Navy and Alfie Parsons became a pilot in the RAF. It has not been possible to identify everyone in the parish who served their country.

In the autumn of 1939 a house-to-house collection was made by members of the Church Council so that a small gift could be sent to each man from the parish who was in the Armed Forces. This was repeated each year during the war and letters of welcome were sent to each man on his return at the end of the war and as a token of appreciation each was also given a leather wallet.

The memorial tablet in the church lists the four men who did not return.

Maurice Atkins, son of Charles and Ada Atkins, was a Lance Corporal in the Royal Army Medical Corps. He died following a bombing raid on 5 October 1944 aged 30 at Eindhoven where two British General Hospitals were located at the time. He is buried at Eindhoven.

Neville Hawkey was a Captain in the 5th Battalion the Dorsetshire Regiment when he was killed near Bayeux in France, on 12 July 1944, aged 32. He is buried at Bayeux. His wife lived at Egdon Cottage, Higher Bockhampton during the war.

Walter Symes, son of James and Mary Symes and husband of Charlotte, was a Royal Marine serving on a merchant ship when he lost his life on 29 May 1941 aged 41. His name appears on the Portsmouth Naval Memorial.

Eric Trent from Lower Bockhampton was an Able Seaman serving on HMS *Holcombe* when it was torpedoed by a German U-boat on 12 December 1943. His name also appears on the Portsmouth Naval Memorial.

Not included on the memorial in St Michael's Church because of the circumstances of his death is Roderick 'Bob' Holt. During the 1930s he worked as a member of the household staff for Cecil and

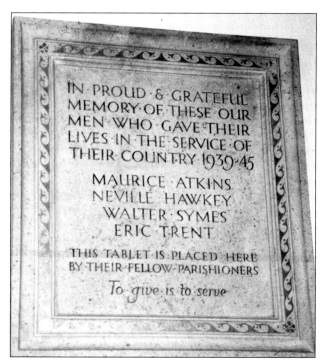

The memorial in St Michael's Church to the men of the parish who lost their lives during the war.

Dorothy Hanbury at Kingston Maurward. He was the son of William and Marion Holt of Dorchester and enlisted in the summer of 1940 as an Aircraftsman in the Royal Air Force Reserve. Whilst undergoing training at Harrogate he returned to Dorset on leave when he contracted rheumatic fever and died in November 1941. He was buried at Stinsford in the Hanbury extension of the cemetery at the invitation of Lady Hanbury who also attended his funeral.

Chapter 16
Parish Social Life

Many of the group activities that once took place in the parish have almost disappeared. We all tend to live rather different lives now compared to the past when many people lived in the same place for all or a large part of their lives and worked in the parish too. Until the 1950s most wives and mothers were at home all day rather than working elsewhere and the children could go to school at Lower Bockhampton at least until they reached the age of 11. Everybody knew everybody else and their families too and as a result social lives were often continuations of relationships in their working lives. Of course there were no televisions, computers or much travel to compete with the social activities which were very popular and well supported.

The Mellstock Hut

For many years the social life of Lower Bockhampton and the rest of the parish was centred on the Mellstock Hut, originally called the Bockhampton Reading-Room and Club. It was opened by Thomas Hardy in December 1919 as a memorial to the 75 men of the parish who fought in the First World War. Cecil Hanbury had paid for the building and provided the site at the north end of the village. In the speech he made at the opening, Thomas Hardy referred to the lively dancing parties which had taken place during Christmas festivities in the past called a 'Jacobs Join' when all the guests contributed towards the cost of the entertainment, usually half a crown (12½ pence). He pointed out that the man who used to host the parties lived in a cottage that had stood exactly on the site of the new club, thus dancers would be carrying on the tradition. That man was Robert Reason the shoemaker, the model for Robert Penny in Thomas Hardy's novel *Under the Greenwood Tree*. As part of the celebrations a dance was held and the first dance, the 'Sir Roger de Coverley' was led by Thomas Hardy and his partner Ellen Vincent, nanny to the Hanbury children.

The Hut, was the venue for meetings of clubs and village groups as well whist drives, shows, parties, the occasional wedding reception and a youth club. It is said that one or two socials during the run-up to D-Day were complicated by fights between white and black American soldiers but these were sorted out by the US Army Military Police.

Following the sale of the estate to Dorset County Council by Lady Hanbury in 1947 new arrangements had to be made for the Hut which had been sold with the estate. Initially the parishioners were allowed to

One of few photographs of the Mellstock Hut in the 1950s with the cottage called 'Bockton' behind Tom Rimmer and Steve Steadman. The house 'Martins' was built on the site of the hut in the 1960s.

141

Left: *Charles Atkins, a member of the Rabbit Club, in his garden at Lower Bockhampton with his prize-winning rabbits.*

Below: *Kingston Maurward Cricket Team and visitors, 1927. Back row includes: Gerald Stockley (gardener), Fred Stemp (gardener), Algy Mayo, Alfred Jenkins (head gardener), Charles Atkins (gardener), Bert Crabbe; middle row, standing: ?; seated: Colonel John Belguy of Bockhampton House, George Mayo of Coker's Frome, Cecil Hanbury and Dorothy Hanbury of Kingston Maurward, Revd Cowley (vicar of Stinsford parish); front row: ?, ?, ?, Tommy Hanbury, ?, ?.*

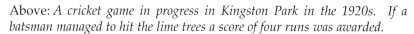

Above: *A cricket game in progress in Kingston Park in the 1920s. If a batsman managed to hit the lime trees a score of four runs was awarded.*

Right: *Alf Pride, who lived in the Terrace at Lower Bockhampton, ready for one of the cricket matches in Kingston Park, c.1945.*

continue using it free of charge but in March 1948 a lease for five years at 2s.6d. a year was suggested to the parish. The parishioners offered to purchase the Hut but this was refused and instead the five-year lease was agreed.

In late 1948 the Hut was refurbished in a 'make do and mend' approach, probably all that was possible due to the shortage of materials in the aftermath of the war. Everyone did their best to gather together the materials that were needed. Mr George Wakely of Bhompston Farm handed over a Valor stove to help heat the Hut whilst Mr Charlie Miller offered a drum for storing paraffin for the stove. The whist drive tables were overhauled by the 'Gentlemen of the Committee' with Mr Gerald Stockley acting as 'O.C.' (officer commanding!). Meanwhile it was proposed that the ladies of the Mellstock Hut Committee 'see about the material for new curtains'. It was agreed that the outside could be smartened up by volunteers who included Revd Taylor and Messrs C. Atkins, R. Dean, C. Miller and G. Stockley. The unnamed chairman was asked to buy ten gallons of creosote, five gallons of tar and two pounds of felting nails. George Wakely offered to provide a roll of roofing felt.

Gerald Stockley, who was often Master of Ceremonies at dances, and Mr Atkins suggested to the committee that a licence should be taken out with the Phonographic Society for the radiogram and a scale of hire charges was agreed: a full dance organised by the parish £1, a whist drive dance 10s., but outsiders would pay £1.5s.0d. and £1. respectively. Denis Dunford and his sister Doris remember that Gerald Stockley was usually in charge of the radiogram and presumably the 78 r.p.m. records.

In 1956 the Hut was offered at a peppercorn rent by the Dorset Farm Institute, repairs being the responsibility of the Men's Club and parish, but understandably the parish preferred to pay a fixed rent with the Institute being responsible for repairs! A compromise was found: a rent of £20 and lease for 15 years with repairs to the value of £175 being carried out by the Institute. However, in 1957 the Hut failed to meet fire safety regulations and had to be demolished. By the early 1960s the house called Martins was built on the site.

Efforts were made to find a site for a new village hall. In 1961 the school closed and the Parish Council discussed the possibility of the canteen being purchased for village activities though nothing came of this idea. By September 1973 three possible sites for a new hall had been identified: opposite Knapwater bungalows, adjoining the house called Martins near the site of the original Hut or next to Yalbury Cottage by the chestnut tree, since felled. The Parish Council suggested that the Dorset College of Agriculture, previously the Dorset Farm Institute, should be asked to sell or lease a quarter of an acre of land either opposite Knapwater or next to Martins. Plans were made to get tenders for a building in May

1974 and the first, received in September, estimated the cost at £9,000. In the following year the college offered a lease for half an acre of land at £35 a year. A formal referendum on the need for a village hall was held in the parish, the outcome being 46 'for' and 38 'against'. This was judged to be inconclusive and as a result no grants could be applied for, which brought to an end hopes for a new hall. Ironically planning permission was granted soon after. The parish is still without a community meeting-place.

The Rabbit Club

Keeping rabbits was very popular in the first half of the twentieth century and many people entered their rabbits in competitions at Rabbit Shows held in the Hut. George Wakely from Bhompston Farm was Show Secretary. Charles Atkins of Lower Bockhampton sent some of his best rabbits to London by train from Dorchester South Station, which were delivered to shows and returned afterwards. Bill Rimmer kept a breed called Flemish Giant while Alf Pride preferred the Old English breed. Competition could be very fierce – fierce enough to induce a little subterfuge on occasion. One of Alf Pride's Old English rabbits was almost perfectly marked except that it had one white foot which should have been black. An application of black boot polish was thought to improve its chances but unfortunately the rabbit did not co-operate and licked off the polish before the judging took place!

Kingston Park Cricket Club

The club was a founder member of the Dorchester and District Evening League. It seems it was a force to be reckoned with in the 1930s and the club won the League's Knock Out Cup in 1940. There was always a programme of friendly matches with local villages. Several players were amongst the staff of Birkin House and Kingston Maurward House. Bill Hold was one of the best pace bowlers in the district. Other members included: ? Wallis, Boy Bartlett, Fred Atkins, Fred Stemp, Harry Childs, Walter Haskey, Frank Taylor, Sam Corbin, Gilbert Drake and Len Barter.

Kingston Park Lawn Tennis Club

An article in *The Field* magazine of 1939 claimed that this club had been in existence for 80 years. It is unclear if the club always had its tennis-courts in the same place but by 1936 they are shown on a map just to the east of the grounds of Birkin House. The club was a private one patronised by the great and the good, including Sir Cecil Hanbury, Dr John Graham-Jones of Bockhampton House as well as Major H.O. Lock of Dorchester and Captain W.F. Martin of Came House, although the magazine article states that tennis was provided for 'all sections

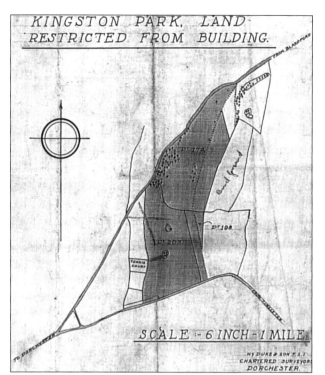

A plan issued as part of the sale of land on the Kingston Maurward estate in 1938 which by chance shows the tennis-court to the east of Birkin House. The 1901 Ordnance Survey map shows there was a pavilion on the site.

Below: This rule card of 1936 shows that the Tennis Club was very much for the middle and upper classes from the Stinsford area but also from further afield. It was also a popular club for people from Dorchester.

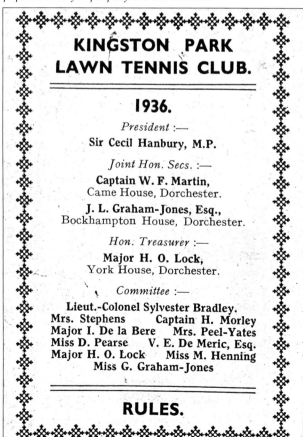

KINGSTON PARK LAWN TENNIS CLUB.

1936.

President :—
Sir Cecil Hanbury, M.P.

Joint Hon. Secs. :—
Captain W. F. Martin,
Came House, Dorchester.

J. L. Graham-Jones, Esq.,
Bockhampton House, Dorchester.

Hon. Treasurer :—
Major H. O. Lock,
York House, Dorchester.

Committee :—
Lieut.-Colonel Sylvester Bradley.
Mrs. Stephens   Captain H. Morley
Major I. De la Bere   Mrs. Peel-Yates
Miss D. Pearse   V. E. De Meric, Esq.
Major H. O. Lock   Miss M. Henning
Miss G. Graham-Jones

RULES.

A tennis match in progress.

of the community of both sexes'. The club was certainly very popular with players from Dorchester who made good use of the courts, particularly on Thursday afternoons which was 'half-day closing' in those days.

In 1939 the club had difficulty in getting a lease of more than three years for the tennis-courts, which could be the reason why no further trace of the club has been found.

The Mellstock Branch of the Women's Institute

The branch was founded by Mrs Aileen Graham Jones in 1936. Her husband designed the branch banner which was later embroidered by Mrs Medway, wife of the vicar.

At a WI whist drive and dance at the Hut during the war a military band played and prizes for spot waltzes and foxtrots were won by Miss Gladys Blackaller with Mr Wilson and Mr Cecil Samways and Mrs Eva Samways from Higher Bockhampton.

An undated newspaper cutting from the Second World War period reports a concert held to raise funds, organised by Mrs Parsons from Higher Bockhampton with her daughter Doris and other members. At the concert there were piano solos by Master Victor Crabbe and Miss Trixie Wallis both from Lower Bockhampton and Cecil Samways led community singing with his accordion.

At another meeting tea was provided for members and friends, followed by games. Musical parcels was won by Mrs F. Thorne and at a short whist drive winners were Mrs Ethel Dunford, Mrs Crabbe, Mrs F. Thorne, Mrs Rimmer and Miss Dorothy Jones. Prizes were given by the president and a surprise parcel, given by Mrs Crabbe, went to Miss Doris Dunford of Stinsford.

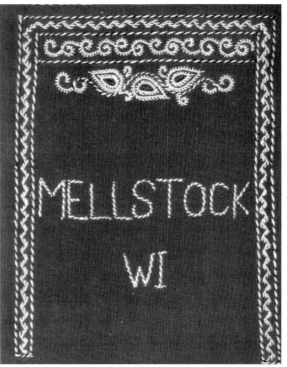

The embroidered banner of the Mellstock Women's Institute. Meetings were held at the Mellstock Hut until the late 1950s and afterwards at Bockhampton House, home of their secretary Mrs Illingworth.

Some fine Dorset featherstitching on the cover of this commemorative book 'Our Village Today – Jubilee scrapbook 1965' made by members of the Mellstock WI. The book is red with black and white stitching.

Members of the Mellstock WI at a Christmas party in the 1960s many wearing specially decorated hats. Standing left to right: Mary Ross, Mrs Beer?, ?, Daphne Vulliamy, Mrs Tindall, ?, Mrs Pope of Wrackleford, Jane Symes and Peggy Kingman cutting the cake, Nell Hansford, ?, ?, Mrs House; seated: Mrs Kilroy of West Stafford, ? of West Stafford, Ethel Dunford, Ada Atkins, ?.

Members of the WI and friends at a special meeting at Milton Abbey where they dressed as 'The Hardy family', 1960s. The cast was, left to right, standing: Denis Dunford as Henry Hardy (though Henry was actually younger than Thomas), Robert Kingman as Thomas Hardy, Peggy Kingman as Thomas Hardy senr, Mrs Stanley Jones as his aunt; seated: Jean Linnington as one of Hardy's sisters and Jane Symes as his mother.

For some events members' families were called upon to join in. For example, when WI branches in Dorset met at Milton Abbey in the 1950s the theme was 'The Family' and a group from the Mellstock branch chose to dress up as the Hardy family.

In 1965 the WI movement celebrated its golden jubilee and the Mellstock branch put together a scrapbook about the parish and the group. It has a red fabric cover embroidered in Dorset Feather Stitch. Mrs Peggy Kingman attended a Garden Party at Buckingham Palace held as part of the celebrations.

Links with Bockhampton House were maintained despite a change of ownership as Mrs Paddy Illingworth hosted meetings there when Mrs Graham Jones left the parish but the last meeting of Mellstock WI was in November 1975.

Coronation Celebrations, 1953

With the prospect of the coronation in June a meeting was held at the Mellstock Hut in February 1953 to decide how the parish should celebrate the event. The inevitable committee was formed with a representative from each hamlet: Mr Beer for Lower Bockhampton, Mr Wakely for Bhompston, Mr Parsons for Higher Bockhampton and Mr Middleton for Higher Kingston. Mrs Nobes the schoolteacher was asked to act as Honorary Secretary and her husband, Captain Nobes, Mr and Mrs Stockley, and the Revd Medway were also members. A Ladies Committee was also formed which included: Mrs Stanley Jones, Mrs Mayo, Mrs Beer, Mrs Buckerell, Mrs Stockley, Mrs Pulford, Mrs Higginson, Mrs Wyndham Hull, Mrs Graham Jones, Mrs Parsons, Mrs Medway, Mrs Symes and Mrs Hyde.

To raise funds for the celebrations lucky draws were planned at whist drives and prizes were offered by members of the committee. These included a chicken, butter, a cake, honey, a picture, a handwoven scarf, a bottle of sherry, a basket of fruit, a bottle of port and eggs. The committee's aim was to raise £60 to cover the costs of the day. The Ladies Committee offered to make cakes and sandwiches to be served at the whist drives.

It was agreed that every child under 15 should be presented with a coronation mug and a quote of £6.8s.0d. was obtained for 72 mugs. Aileen Graham Jones offered her garden at Bockhampton House as the site for the marquee which was to be the centre of the day's activities. A television was set up so that everyone could watch the ceremony at Westminster Abbey. Despite it being a rather grey and damp day the celebrations were reported as a great success in the *Evening Echo*.

After the event £9 remained unspent and suggestions were made as to how this should be used. These included levelling the village playing-field, a bus shelter at Stinsford, a summer treat for children and water to be laid on inside the village hall. The final choice was none of these. Instead it was decided that a walnut tree should to be planted near Bockhampton Bridge in Aileen Graham Jones's paddock. She reassured the group that the tree would remain the property of the parish even though it was planted on her land. In due course three trees were planted with a plaque beside each. Two were removed during the 1970s but the remaining tree thrives today, with the walnuts much enjoyed by the squirrels and passers-by.

The parish celebrated the Queen's silver jubilee in 1977 with a tea party at Kingston Maurward House. This was also the case for the wedding of Prince Charles and Lady Diana Spencer in 1991.

The Hardy Social Club

The club was set up in 1974 and the minute book begins by declaring that members were to be 'responsible adults in Stinsford parish', each paying 20 pence a year membership. For the first Christmas a special meeting took place and Christmas cake, coffee, sandwiches and mince pies were enjoyed. Whist drives, slide shows, bingo, a visit to Ungaretti's Chocolate Factory in Dorchester and coach trips were planned for the coming year. The club met at various venues, including the College of Agriculture, Bockhampton House, The Cottage and Yalbury Cottage hotel and restaurant. Clare Carey who was warden for the Knapwater bungalows organised the later meetings and activities. The minute book gives no reason for the demise of the club in 1981.

CORONATION DAY 2nd JUNE, 1953

To ALL HOUSEHOLDERS and their families of STINSFORD PARISH
You are invited to spend Coronation Day at
BOCKHAMPTON HOUSE

Every one is Welcome, including your visitors.   Everything is free.

THE GARDENS of Kingston Maurward Farm Institute will be open to view from 2.30 to 6 p.m.

11 a.m.	Short Service in marquee conducted by the Vicar.
11.15	Coronation Service relayed from Westminster Abbey.
1.15	Buffet Lunch with beer, cyder and soft drinks. Formal TOAST of "THE QUEEN."
2.15	Parade of Decorated Bicycles
2.30	Sports
4 o'c	Tea
5.30	Fancy Dress Parade) Followed by Distribution of Prizes Coronation Hat Parade) and Coronation Mugs.
6.30	Drive for the Old People around the decorated streets of Dorchester.
7.15	Whist Drive and Dancing in the marquee. Refreshments provided.
11 p.m.	NATIONAL ANTHEM.

COMPETITIONS

It is hoped that there will be as many entries as possible for the following Competitions.

Decorated Window (exterior). Judging, 1st June after 6 p.m. by a panel of Ladies from Dorchester.

Decorated Bicycle - boy or girl.
Fancy Dress for Children - all ages, dressing-room available.
Home-made Coronation Hat - to be worn by the maker; open to ladies and gentlemen.

Mrs A.H. Higginson and Mrs H. Gooch have kindly consented to judge Competitions and present the Prizes.

In order to obtain some idea of numbers for the catering for lunch and tea, please fill in the slip below, tear off, and send to the Hon. Secretary: Mrs Nobes, School House, Bockhampton by Monday, 18th May, 1953.

The Committee would welcome any contribution, however small, from those who have not already subscribed to the Coronation fund, either in money or kind. The Hon. Treasurer is Capt. Nobes, School House, Bockhampton.

- -

	LUNCH	TEA
Number of adults		
" " children under 5		
" " " over 5		
Entries for Decorated Window		
" " " Bicycle		
" " Fancy Dress		
" " Coronation Hat		
Name		

Programme for Coronation Day celebrations in the parish, 2 June 1953.

As part of the celebrations for the coronation on 2 June 1953 children from the parish took part in a fancy-dress competition at Bockhampton House. Derek Pride from Lower Bockhampton went as a soldier wearing his father's medals and won third prize in the 'over seven years' group. First prize went to John Wyatt and second to Dennis Key.

THOSE WHO WON PRIZES AT STINSFORD

STINSFORD'S celebrations proved a great success. The large number of prize-winners included the following:—

Decorated window: 1, Mrs. Atkins; 2. Mrs. Medway; 3, Mrs. Pride; h.c., Mrs. Beer, Mrs. Farr, Mrs. M. Graham Jones, Mrs. Rogers, Mrs. Symes.

Coronation hats.—Women: 1, Mrs. M. Graham Jones; 2, Mrs. Pulford; 3, Mrs. Pride. Men: 1, Mr. Caddy; 2, Mr. Pride; 3, Mr. Atkins.

Decorated bicycles. — 1, Evelyn Tizzard; 2, Jean Bowles; 3, Paul Buckrell; h.c., Diane Thomas, Doris Dunford and Peter Goldsworthy.

Fancy dress.—Seven and under: 1, Glyn Thomas; 2, Jennifer Jones; 3, Stewart Dean. Over 7—Boys: 1, John Wyatt; 2, Dennis Key; 3, Derek Pride. Girls—1, Janet Tanner; 2, Jean Bowles; 3, Shirley Wyatt.

Sack race. — Under 8: 1, Bert Jeanes; 2, Jennifer Jones; 3, Ian Pulford. Over 8: 1, Shirley Thorne; 2, Peter Goldsworthy; 3, John Wyatt.

Egg and spoon.—1, Graham Ball; 2, Michael Caddy; 3, Diane Thomas. Potato race.—Under 9: 1, Graham Ball; 2, Diane Thomas; 3, Shirley Wyatt. Over 9: 1, George Hendrick; 2, Wilf Tizzard; 3, Doris Dunford.

Obstacle.—1, Peter Goldsworthy; 2, John Wyatt; 3, George Hendrick. Flower pot.—1, Derek Pride; 2, Margaret Key; 3, Shirley Wyatt. Three-legged.—Under 8: 1, Pat Hendrick and Ian Pulford; 2, June Grace and M. Key; 3, Mary Ross and Jennifer Jones. Over 8: 1, Wilf Tizzard and Geo. Hendrick; 2, Derek Pride and John Wyatt; 3, Janet Tanner and Shirley Thorne.

Slow bicycle. — 1, Peter Goldsworthy; 2, Dennis Key; 3, Janet Tanner.

Whist first prizes were won by Mrs. Dunford and Mr. G. Bowles.

Coronation day prize winners announced in the Evening Echo.

Left: *Celebrating the silver jubilee, 1977. Amelia Farr (left) whose husband Frank had worked at Stinsford and the Farm Institute and was a well-known bell ringer in Dorset. Left to right, standing: Fred Kellaway (bricklayer on the estate maintenance team), Maureen and Tom Rimmer of Lower Bockhampton; seated, right: Eve 'Dolly' Kellaway (wife of Fred) with unknown little girl.*

Right: *Residents of Knapwater bungalows celebrating the jubilee. Left to right: Bill Dunford (retired dairy-man), Elsie (wife of Harry Fost, a caretaker at the Farm Institute), Ethel Dunford (Bill's wife), Mrs and Mr Jeanes who retired to Knapwater from Higher Kingston and Bert Crabb (retired tractor driver).*

Left: *Celebrating the silver jubilee, 1977.* Left: *David Pain from Lower Bockhampton, ?, ?, Steve and Pat Pollard from Higher Bockhampton, unknown little girl.*

Below left: *The silver jubilee. Left to right: Josh Hull (caretaker), Mr Jeanes, Mrs Jeanes and Kate Wyatt from Lower Bockhampton.*

Below, right: Left to right: *Annabel Evans from the Old Manor House ?, ?, Fred Bowles who worked on the College farm.*

Playing in and around the river – a favourite pastime for many children. This photograph was taken c.1950 in the meadows next to Bockhampton Bridge.

Above: *Royal wedding celebrations held at Kingston Maurward in 1981 with Jamie Pinnow as Robin Hood. On the right Margaret Webb who lived in the Old Post Office, Lower Bockhampton.*

Below: *An unknown knight, whose name perhaps began with 'T' and a dynamic Robin Hood (Jamie Pinnow), 1981.*

Football in the playing-field in 1942 or 1943. Opposite is the schoolteacher's house with the head gardener's cottage in the background to the right. Left to right: Peter Crabbe, Phil Stockley, David ?, Peggy James, Raymond Evans, Alan Stockley.

Children's Social Activities

Many people remembering their childhood in the parish mention the freedom they enjoyed, particularly during the school holidays when they spent whole days out in the fields, along the river and in the water-meadows without this being a worry to their parents. There were several favourite places for paddling and swimming, including a pool that was across the meadows from the bottom of the Cow Path, which ceased to exist when the river was dredged in the 1960s. The others were the swimming hole and the river itself on the other side of the road. Both these spots are on the southern edge of the parish just off the road to West Stafford.

149

A Sunday school outing to the seaside, early 1950s. Left to right: *Joan Ball, Graham Ball, Ivor Parker, Derek Pride.*

Fishing for tadpoles and sticklebacks with jam jars was popular in the spring and more serious fishing for eels near the weirs, which could be taken home for a tasty tea. Some children were adept at catching trout by clever use of a Wellington boot put in the water in front of the trout. With luck the fish moved into the darkness of the submerged Wellington which was quickly scooped up, complete with fish! Older boys have told how they were able to tickle trout and salmon – no names disclosed!

Football in the playing-field at Lower Bockhampton and go-karting were popular with the boys and one or two girls as well. The karts were made from old pram wheels with a seat made from offcuts of wood. All that was needed to complete the kart was a length of washing line with which to steer.

Games with 'bows and arrows' made from bamboo growing in the park were popular with some of the Read children living at the Old Manor House and thankfully nobody appears to have come to grief.

For a time there was a Youth Club led by Mr Ross, who worked as a groom at Stafford House. It met at the Mellstock Hut and was run with funds raised by parents through whist drives.

Bockhampton Show – Bockhampton and District Horticultural Association

This association is the one group that is still active at the time of writing. The first show was held in 1942 in the Mellstock Hut under the auspices of the

Women's Institute and was established in response to the Dig for Victory campaign encouraging people to grow more food during the war.

Until 1948 the Horticultural Shows at Lower Bockhampton took place in Parsons' Field, now the site of Spring Glen, and at Bockhampton House. In 1955 the title of the show was changed to Stinsford, West Stafford and District Horticulture and Flower Show. Shows attracted about 500 entries each year.

Stafford House was the 1956 venue, at the invitation of Sir Philip Grey Egerton and the association was renamed again to Stinsford, West Stafford and Woodsford Village Produce Association. The entries increased to 570 but despite this it proved to be the last show for some years. Some 13 years later in 1969 the association was revived with its present title and the show was held again at Bockhampton House, then the home of Mrs Paddy Illingworth who with George Wakely of Bhompston Farm was largely instrumental in the association's revival. The Old Manor House was the venue for the show in 1971 before a long-term home was found in the Horticultural Classrooms at Kingston Maurward College.

In August 2000 the association organised a special millennium event called 'Stafford and Stinsford 2000' which took place in the grounds of Stafford House at the invitation of the owners at the time, Mr and Mrs John Smith. The show was set up in a large marquee and local organisations from West Stafford and Stinsford contributed displays and exhibitions. The event was opened by two children, Sophie Kendall-Price from Lower Bockhampton and Christopher Wilson from West Stafford. The afternoon was a great success attracting a large number of visitors and was followed by an extremely popular musical evening of 'Songs from the Shows'. A cheque for

After opening the BDHA Show marquee, Sophie Kendall-Price from Lower Bockhampton and Christopher Wilson from West Stafford are presented with commemorative millennium crowns by Dr David Vulliamy, 19 August 2000. Left: *Mike Cosgrove (show secretary), Sophie Kendall-Price, Christopher Wilson, Dr David Vulliamy (president), Daphne Vulliamy and Trevor Craven (general secretary).*

Left: *Patrick Rimmer and Charles Atkins photographed as winners of the junior and adult 'Best kept garden' competition, c.1970. They are standing in Charles Atkins' garden in the Terrace, Lower Bockhampton. All but one of the large trees in the background are now gone.*

Right: *Bockhampton and District Horticultural Association show held at Kingston Maurward, 1987. The judge of the handicraft section with steward Pat Cosgrove (right).*

Left: *A well-attended BDHA Summer Show held at Kingston Maurward, 1998.*

Below: *Crowds enjoying the summer sunshine at the millennium celebration 'Stafford and Stinsford 2000' which incorporated the BDHA Summer Show and other exhibits and was held in the grounds of Stafford House, 19 August 2000.*

Inside the BDHA marquee during the judging of exhibits and before the crowds arrived, 19 August 2000. In the foreground is a fine selection of sponge cakes, while behind is the exhibition of local history arranged by Claire Kendall-Price and Kay Kearsey.

£2,000, the profits from all the day's activities, was later presented to the Joseph Weld Hospice.

The association shows continued in the courtyard classrooms of the college for 2001 and 2002 but these proved to be rather unsuitable and since 2003 West Stafford Village Hall has been the venue, with a small marquee in the car park.

Another popular event which raises funds for the association is the plant sale held at Bridge Cottage, Lower Bockhampton in May each year. Donated plants are sold at very reasonable prices and there is always time for a cup of tea or coffee and a chance to catch up with neighbours past and present. Somehow the sun almost always shines!

At a 'Thank you' evening held at West Stafford Village Hall Dr David Vulliamy presented a cheque for £2,000 to Caroline Nickinson of the Joseph Weld Hospice Trust, the proceeds from the millennium event, September 2000. Left to right: Trevor Craven, Dr David Vulliamy, Derek Pride, Peter Watson, Eric Rose, Caroline Nickinson, Mike Cosgrove.

A reunion at the Stafford and Stinsford 2000 millennium event in July 2000. Hilda Burnett (previously Lee) who had lived in Lower Bockhampton in the 1930s met Cyril and George Atkins who were both born and lived in the village all their lives. In the background are Kay Kearsey and Claire Kendall-Price who produced the display of parish history.

The annual BDHA plant sale held in the garden of Bridge Cottage, Lower Bockhampton, May 2005. Always well attended, it is now the only social event in the hamlet.

Above: *Refreshments at the plant sale, 2005. From left: John Grant, Audrey Grant, Marion Mussell, Olive Davis, Derek Pride and Bernard Mussell.*

Above: *Visitors to the sale, May 2005. From left: Peter Watson from West Stafford; Daphne Vulliamy, Kate Webb, David Vulliamy, Markus Stickelberger and others.*

Right: *Jean Wakely from Bhompston* (left) *and Marian Mussell, who used to live at Knapwater, catching up on local news at the annual plant sale, 2005.*

And finally...

Stinsford Parish Council

On 4 December 1894 a well attended meeting was held at the school to form a Parish Council. Present were: Jas. S. Hull, J. Collins, Revd L.H. Mitchell, J. Clark, H. Hall, R. Miller, W. Veasley, Jos. S. Hull, G. Way, H. Hardy, A. Dare, W. Hull, J. Udall, T. Way, W. Gale, A. Croft, S. Squibb, G. Rolls, Levi Clark, W. Woodland, F.S. Dawe, J. Trent, S. Whittaker, E. Wills, J. Lush, W. Damen, R. Burt, W. Thomas, W. Bartlett, J. Samways, G. Rendall, R. Churchill, J. Bishop, W. Burden, G. Hansford, A. Crabb, W. Whittle, C. Squires, A. Tizzard, C. Corbin, G. Willcox, W. Vallens, J. Richards, J. Bowles, John Riggs, Esau Curtis, E. Hansheen, C. Christopher, W. Amey, G. Sturmey, J. Frost, J. Gale, J. Cox, W. Purseglove, C. Elsworth and E.T. Clark (candidate). As would be expected in 1894 all those present at the meeting were men.

Revd Mitchell was elected chairman and 12 nomination papers were handed in. The election of members was by a show of hands. The successful candidates were Reginald Thornton of Birkin House; James Symes Hull, farmer of Higher Kingston; Mrs Gertrude Fellowes of Kingston House; Stephen Whittaker, shoemaker of Lower Bockhampton; Edward Clark; Joseph Symes Hull, farmer of Stinsford; Edward Wills. However, Mr Elijah Dare, headmaster of the school and an unsuccessful candidate, demanded a poll of the whole parish, which took place on 17 December. The results were rather different, the successful candidates being: James Symes Hull, Mrs Gertrude Fellowes, John Bowles of Stinsford, Edward Clark, Reginald Thornton, John Mayo of Coker's Frome and Joseph S. Hull.

The minute books, which survive from 1938, show that the subjects discussed by parish councillors each year are very similar to those of today: the playing-field in Bockhampton, from 1944 planning applications, lack of a bus service and bus shelter, the state of the river path, litter, footpaths and speeding traffic.

In the 1960s there was much discussion about the need for 'old people's bungalows' for about nine couples, mostly living in tied cottages who 'could not cease work until they found other accommodation'. The Knapwater bungalows were eventually completed in 1972.

The Parish Council has existed for 113 years, to represent the views of the residents to the District and County Councils and organisations such as the police, to improve facilities and protect the environment. No doubt it will continue to do so thanks to all those who have served and serve now as parish councillors and parish clerk.

Stinsford Parish Council meeting in the Old Library, Kingston Maurward College, November 2007. Left to right: *Andrew Thomson, Hugh Grenville-Jones, David Pain, George Armstrong, Vanessa Gifford (parish clerk), Pat Pollard, Chris Nolson.*

✦

The 'embowered lane' in Thomas Hardy's Under the Greenwood Tree, *the river path to Bockhampton at the junction with Church Lane, 1930s. The kissing gate has gone now but thankfully the rest is unchanged and still tranquil.*

Subscribers

Mr and Mrs Derek Albutt, Lower Bockhampton, Dorset

Will and Vron Aplin, Dorchester

George and Susanne Armstrong, Lower Bockhampton, Dorset

Julian Bailey, Stinsford

Graham C. Ball, Poole, Dorset

Les Blackaller, Dorchester

Richard and Sue Booton, Stinsford

Susan Brewer, Perranporth, Cornwall

Sharon T. Brooks (née Conroy), Dorchester, Dorset

In memory of Jack Buckrell, Farm Bailiff at the Dorset Farm Institute, Kingston Maurward, from 1947 to 1960, and his wife Doris Buckrell

Anne and Dick Chadney, Stinsford

Douglas and Pamela Chainey, Stinsford

Trevor J. Christopher, Fareham, Hampshire

A.C. Churchill, Hindon, Wilts

Shirley P.G. Churchill (née Wyatt), Dorchester, Dorset

Michael Clarke, Stinsford, Dorset

Margaret R. Conroy (née Slade), Charminster, Dorset

Marion P. Cooper, Dorchester, Dorset

Copplestone family, Lower Bockhampton

Mr R. and Mrs J. Cosgrove, Dorchester, Dorset

Philip and Paula Cosgrove, Balerno, Midlothian

Peter W. Coxon, Bruton, Somerset

Sheila Crick (née Atkins)

Pat and Tony Daniels, Poundbury, Dorchester, Dorset

Ann Davies, Bretforton, Worcs

Helen Demery, Llanbadoc

Beatrice Dennis, Puddletown, Dorset

Robin James Dodd, Derby

Dennis A. Dunford, Weymouth, Dorset

Mr Paul M. Dunn, London

Pamela M. Eccles, Dorchester

E.S. and M.J. Edwards, West Knighton

Dr Clive Richard Ellerby, Poundbury, Dorchester

Allan and Barbara Ferris

Dr Tony Fincham, Dorchester

Lainy Fleming, Lower Bockhampton, Dorset

Mrs Brenda Flint, Wimborne, Dorset

T. (John) Foot, Stinsford, Dorset 1935-56

Mr D.J Forrester, Charlton Down

Mr B.P Forrester, Bishopthorp, York

Sylvia C. Goddard, Bedfordshire

D.T.C. Hanbury

Shirley Harris, Crossway, Dorset

Alan Hodge, Owermoigne, Dorset

Christa Holm, Bockhampton, Dorset

Mr D.J. Holt, Wrexham

Harry and Celia Hounsell, Lower Bockhampton

Mr and Mrs R.W. Huggins, Stinsford, Dorset

Wendy Hunt, Dorchester

Oliver Hurden, J.P., Fareham, Hants

Paddy Illingworth, Lower Bockhampton, Dorset

Mr B. Jeanes, Milborne St Andrew, Blandford, Dorset

Mr and Mrs T. W. Jesty

Sandra Jesty, Born Stinsford

Ron and Dorothy Karley, Lower Bockhampton

Ian Karley, Lower Bockhampton

Tim Kearsey

Roy and Eve Kellaway, Lower Farm, Lower Bockhampton

Mr and Mrs John Kennedy, Charminster

Deborah Kingman, Norris Mill

Mark Kingman, Norris Mill

Kingston Maurward College

Nicholas G. Lee, Stinsford and Lower
  Bockhampton

Derek Mayo Lewis, formerly of Sutton
  Courtenay, Oxon

Alison and Mark Lewis, Stinsford, Dorset

Helen Lewis (née Mayo), formerly of Frome
  Whitfield and Cokers Frome

Jacqueline Lindsay (née Dart), Malmesbury,
  Wilts

Tim and Bridget Loasby, Kingston Maurward

Mrs P. M. Lockyer, Dorchester

Marion Marsh, Stinsford, 1922-33

Simon and Rebecca Marshall, Lower
  Bockhampton, Dorset

Mrs Victoria E. Martenstyn, Nottinghamshire

L.J. Mayo, Dorchester

Peter Mayo, France

Anita Mayor (née Lewis), Watlington, Oxon

Wayne McIntyre Eaves, North Trigon Farm

Ian Methven, Mickleover, Derby

Simon Mills, Dorchester, Dorset

R. H. Moore, Exelby, N. Yorks

Mrs Diane E. Morgan, Ringwood, Hants

Bernard and Marion Mussell, Dorchester,
  Dorset

Miss Susan Mussell, Dorchester, Dorset

Nick Needham, Buckland Newton, Dorset

Peter and Christine Nolson, Stinsford

Marian O'Hagan in memoriam

David and Lynda Pain

Neil Parsons, Newquay, Cornwall

Charles and Judith Pettit, Shenington, Oxon

Bob Pinnow

Harry Polley, Dorchester

Derek A.J. Pride, Born 17/5/41 at Lower
  Bockhampton

Mr D. and Mrs A. Prior, Dorchester, Dorset

Pete and Jenny Read, New Zealand

C. Read, Old Manor House

Dennis and Doris representing the Dunford
  and Parker family,

Mina M. Rich

Louise Rich (née Crick), Crawley, West Sussex

Nigel Rich C.B.E, London SW7

Joanne Richardson (née Lewis), Gisborne,
  New Zealand

Tom and Maureen Rimmer, Lower
  Bockhampton

Bridget Roser (née Lewis), Melbourne, Australia

Gertrude Russell, Portsmouth

Ruston family, Stinsford, Dorset

Bob and Peter Salway, So'ton evacuees. Lived
  with Mr and Mrs Davis, Talbothays Cotts,
  owned by Kate Hardy

Ruth and John Sharman, Stinsford

Joanie Sharp, Congresbury, Bristol

Jan Simmons, Charminster, Dorset

'Skip'

John D. Smith (descendant of the Matthews
  family, who were married at Stinsford Church)

Mr Jeffry St. Aubyn, Higher Kingston

Major Jack St. Aubyn, Higher Kingston

Geraldine R. Stevens (née Wyatt), Weymouth,
  Dorset

Vivienne A. Stoat (née Lee), Stinsford and
  Lower Bockhampton

David Strong, Anne Bartlet and George Strong

Markus Stuckelberger, The Old Post Office,
  Lower Bockhampton

Peter and Sarah Studley, Weymouth, Dorset

The Symes family

Ray and Angela Thomas, West Stafford, Dorset

June Thompson (née Hill)

Andrew Thomson, The Old Manor,
  Kingston Maurward

Shirley Thorne, Kingston Maurward

The Tizzard family

The Hon. Mrs Townshend, Melbury, Dorset

D. Turner, Lower Bockhampton,
  Dorset 1927 - 1938

W. J. Vallance, West Stafford

Rob Van der Hart, Ringstead Bay

Dr and Mrs D. Vulliamy, Bockhampton, Dorset

Tony and Jean Wakely, Bhompston

A.J. Warren, Bridport, Dorset

Mrs J. Warren-Peachey, Dorchester, Dorset

Kate Webb, The Old Post Office, Lower
Bockhampton

M. W. West, Aston, Sheffield

Elizabeth Wills, Lower Bockhampton, Dorset

Jim and Diana Wilson, Stinsford and Lower
Bockhampton, 1961-76

Christine and Michael Woodward, Leicester

Claire and Craig Woolgar, Guildford, Surrey

A.F. Wyatt, Dorchester, Dorset

John Wyatt, Lived in Lower Bockhampton

Timothy G. Wyatt, Frampton, Dorset

David L. Wyatt, Dorchester, Dorset
Yalbury Cottage, Lower Bockhampton

Further Titles

*For information regarding up-to-date availability,
please check our website at www.halsgrove.com*

The Book of Addiscombe • Canning and Clyde Road
Residents Association and Friends
The Book of Addiscombe, Vol. II • Canning and Clyde
Road Residents Association and Friends
The Book of Ashburton • Stuart Hands and Pete Webb
The Book of Axminster with Kilmington • Les Berry
and Gerald Gosling
The Book of Axmouth & the Undercliff •
Ted Gosling and Mike Clement
The Book of Bakewell • Trevor Brighton
The Book of Banff • Banff Community Group
The Book of Bampton • Caroline Seward
The Book of Barnstaple • Avril Stone
The Book of Barnstaple, Vol. II • Avril Stone
The Book of Beaminster • Beaminster Museum
The Book of The Bedwyns • Bedwyn History
Society
The Book of Bere Regis • Rodney Legg and John
Pitfield
The Book of Bergh Apton • Geoffrey I. Kelly
The Book of Bickington • Stuart Hands
The Book of Bideford • Peter Christie and Alison Grant
Blandford Forum: A Millennium Portrait • Blandford
Forum
Town Council
The Book of Bitterne • Bitterne Local Historical
Society
The Book of Blofield • Barbara Pilch
The Book of Boscastle • Rod and Anne Knight
The Book of Bourton-on-the-Hill, Batsford and Sezincote
• Allen Firth
The Book of Bramford • Bramford Local History
Group
The Book of Breage & Germoe • Stephen Polglase
The Book of Bridestowe • D. Richard Cann
The Book of Bridgwater • Roger Evans
The Book of Bridport • Rodney Legg
The Book of Brixham • Frank Pearce
The Book of Brundall • Barbara Ayers and Group
The Book of Buckfastleigh • Sandra Coleman
The Book of Buckland Monachorum & Yelverton •
Pauline Hamilton-Leggett
The Book of Budleigh Salterton • D. Richard Cann
The Book of Carharrack • Carharrack Old
Cornwall Society
The Book of Carshalton • Stella Wilks and Gordon
Rookledge
The Book of Carhampton • Hilary Binding
The Parish Book of Cerne Abbas • Vivian and
Patricia Vale
The Book of Chagford • Iain Rice
The Book of Chapel-en-le-Frith • Mike Smith
*The Book of Chittlehamholt with
Warkleigh & Satterleigh* • Richard Lethbridge
The Book of Chittlehampton • Various
The Book of Codford • Romy Wyeth
The Book of Colney Heath • Bryan Lilley
The Book of Constantine • Moore and Trethowan
The Book of Cornwood and Lutton • Compiled by
the People of the Parish
The Book of Crediton • John Heal
The Book of Creech St Michael • June Small
The Book of Crowcombe, Bicknoller and Sampford Brett •
Maurice and Joyce Chidgey
The Book of Crudwell • Tony Pain
The Book of Cullompton • Compiled by the People
of the Parish
The Second Book of Cullompton • Compiled by the
People
of the Parish
The Book of Dawlish • Frank Pearce
*The Book of Dulverton, Brushford,
Bury & Exebridge* • Dulverton and District Civic
Society
The Book of Dunster • Hilary Binding
The Book of Easton • Easton Village History
Project
The Book of Edale • Gordon Miller
The Ellacombe Book • Sydney R. Langmead
The Book of Elmsett • Elmsett Local History Group
The Book of Exmouth • W.H. Pascoe
The Book of Fareham • Lesley Burton and
Brian Musselwhite
The Book of Gerrans & Portscatho • Chris Pollard
The Book of Grampound with Creed • Bane and Oliver
The Book of Gosport • Lesley Burton and
Brian Musselwhite
The Book of Haughley • Howard Stephens

The Book of Hayle • Harry Pascoe
The Book of Hayling Island & Langstone • Peter Rogers
The Book of Helston • Jenkin with Carter
The Book of Hempnall • Maureen Cubitt
The Book of Hemyock • Clist and Dracott
The Book of Herne Hill • Patricia Jenkyns
The Book of Hethersett • Hethersett Society
Research Group
The Book of High Bickington • Avril Stone
The Book of Homersfield • Ken Palmer
The Book of Honiton • Gerald Gosling
The Book of Ilsington • Dick Wills
The Book of Kessingland • Maureen and Eric Long
The Book of Kingskerswell • Carsewella Local
History Group
The Book of Lamerton • Ann Cole and Friends
Lanner, A Cornish Mining Parish • Sharron
Schwartz and Roger Parker
The Book of Leigh & Bransford • Malcolm Scott
The Second Book of Leigh & Bransford • Malcolm Scott
The Book of Litcham with Lexham & Mileham • Litcham
Historical and Amenity Society
The Book of Llangain • Haydn Williams
The Book of Loddiswell • Loddiswell Parish History
Group
The Book of Looe • Mark Camp
The New Book of Lostwithiel • Barbara Fraser
The Book of Lulworth • Rodney Legg
The Book of Lustleigh • Joe Crowdy
The Book of Lydford • Compiled by Barbara Weeks
The Book of Lyme Regis • Rodney Legg
The Book of Manaton • Compiled by the People
of the Parish
The Book of Markyate • Markyate Local History
Society
The Book of Mawnan • Mawnan Local History Group
The Book of Meavy • Pauline Hemery
The Book of Mere • Dr David Longbourne
The Book of Minehead with Alcombe • Binding and
Stevens
The Book of Monks Orchard and Eden Park • Ian
Muir and Pat Manning
The Book of Morchard Bishop • Jeff Kingaby
Mount Batten – The Flying Boats of Plymouth •
Gerald Wasley
The Book of Mulbarton • Jill and David Wright
The Book of Mylor • Mylor Local History Group
The Book of Narborough • Narborough Local
History Society
The Book of Newdigate • John Callcut
The Book of Newtown • Keir Foss

The Book of Nidderdale • Nidderdale Museum Society
The Book of Northlew with Ashbury • Northlew
History Group
The Book of North Newton • J.C. and K.C. Robins
The Book of North Tawton • Baker, Hoare and Shields
The Book of Notting Hill • Melvin Wilkinson
The Book of Nynehead • Nynehead & District
History Society
The Book of Okehampton • Roy and Ursula
Radford
The Book of Ottery St Mary • Gerald Gosling and
Peter Harris
The Book of Paignton • Frank Pearce
The Book of Penge, Anerley & Crystal Palace •
Peter Abbott
The Book of Peter Tavy with Cudlipptown • Peter
Tavy Heritage Group
The Book of Pimperne • Jean Coull
The Book of Plymtree • Tony Eames
The Book of Poole • Rodney Legg
The Book of Porchfield & Locks Green • Keir Foss
The Book of Porlock • Dennis Corner
The Book of Portland • Rodney Legg
Postbridge – The Heart of Dartmoor • Reg Bellamy
The Book of Priddy • Albert Thompson
The Book of Princetown • Dr Gardner-Thorpe
The Book of Probus • Alan Kent and
Danny Merrifield
The Book of Rattery • By the People of the Parish
The Book of Roadwater, Leighland and Treborough •
Clare and Glyn Court
The Book of St Audries • Duncan Stafford
The Book of St Austell • Peter Hancock
The Book of St Day • Joseph Mills and Paul Annear
The Book of St Dennis and Goss Moor • Kenneth
Rickard
The Book of St Ervan • Moira Tangye
The Book of St Levan • St Levan Local History
Group
The Book of St Mawes • Chris Pollard
*The Book of Sampford Courtenay
with Honeychurch* • Stephanie Pouya
The Book of Sculthorpe • Gary Windeler
The Book of Seaton • Ted Gosling
The Book of Sennen • Alison Weeks and
Valerie Humphrys
The Book of Shaugh Parish • Don Balkwill
The Book of Sidmouth • Ted Gosling and Sheila
Luxton
The Book of Silverton • Silverton
Local History Society

The Book of South Molton • Jonathan Edmunds
The Book of South Stoke with Midford • Edited by
Robert Parfitt
South Tawton & South Zeal with Sticklepath • Roy
and
Ursula Radford
The Book of Sparkwell with Hemerdon & Lee Mill • Pam
James
The Book of Spetisbury • Ann Taylor
The Book of Staverton • Pete Lavis
The Book of Stinsford • Kearsey & Cosgrove
The Book of Stithians • Stithians Parish History Group
*The Book of Stogumber, Monksilver, Nettlecombe
& Elworthy* • Maurice and Joyce Chidgey
The Book of South Brent • Greg Wall
The Second Book of South Brent • Greg Wall
The Book of Studland • Rodney Legg
The Book of Swanage • Rodney Legg
The Book of Tavistock • Gerry Woodcock
The Book of Thatcham • Peter Allen
The Book of Thorley • Sylvia McDonald and Bill
Hardy
The Book of Tiverton • Charles Noon
The Book of Torbay • Frank Pearce
The Book of Truro • Christine Parnell
The Book of Uplyme • Gerald Gosling and Jack
Thomas
The Book of Veryan & Portloe • Diana Smith and
Christine Parnell

The Book of Watchet • Compiled by David Banks
The Book of Watchet and Williton Revisited •
Maurice and Joyce Chidgey and Ben Norman
*The Book of Wendling, Longham and Beeston with
Bittering* • Stephen Olley
The Book of West Coker • Shorey, Dodge & Dodge
The Book of West Huntspill • By the People
of the Parish
The Book of Weston-super-Mare • Sharon Poole
The Book of Whippingham • Sarah Burdett
The Book of Whitchurch • Gerry Woodcock
Widecombe-in-the-Moor • Stephen Woods
Widecombe – Uncle Tom Cobley & All • Stephen
Woods
The Book of Willand • James Morrison and
Willand History Group
The Book of Williton • Michael Williams
The Book of Wilton • Chris Rousell
The Book of Wincanton • Rodney Legg
The Book of Winscombe • Margaret Tucker
The Book of Witheridge • Peter and Freda Tout
and John Usmar
The Book of Withycombe • Chris Boyles
Woodbury: The Twentieth Century Revisited • Roger
Stokes
The Book of Woolmer Green • Compiled by the
People of the Parish
The Book of Yetminster • Shelagh Hill